Teens, Social Media, and Image Based Abuse

"This landmark study is vital reading for everyone interested in understanding young people's experiences of image-based sexual harassment and abuse and the steps we can take to reduce its prevalence and harms. As countries around the world debate how to reduce online harassment and abuse experienced by young people, this detailed and incisive book provides a roadmap. It ensures we better understand how young people are living their lives, as well as recommending nuanced and holistic responses."

—Clare McGlynn, *Professor of Law, Durham University, UK*

"It is a stark hypocrisy of public debates about social media that teens commonly experience unwanted dick pics and other abusive images while polite society turns the other way. This book's rich accounts of young people's digital lives, honestly told in their own voices, will surely fuel improvements by regulators and industry. If not, we are all culpable."

—Sonia Livingstone, *Professor of Social Psychology, LSE, UK*

"*Teens, Social Media, and Image-Based Abuse* provides an unapologetic, and at times challenging, insight into the real lives of young people as they navigate sexual safety in a digital world. Not only do the authors bring their world-leading expertise to this issue, but they challenge readers' to genuinely listen and engage with what teens want adults to know about both the problem, and its solutions. The result is an eminently accessible book that bridges the divides between lived experience of image-based abuse, conceptual frameworks in the field, and critical recommendations for policy and changemakers. Most importantly, the authors provide a much-needed antidote to the continuing influence of abstinence-based sex education, which fundamentally fails to equip young people for the rapidly shifting digital worlds they live in. Instead, the authors' call for a digital sex education that empowers young people, teachers and parents to transform online sexual cultures based on respect, care and consent. This book will be an invaluable resource for researchers, educators, policymakers, and anyone who is committed to a future free of sexual harassment and abuse."

—Anastasia Powell, *Professor of Family and Sexual Violence, RMIT University, Australia*

"Young people's technology use is often regarded with fear and suspicion by adults. This is especially true when sex and consent are involved; adults would often rather 'bury their head in the sand' than grapple with the realities of what teenagers face. As Jessica Ringrose and Kaitlyn Regehr show in their excellent *Teens, Social Media, and Image-Based Abuse*, this attitude leaves teenagers without guidance, navigating sexual harassment and online sexual materials without adult help. This is especially problematic for girls, who are far more likely to receive unwanted sexual material and be pressured to share nude images. Ringrose and Regehr use the voices of a highly diverse group of UK teenagers to show that their digital and social realities may be unpalatable to adults, but this does not make them any less real. By foregrounding the experiences of teenagers, the book shows empirically that it is better sex education, not ignorance or prohibition, that will empower youth to fight image-based harassment, sexual double standards, and other injustices enabled by social platforms. Our public policy must be guided not by moral panic, but by empirical research—like this book—that prioritizes the thoughts and feelings of youth themselves. A must-read for scholars, parents, and policymakers committed to fighting sexual inequality and online abuse."

—Alice E. Marwick, *Senior Faculty Researcher, University of North Carolina, USA*

"This is a brave, purposeful, and socially urgent book. Drawing from significant data, Ringrose and Regehr amplify teen voices on the digital issues that are affecting them the most. In this age of anxiety about kids and smartphones, *Teens, Social Media, and Image-Based Abuse* is a sane and lucid tonic that unpacks complicated issues around teens and social media. Highly readable and informative, it will change the way you think about the social media landscape."

—Tanya Horeck, *Professor of Film and Feminist Media Studies, Anglia Ruskin University, UK*

Jessica Ringrose · Kaitlyn Regehr

Teens, Social Media, and Image Based Abuse

palgrave
macmillan

Jessica Ringrose
Institute of Education, UCL's Faculty
of Education and Society
University College of London
London, UK

Kaitlyn Regehr
Department of Information Studies
Digital Humanities University College
London
London, UK

ISBN 978-3-031-92321-0   ISBN 978-3-031-92322-7   (eBook)
https://doi.org/10.1007/978-3-031-92322-7

This work was supported by University College London.

© The Editor(s) (if applicable) and The Author(s) 2025. This book is an open access publication.

Open Access This book is licensed under the terms of the Creative Commons Attribution-NonCommercial-NoDerivatives 4.0 International License (http://creativecommons.org/licenses/by-nc-nd/4.0/), which permits any noncommercial use, sharing, distribution and reproduction in any medium or format, as long as you give appropriate credit to the original author(s) and the source, provide a link to the Creative Commons license and indicate if you modified the licensed material. You do not have permission under this license to share adapted material derived from this book or parts of it.
The images or other third party material in this book are included in the book's Creative Commons license, unless indicated otherwise in a credit line to the material. If material is not included in the book's Creative Commons license and your intended use is not permitted by statutory regulation or exceeds the permitted use, you will need to obtain permission directly from the copyright holder.
This work is subject to copyright. All commercial rights are reserved by the author(s), whether the whole or part of the material is concerned, specifically the rights of translation, reprinting, reuse of illustrations, recitation, broadcasting, reproduction on microfilms or in any other physical way, and transmission or information storage and retrieval, electronic adaptation, computer software, or by similar or dissimilar methodology now known or hereafter developed. Regarding these commercial rights a non-exclusive license has been granted to the publisher.
The use of general descriptive names, registered names, trademarks, service marks, etc. in this publication does not imply, even in the absence of a specific statement, that such names are exempt from the relevant protective laws and regulations and therefore free for general use.
The publisher, the authors and the editors are safe to assume that the advice and information in this book are believed to be true and accurate at the date of publication. Neither the publisher nor the authors or the editors give a warranty, expressed or implied, with respect to the material contained herein or for any errors or omissions that may have been made. The publisher remains neutral with regard to jurisdictional claims in published maps and institutional affiliations.

Cover credit: Isaac Ruiz – estudio calamar

This Palgrave Macmillan imprint is published by the registered company Springer Nature Switzerland AG
The registered company address is: Gewerbestrasse 11, 6330 Cham, Switzerland

If disposing of this product, please recycle the paper.

Jessica would like to dedicate this book to the memory of her mother Karen Ringrose who died while we were putting the finishing touches on this book. Her enduring spirit propels us to stamp out sexual abuse and fight for the rights and agency of all survivors.

Acknowledgements

We would like to start by thanking all the young people who participated in our research. By volunteering to work with us and share their views they have enabled us to gather a rich array of youth experiences on social media. We are especially grateful that they offered us such frank insights and careful considerations about the problems they encountered online and at school, coming up with lots of ideas about how to improve things, which we've aimed to document in this book, staying as close to their views and perspectives as possible. We'd also like to thank the school staff that supported the research facilitating our research visits, giving us the physical spaces to conduct the interviews, which we saw in some sites was not easy given the lack of resources, including classroom space, available in some of the state schools.

We are thankful for the University of Kent internal impact funding for the project "Gender, Social Media and Young People's uses of Digital Technologies," which supported the first qualitative phase of this research. We are very grateful to have partnered with the School of Sexuality Education (SSE) on this research. We would particularly like to thank Amelia Jenkinson, founder and former CEO of SSE and Sophie

viii Acknowledgements

Whitehead, former head of policy at SSE and doctoral candidate, who supported research interviews and preliminary data analysis. Also thanks to SSE Facilitator Nathaniel Cole who helped conduct some interviews with boys. SSE also worked closely with the schools to offer additional supports in any cases where safeguarding issues were raised, and we are very thankful for their ethical commitment to protect youth from harm.

We acknowledge and thank the UCL/University of Toronto Partnership Grant "Youth Sexting: Sharing Networked Image Practices (SNIP) mAPPing," with Professor Faye Mishna at University of Toronto, which enabled us to replicate our study in Toronto. Although these findings are not covered in this UK specific book, it was through this follow-on project that we met Canadian researcher, Betsy Milne who further supported the UK data analysis, and helped shape the findings into a popular report which reached a wide stakeholder audience influencing the online safety bill and the creation of a new cyberflashing offence. Thank you to Betsy!

We'd also like to thank the UCL Social Science Plus for awarding funding for the project: Children and unsolicited sexual images on Social Media Apps: Developing Better Digital Defences and Literacy with Dr. Enrico Mariconti, UCL Computer Science, who helped design our survey and to research assistant Somaya Alwejdani who analysed the survey results generating important statistical findings for us.

We are grateful to Margaret Mulholland from Association of School and College Leaders who worked with us to streamline the research into a popular report and to host some of the resources associated with this project on the ASCL website. https://www.ascl.org.uk/ibsha.

We would like to acknowledge the Department of Education, Society and Practice, at IOE, UCL's Faculty of Education and Society, who provided editing support for our manuscript.

Jessica would like to thank her partner José and cat Rocky for their patience and love during the prolonged period of germinating and birthing this book into existence.

Contents

1 An Introduction to Social Media, Platform Economies,
Consent, Images and Abuse   1

2 South East Community College: Youth Social Media
'Produsers' and the Apps Opening the Floodgates
to Non-consensual Sexual Images   25

3 Lion's Co-educational Independent Boarding School:
How Highly Selective School Status Shapes Digital
Sexual Cultures and Identities   63

4 Outer North Academy: Geolocational Risk and Tech
Facilitated Violence: Responding to Cyberbullying,
Racism and Child Sexual Exploitation at School
and in Neighbourhoods   83

5 Central Comprehensive: Religion, Honour, Digital
Sexual Double Standards and Victim Shaming
and Blaming   123

x   Contents

6   Stags School for Boys: Elite Masculinities, Nudes
as Homosocial Currency and Mastering Your Digital
Footprint   149

7   North West Secondary: Snapscore Micro-Celebrity,
WhatsApp Wanking, & Sex Subscriptions Porn Push:
Barriers to Platform and School Reporting   181

8   Swans School for Girls: Performing High Achieving
Femininities: Sexy Selfies and Digital Dating
Dynamics in an All-Girls School   217

9   Conclusion: Image-Based Sexual Harassment
and Abuse Affects Everyone So How Can We Best
Support Young People?   261

Index   289

List of Figures

Fig. 2.1	Group of seven fifteen year old girls engaging with the creative research methodologies and visual prompts of advertising images, drawing on the social media app templates	29
Fig. 2.2	Templates for participants to use in drawing social media images	32
Fig. 2.3	Chantelle's drawing 'He got blocked like the speed of light', 'explicit content 3 hours ago'	43
Fig. 2.4	Janelle's mind map for better sex education	58
Fig. 2.5	Examples of warnings drawn on the templates	59
Fig. 3.1	Julia's drawing of posting surfing experience, using Snapchat filters and 'mug shot' on her private account with just friends	71
Fig. 4.1	Year 7 drawing of a home and warning not to put images with identifiable location on social media	89
Fig. 4.2	Venus's drawing of 'Shouting out yourself'	94
Fig. 4.3	Venus's Better Sex Education List—Everyone is equal, no group chats! causes problems, What age you think we should have a boyfriend, LGBT, Racism	119

xii   **List of Figures**

Fig. 5.1   Nadia's drawing—'do not' instructions' about Instagram
and Snapchat   128
Fig. 5.2   Kaleisha's image of anonymous, faceless dick pics   130
Fig. 6.1   "Take off my pants!!" Instagram DMs from Premium
Subscription Accounts   154
Fig. 7.1   Sierra's drawing of 'send one back babes' getting nudes
from 'people who add you that you don't know'   185
Fig. 7.2   Liv's drawing of woman taking a mirror 'belfie' or butt
selfie; and 'wanna see me cum!' an 'older person' sending
her a dick pick with the message   186
Fig. 7.3   Talia's drawings of image of transactional dick pic,
with tounge and droplets emoji 'ride me; now its your
turn'   190
Fig. 7.4   Kira's drawing of masturbation videos   191
Fig. 7.5   Anthony's drawing of a post from xox,xox,xox account:
'follow for some nudes/send some news (sic),' which he
describes as: 'Porn Bot account asking for followers'   205
Fig. 7.6   Jordan's drawing of Belle Delphine selling bath water
and premium Snapchat accounts as 'prostitution'   209
Fig. 7.7   Danny's drawing: "Bruh; Me and the Boys on Social
Media, 'Students should be advised to not get too
personal on social media'; 'Memes shouldn't be
restricted it wouldn't be fun'; 'Students should be told
of the consequences,' 'Sensitive content NSFW (Not
Safe for Work) Content.'   211
Fig. 8.1   Grace's drawing of Lily's mirror selfie with Snapchat dog
ears filter in vest top   223
Fig. 8.2   Charli's drawing of scribbles to focus on body parts   225
Fig. 8.3   Charli's drawing of mirror butt selfie (belfie) and figure
covering naked breasts with hands   226
Fig. 8.4   Ruby's drawing: 'Don't feel pressured to have pictures
of yourself in underwear because it's how you're 'meant
to look' or because someone tells you to   227
Fig. 8.5   Samantha's drawing of 'Abs, Jaw line, Collar bones. I
want people to be taught about asking for pics rather
than how to respond   232

List of Figures xiii

Fig. 8.6 Janice's drawing: stick figure of a boy doing front double bicep pose: 'posing in front of the mirror at the gym showing muscles they don't have'. Underwear showing, v-line, faint 6-pack 'they take photos in their room, shine a light and make it black and white to highlight their abs'. Tips: *Never send anything to anyone you wouldn't send to your dad   233

Fig. 8.7 Milly's drawing of jaw line image, 'boys competition on who can get the most/fastest replies to a picture before sending an unsolicited dick pic and asking for nudes. Don't respond   235

Fig. 8.8 Tamara's drawing of boys sending dick pics as 'banter'; shameful for girls to save them. Girls should be taught you don't need male attention   236

Fig. 8.9 Grace's drawing of 'dick pick from weird boy in Ireland'   239

1

An Introduction to Social Media, Platform Economies, Consent, Images and Abuse

On Saturday 17 November 2018, Jessica and two sex education facilitators attended a Feminism in Schools conference in south London. They were scheduled to deliver workshops on 'rape culture' at school along with several groups of secondary-school aged children. They had anticipated hearing concerns around online misogyny and sexism, sexual double standards and slut shaming. What they had not expected was the overriding prevalence of a specific form of image-based sexual harassment, common amongst millennials: the unsolicited dick pic. Across all the workshops they facilitated that day were these refrains in relation to receiving unwanted sexual images online:

'Reporting is hard… Because it is normal.'

'Ignoring it is better, or using humour.'

'Blocking them's easier.'

'But even if you do block the person [they] can make up another account.'

© The Author(s) 2025   **1**
J. Ringrose and K. Regehr, *Teens, Social Media, and Image Based Abuse,*
https://doi.org/10.1007/978-3-031-92322-7_1

The young people's statements about the challenges of reporting, and the individualised strategies used to manage these online encounters, highlighted to us the enormous challenges of navigating these new forms of social media intimacy. It also drove home how image-based sexual harassment and abuse appeared to be largely taken for granted and normalised.

Responding to these challenges early the next year in 2019, we embarked upon a research project to explore young people's image-sharing practices, including documenting unwanted sexual images they received on social media platforms, and understandings of and responses to image-based sexual harassment. Taking seriously young people's feelings of resignation, frustration and despair around the normalised lack of consent on social media, we wanted to explore these issues and find solutions.

A wealth of research has shown that young people are often left to navigate social media driven risks and when things go wrong on their own, without adult support (Hasinoff, 2015). Many times, there is a gaping void between what is taught in schools around these issues, and what young people want to learn about and need to know in order to protect themselves in a rapidly transforming context of mobile technology, platforms and apps. New legislation and education-based interventions have been slow and typically unable to keep pace with fast changing technologies and the implications they bring.

This book seeks to address these problems. Many adults find this topic difficult, unpalatable, and many would prefer to ban children from technology than address the very real social issues of power and control that underpin the possibilities of abuse online. This leaves children alone, without support and paradoxically without ways to protect themselves from abuse. We wanted to change this by listening to teens about what they are facing online and developing strategies that will support them effectively. This book will explore our extensive research into this topic in depth, looking at how young people use social media, how they produce, consume and share sexual images, and how they understand and respond (or not) to image-based sexual harassment and abuse.

The Research: A 'Snap'shot of Findings

The study detailed in this book is grounded in nearly two decades of research on how youth use social media. Jessica started studying these issues back in 2007, when social media was referred to as social networking sites (SNSs). Studying the youth dominated site BEBO she looked at how teens were navigating sexual relationships and crafting new digital identities online (Ringrose, 2010; Ringrose & Eriksson Barajas, 2011). In 2011, she led one of the first studies on youth "sexting" in England, commissioned by the National Society for the Prevention of Cruelty to Children. That study found sexual double standards were shaping youth digital relationships in profoundly gender inequitable ways.

In the spring of 2019 we began collecting the views of 486 young people aged 11–21 years in England with the aim of following up on how the social media landscape had transformed in the ensuing decade. First, we interviewed 150 teens and young adults in qualitative focus groups in seven diverse schools and one university setting,[1] across the UK. We developed a suite of creative methodologies to focus on what, when, why and how young people share images based on their use of particular platforms and apps on their mobile devices. We followed this up with a survey with 336 youth in the summer of 2020 during the height of the Covid lockdowns, exploring whether the trends in the qualitative data were borne out in a larger sample. The survey confirmed many of our qualitative findings, and we saw a continuation of some of the depressing trends around the normalised sexism and sexual violence online from 2011. What had changed nearly 10 years later was the technological platforms, as had some of the elements of tech facilitated sexual harassment and abuse.

Taken as a whole, what we found was that young people both love and worry about their mobile devices and social media platforms. As

---

[1] While we do not include the findings from the university students in this book, they offered important insights into how the trends continued to impact youth beyond their compulsory school years.

one girl, Venus,[2] who we will learn about in Chapter 4, told us: 'social media both helps us and harms us'. We found age-old dynamics around (hetero)sexual pressure and coercion, primarily of girls. Solicitation of nudes is a common feature of youth digital sexual culture, and in a continuation of traditional sexual double standards, girls who create sexual images are slut-shamed, while boys continue to be socially rewarded by peers for possessing and sharing girls' nudes, in line with normative ideals of heterosexual masculinity as aggressive and predatory. The survey confirmed the results of the focus groups, with 41% of girls reporting having been asked to send a sexual image, compared to only 17.5% of boys. In addition, 44% of girls felt pressured to send a nude image compared to only 12% of boys. We were also able to determine from the survey that the social media platform Snapchat accounted for 60% of solicitation for nudes, and 33% of image-based sexual abuse, which aligned with our qualitative findings.

What differed dramatically from the 2011 research was the new centrality of images of male genitals (dick pics) that arose in the 2019–2020 research. Stories of unwanted male genital images dominated our conversations with girls in the focus groups, where a shocking 75% of girls reported having received an unwanted penis image, which is now classified as cyberflashing (McGlynn & Johnson, 2021). We outline the qualitative methodology further in the following chapter.

The survey confirmed what we had found in our interviews, albeit with lower overall numbers than the in-depth investigations revealed. We found 37% of girls had received unwanted sexual pictures or videos online, with 32% of girls receiving unwanted dick pics. In contrast, only 20% of boys had received unwanted sexual images online, and only 5% of boys had received an unwanted dick pic. To be clear this means that amongst young people under 18 years of age, girls are *over six times* more likely to be cyberflashed than boys. Furthermore, 80% of girls

---

[2] Our study received approval from our university research ethics committee. We follow strict ethical protocols around anonymity and confidentiality of all data, including using pseudonyms for the names of the schools, teachers and students as well as altering some elements of the schools so they are not identifiable. We have also removed all identifying elements from the images in this book, which were either shared with us (after gaining informed consent from parents and children) or drawn as part of conducting our research.

1 An Introduction to Social Media, Platform Economies ... 5

in the survey reported feeling 'disgusted' and 58% felt 'confused' when receiving dick pics. We will delve into the complex feelings of both girls and boys around dick pics in much greater depth in our school-based research chapters documenting the in-depth experiences of the young people we worked with. Once again, Snapchat was the most common platform where unwanted images were received, with a whopping 62% of unsolicited sexual images and/or videos received while using Snapchat. This was followed by 21% via Instagram, 8% via Whatsapp, 3% on Tiktok, and a mere 1% via Facebook, likely because few teens now use the 'dinosaur' Facebook (see text box 1).

> **Facebook**: Founded by Mark Zuckerberg and Friends in 2004, Facebook grew around the varsity context of the early 00s. In 2009, Facebook pioneered the "like button" which streamlined interactions and would mark the beginning of ranked, personalised news feeds (Lapowsky, 2024). "Liking" was subsequently used to determine which posts were prioritise on users' feeds, a system which became increasingly complex, and is now based on thousands of data points made up of online interactions, reactions and comments (Barrett, 2024). In recent years we've seen a rise of public awareness around issues of privacy, data harvesting, targeted advertising and algortyhims on Facebook. We found Facebook was barely mentioned in our study because of low rates of use by young people.
>
> **Instagram**: Launching in 2010, Instagram was developed in relation to the poor camera technology of early smartphones. The photo sharing application developed filters to alter photos' appearance and doing so, the app copied the look and feel of "instant" polaroid cameras (BBC, 2024). Early app usage was based around capturing moments of spontaneity rather than an overly polished aesthetic. However, as the application grew after being purchased by Facebook in 2012, and as the filters available became more and more sophisticated, the focus on experience moved towards appearance and high production qualities. The focus in our research is upon how Instagram can enable young people to be targeted through group chats and advertising. In 2024 Instagram introduced teen accounts to increase

the privacy functions of the app, but critics remained concerned that advertising revenue and targeting would remain problematic features of the app. Insgtagram was widely used in our study and the main problem it presented was porn push.

WhatsApp: The instant messaging service was launched in 2009. It is a—if not *the*—primary means of Internet communication and allows users to send text, voice messages, make voice calls and video calls. It has a group functionality, which gives the possibility of group chats amongst large community groups or entire school groups, a function that can enable non-consesual mass sharing of images. In 2014 Facebook purchased the messaging platform for 19.3 billion USD. In our study WhatsApp is mentioned as a platform where images can be shared widely without the users knowledge.

Snapchat: Originally called *Picaboo*, Snapchat launched their app on the Android store in 2012. Snapchat took the idea of photo sharing to a much more personal level and allowed a disappearing function, making images only available for a short time, after which they become inaccessible to recipients. The app embraces ephemerality and has now evolved beyond person to person sharing to include "stories", add supported content and a password protected folder "My Eyes Only". Snapchat has been popular amongst younger generations, particularly for under 16s. Snapchat is the most problematic platform in our study, with 62% of unwanted sexual content received on this app. We explore in this book how the widescale use of the platform by youth and the features create this risky context. The app features include gamified functions encouraging increased time on the app and even addiction, anonymity of perpetrators of harassment and violence, ephemerality of content (disappearing media) which discourages reporting, and spreadability of content through hacking snapchat features. Snapchat consistently denies accountability for online harm despite repeated reports of child sexual exploitation on the app (Rahman-Jones, 2024). Based on results from our study, Snapchat is the worst offendor enabling image-based sexual harassment and abuse, and should potentially be banned for young people until it creates better measures to support children and young people staying safe online.

1 An Introduction to Social Media, Platform Economies ... 7

> **TikTok**: Released in 2016, the Chinese owned video-sharing platform, TikTok has seen a rapid rise to success particularly amongst teens and young people. The platform is characterised by fast pasted moving image content and algorithms that are highly reactive. Recent information has highlighted how efficient TikTok is at attention grabbing tactics leading to issues with additive use. TikTok was just becoming more popular at the time of our study but research indicates that while the platform may be addictive for youth, (Bressner, 2024) it presents less of an issue for image-based sexual abuse because its based on a recommender algorithm to promote popular feeds and influencer material than private image exchange.

We found that Snap Inc. (formerly Snapchat) the app built around disappearing images, was the most used and the most problematic for the young people in our study. For the uninitiated into this mostly youth dominated platform, Snaps are photos sent that only last 10 seconds and then disappear. Young people are the main users of Snapchat, with the site claiming its app 'reaches 90% of 13–24 years olds and 75% of 13–34-year-olds across the UK' (Snap inc., 2024). We found a range of unique functions that make it particularly desirable to young people, including features such as bitmoji avatar profile images, snapmap, snap scores, streaks, quick adds and more. For instance, we learned about the Snapchat appearance and aesthetic creating a particular set of practices, a 'vernacular' or a particular set of rituals and habits and insider *language* of the app, that was an ingrained part of young people's digital cultures.

Snapchat was largely viewed as helpful, fun and exciting by the young people participating in our research, because it enabled them to increase their networks and connectivity through new processes and affordances. By connecting users with a wide network of unknown and semi-known users, Snapchat increases the visibility of young people's profiles. Of course, this carries the risk of unknown predators contacting them through a variety of means, which some young people had also experienced first-hand. As we noted, the survey confirmed Snapchat was the most common platform used for all forms of image-based sexual harassment and abuse, accounting for 62% of unsolicited sexual images/videos, 60% of solicitation for nudes and 33% of image-based sexual abuse.

Our survey also allowed us to dig into the age and profiles of the senders of unwanted sexual content. We found 42% of recipients of unwanted sexual images claimed that they did not know the age of the sender. This was likely the result of the available anonymity of the platforms used—particularly, the ability for users to hide their age, amongst other identifying characteristics. Of the recipients who did know the age of the sender, more than half (56%) of the unwanted sexual images were received from youth senders (i.e. under 18 years old) with the remainder (43%) from adults. We also found, however, that young people felt that a large amount of unwanted content they were receiving (61%) was coming from either unknown senders or bots. This is important as we can see that it is not a known or even human contact that spreads the unwanted sexual content but could be part of the algorithm of the platforms. Young people can be a target for sexualised content on a platform like Snapchat, but also on Instagram, where the affordances can be used to create a sense of intimacy. The young people told us they were frequently exposed to bots trying to access weaknesses in the user or to attract views and clicks to move the user to paid content.

Indeed, we found that Instagram also creates various opportunities for perpetrators to engage in image-based sexual harassment and abuse. Despite young people generally having more caution around the images they posted on Instagram because of the permanence of the images (the archival nature of the site) (Tiidenberg, 2018), we found that the message request function allowed for mass numbers of young people to be bombarded with sexual group message content. This was gendered: we found this was where boys experienced what they called 'catfishing', which leads to sextortion, but also what we came to call 'porn push'. Boys are sent sexually explicit images of women and girls with links that push them to go to porn sites or to 'subscriptions' services from influencers/gamer girls. According to the survey findings, Instagram was the second most common platform used for image-based sexual harassment and abuse, accounting for 21% of unsolicited sexual images and/ or videos, 21% of solicitation for nudes, and 33% of image-based sexual abuse. Young people across every site and in every age group had received unwanted sexual messages from porn bots on Instagram. Porn bots are automated activities sending links to online porn content. Boys also spoke about content coming through on PS4 and other gaming programs.

Finally, one of the most alarming trends in both the qualitative research and the survey was the lack of supports available to young people in relation to tech facilitated sexual violence, including image-based sexual harassment and abuse. The survey found shockingly low rates of reporting of unwanted images being sent or of being harassed to send images. Over half of the participants reported doing nothing when they had received unwanted sexual content. Nearly one third said 'I don't think reporting works'. Only 5% reported telling their parents/carers and a mere 2% reported it to their school. The near total refusal to report digital sexual violence to parents and schools is concerning and reflects what we found in the qualitative research, which was a lack of adequate relationships and sex education (RSE) that included digital literacy around issues such as digital sexual violence. Taken together, these statistics reveal very low levels of consent in social media platforms, particularly Snapchat. Girls and boys are under different types of pressure and subject to different risks in general. Girls are experiencing more pressure to send images and more images are being sent to girls without their consent. Furthermore, much of the content is from unknown senders through features of the apps that will always open them to risk through wider and wider networks. Finally, young people do not tell adults about these problems, feeling that reporting won't work. This has huge implications for how we teach digital literacy and RSE, as we will explore in the school chapters and more fully in our conclusion.

Defining Image-Based Sexual Harassment and Abuse (IBSHA) and Criminalising Cyberflashing

'Thank you very much, Dr. Regehr, and we are sorry if any of our listeners found the contents of that segment distressing,' is what the presenter said, right before kicking Kaitlyn off a national breakfast show. Their listeners might find it distressing? Our research team was trying to bring public attention to the findings from the public report on image-based abuse of young people online we launched in December 2021 (Ringrose et al., 2021). We were letting people know about the high rates of graphic sexual images, typically of penises, girls were receiving as young as aged 11 in our research. We were trying to advocate for policy to hold social media companies accountable and to give guidance to parents and educators about how to support young people. When Kaitlyn asked the show's producer why the segment had been cut short, he explained that using the word 'dick pic' was not appropriate for breakfasttime programming. Kaitlyn later responded to the incident on Twitter (now X), acknowledging that children receiving unwanted sexual content on Snapchat was 'not appropriate anytime', noting something like 'That's the point. We adults need to stop sticking our heads in the sand and help young people navigate this!' (The exact Tweet is no longer available given Kaitlyn closed her account).

Despite some of these challenges in communicating the findings of our report to the public and encountering some resistance from adults and some refusal to acknowledge the traumatic sexualised experiences of young people, just two months after the launch event, our report became a central research lynch pin informing new national legislation. The government published an announcement stating that perpetrators of cyberflashing could face up to two years in prison under new laws as part of wide-ranging reforms to keep people safe on the internet. The government press release 'Cyberflashing' to become a criminal offence" read "Research by Professor Jessica Ringrose from 2021 found that 32 percent of girls aged 12–18 surveyed had received an unsolicited nude picture of men or boys" (Gov.UK, 2022). The press release hyperlinked directly to our research report. Our research and recommendations were incorporated into the Online Safety Act. This marked a major first step. It showed that just months after a major media outlet claimed our findings were not appropriate for public consumption, they were informing a national government bill, helping to change laws in order to protect kids.

However, the cyberflashing offence does not highlight consent and requires the complainant to prove intent to cause harm, which makes the law nearly impossible to prosecute. Further, education and support for young people on the ground remains negligible and we've seen recent trends to turn back the clock on RSE as part of a moral panic over the sexualisation of youth. We argue that the only way to support young people is through better education and support. We need to break down the stigma around teenage online sexual cultures and practices so that adults can make informed teaching and parenting strategies.

Sexual consent is now a term used across popular cultural contexts such as women's magazines, but is also central to what is advocated for in sex education in schools. Sexual consent conventionally is understood in a highly linear way around articulating yes or no. However, research on adults has shown that affirmative consent models (yes means yes) are problematic and do not consider heterosexualized gender norms and scripts of behaviour where women and girls may be more conditioned to concede to aggressive sexual behaviour on the part of men, or feel less able to articulate needs, wants and desires (Tolman, 2002). Legal constructs of consent may not therefore be able to resolve complex issues of power, inequality and messy ambiguities of consent. Gender norms are therefore central to discussions of consent, particularly in discussions of lack of consent and the arguments about who is responsible for harm (Setty, 2021). The digital domain and social media platforms, open up new pathways to consider around consent (De Ridder, 2017) and in particular with regard to images, the focus of this book.

In our work, drawing on criminological (Henry et al., 2020) and legal research (McGlynn et al., 2017), we use the inclusive term image-based sexual harassment and abuse (IBSHA) to describe a range of practices where images are used to harass and abuse online. This includes being sent unwanted sexual images (e.g. unsolicited dick pics, now a criminal offence of cyberflashing) (McGlynn & Johnson, 2021); unwanted solicitation for sexual images (e.g. pressured sexting, a legal but harmful form of harassment), and non-consensual image-sharing practices beyond the intended recipient (e.g. 'revenge porn', which is a form of legally recognised abuse). Unfortunately, many of the features of the harms we explore are not technically illegal, such as pressuring girls to send nudes; and at the time of the study there was no legal offence of cyberflashing; indeed, our own work was used to create the new offence in 2022, as we'll document more fully in our conclusion. We believe that online sexual harassment is a key component to what is happening amongst young people, and it is often connected to what becomes an identifiable abuse. Take for example a transactional dick pic (Salter, 2016) which we explore in our data chapters. This is when a dick pick is sent with the provocation to send a nude back—'send one back babes' (See Fig. 7.1). This complicated form of harassment and pressure is bound up with a form of online abuse, now identified as cyberflashing. To capture this complexity therefore we will use the acronym of IBSHA throughout the book.

At present IBSHA has not been adequately incorporated into UK Government policies on sexting and sex and relationship education. The current updated government guidance on education regarding "sharing nudes and semi nudes" (Department of Science, Innovation and Technology, 2024) does include a footnote to online sexual harassment guidance we helped design (ASCL, 2021). But the government document still does not adequately cover basic elements of image-based sexual harassment and abuse including cyberflashing, sharing intimate images, upskirting and AI deepfakes. The legal context is one where sharing images of underage young people is criminalised and constituted as child pornography. Despite these laws rarely being applied to young people, this context shapes what schools can tell young people according to their legal responsibilities. Youth are given contradictory messages about nude images and primarily this ends up resulting in abstinence messages— don't sext! Nude images of children are considered child pornography, whereas non-consensual images of adults come under revenge porn or 'intimate image' laws. This also means that services to support IBSHA tend to only be applied to those who are over 18 for instance, under 18s cannot access services through the Revenge Porn Helpline (Robinson, 2020). This is despite research highlighting a higher prevalence of image-based sexual abuse amongst adolescents than adults (Walker & Sleuth, 2017). Instead, young people have to use other services such as Report and Remove.

Educationally speaking, therefore, rather than identify and recognise a vast landscape of tech facilitated sexual violence, including online sexual harassment and image-based abuse, the policy landscape relies on categories of child pornography and child sexual abuse in ways that neglect a focus on how youth can protect themselves from non-consensual treatment of images in their digital cultures, including social media platforms. The criminalisation of all youth sexting has promoted a consistent message that since all underage sexting is illegal it must be uniformly discouraged. The 'stop sexting' abstinence approach to sexting has been found globally to be ineffective (Döring, 2014).

The abstinence approach to sexting also fails to distinguish between consensual and non-consensual practices (Krieger, 2017). For instance, the UK Government Department for Education policies, including the Online Education Hub (Gov.UK, 2022) which provides advice for online safety, says children must be taught 'not to provide content to others that they would not want shared further and not to share personal material which is sent to them' This effectively makes victims who have created images responsible for them being shared, even if the sharing is non-consensual. We push for a shift in direction to always consider how consent operates in order to identify and address image-based abuse.

Moreover, consent is not simply a human intentionality; it is part of the infrastructure of social media platforms. Social media often forecloses the possibility of consent around images. There needs to be a policy push around responsible tech, or what Livingstone and Pothong (2021) call 'safety by design', which takes these issues into account ahead of time and plans and funds support services for youth, including education about how best to manage these new conditions of technological risk. As we will explore in this book, the focus on child sexual abuse and adult predators at the expense of better understanding of both adult and peer-to-peer practices of online sexual harassment and/or image-based sexual abuse was a major barrier to understanding or taking seriously youth experiences across our school settings.

There has been a spate of international research that critiques the victim blaming and girl focused nature of anti-sext education resources and formats (Albury & Crawford, 2012; Hassinoff, 2015). This research has suggested that by focusing mostly on girls' nudes, an understanding of boys' behaviour around sharing images non-consensually, as well as their own practices of sending nudes (dick pics), has been neglected. UK research also found sexting education needs to be developed to incorporate contextual issues linked to power, gender, trust and communication (Jørgensen et al., 2019). The researchers received negative feedback from young people across the board regarding school assemblies as a format for education on 'sexting'. They explained that the group setting did not make them feel comfortable to ask questions, led to episodes of lad banter and slut shaming in some cases, and was overall viewed as completely ineffective. Across all our research in schools and educational settings we also found ineffective sex education, and girls in particular, therefore, felt a lack of accountability and support from adults (both parents and teachers) and a failure to identify or effectively respond when online sexual harassment and abuse is happening. This was what propelled us to write this accessible account of their experiences to help adults to listen and learn from what youth are trying to tell them, as we explain further below.

Child Responsive, Rights Based and Participatory Approaches

'Good morning, Professor Ringrose, I'm the education editor at *The Telegraph*. I am writing about sex education in schools'. This was the opening to an ominous message which appeared in Jessica's inbox in March 2023. The email went on to explain how a Conservative MP had collected evidence on the 'nature and extent of *indoctrinating* RSE (Relationship and Sex Education)' in UK schools. She had cited several examples of sex education materials devised for UK classrooms, which include teaching content that is considered 'age inappropriate by many parents' (email correspondence, March 2nd, 2023). The MP identified research into sex education, including ours, as problematic in that it exposed young people to risk, and called into question any research or education that covers 'sexually explicit' issues with young people. Akin to Kaitlyn being kicked off a radio show, we are again presented with a paradox, the very paradox that drives this book. Children are *already experiencing* non-consensual sexual cultures and content on social media. Is the best response to this, as we asked earlier, to bury our heads in the sand? Or do we follow the ethics of harm reduction and try to find support systems and preventative measures around these practices? Is not the first step for researchers to find out what the nature of these experiences are for young people? To listen to them and to take seriously what they are telling us?

This email would mark the beginning of a new culture war on sex education with potentially dramatic consequences. The report hastened an expedited review of sex education and attempts to turn back the clock decades on sex education in England, with guidance in 2024 suggesting children aged 13 should not learn about contraception because it was too explicit (Adams & Crerar, 2024). Remember, in March 2022 (exactly one year earlier), the UK Ministry of Justice outlined the new cyber flashing legislation using our research as a cornerstone because of abuse experienced by our participants. Flash forward to March 2023, where an MP instigates a pulling back on digital literacy. Move again up to March 2024 when reforms are introduced that place young people back in harm's way due to restrictions on sex education, including content covering sexual violence.

We can clearly see how sex education is a highly political space. The appropriate ways to support young people in developing healthy and safe practices in relation to digital realities is hotly disputed by politicians (even within the same party). As academics, whose research is on the cutting edge of these issues, we agree that guidelines and regulations on best practice in sex education are needed, but this needs to be guided by *evidence*, not moral panic. To limit RSE and digital literacy so substantially is effectively to leave children to navigate this terrain alone, causing harm, rather than alleviating it. Pitting parental rights to protect against children's educational rights is a zero-sum game, which will end up hurting all involved.

We want to be very clear that in many cases what young people shared with us was disturbing to those who are not using the platforms. At times, we experienced our own feelings of shock and horror at some of what young people shared with us, including the casual condoning of sexism and misogyny as completely normal in digital sexual practices, as well as overt examples of image-based sexual abuse. Using our research lens to better understand what is going on in these social media ecospheres, we found that unfortunately, age appropriate does not always exist in the digital terrain. That is the problem. Technology and culture already have young people caught up in a web of non-consensual and unethical practices that need to be carefully unpacked and understood in order to find solutions and support. Indeed, repeatedly, we found that teens did not want to receive some of the content that came across their screens and yet, it is coming into their phones, their homes, their bedrooms in a steady stream. This trend is of course on the rise with more algorithmically fed content on platforms like TikTok.

We are seeing a renewed push from the government to ban phones in schools, but international research on mobile phone bans has pointed out again and again that this is not a realistic solution (Campbell & Edwards, 2024). The abstinence approach to screens is not protective in the long run. Moreover, as long as social media companies remain virtually unregulated, and teenagers are using social media platforms at ever earlier ages (as we show through our research), we have no choice but to confront the reality in which they are living and give them the tools to protect themselves. As such, we propose the concept of child responsiveness, based on the principles of participation and child rights (United Nations Rights of the Child, 1990). This approach takes children and young people's views seriously and prioritises listening to them. It uses a variety of methodologies in order to tap in and capture what young people are experiencing (Kleine et al., 2016). Our unique mAPPing methodology, which we unpack in the chapters to come, was a process that we developed and pioneered, drawing from approaches in media and internet studies as well as child centred, arts-based participatory research, to help us focus on what, when, why and how young people share images based on their use of particular platforms and apps on their mobile devices. This has enabled us to address the gap between adult and child experiences and understandings that we've been pointing to.

This Book

This book takes a sociocultural and platform affordances (Boyd, 2010) approach to show how the imperative for social media companies to make profit opens teens to online harms. We will demonstrate how joining up more and more people and showing them more and more content creates a variety of risky contexts for young people. There are many actors who use these social media spaces to target vulnerable users in order to sell content to them. This could be opportunities for making money, such as when the youngest of our participants, the 11-year-olds, told us that 'companies' have contacted them on platforms like Snapchat and Instagram to say that they think they could be a model and asking them to click onto a site where they can submit images for money. These children's school was in a highly deprived borough of London, meaning that young people were susceptible to money-making schemes on 'the socials', and in this same school we heard from 13-year-old girls about a girl at a neighbouring school creating sex subscription type content with her boyfriend.

Likewise the specific features and functions of differing platforms, their affordances, will encourage gaining more and more contacts and friends, largely through user engagement metrics such as numbers of likes, followers or scores, so that young people turn off privacy settings to gain more contacts and up their metrics, opening themselves up to content that targets them. Social media theorists call this a 'like economy', and we will show how it works, its effects, where simply by opening a Snapchat account young people are sent content they do not want, such as sexually explicit or violent and scary content. Thus, a boisterous group of 13-year-olds in their school library described getting 'mad' content online designed to 'freak them out' about ghosts and dead people. Then, in the same breath as describing ghosts, they also told a story of a 'desperate old man' who was masturbating, contacting them through the video call option on Snapchat.

In another school in a more affluent neighbourhood, a group of 13-year-old boys discussed being targeted by 'bots' on social media platforms that tried to sell them 'sex subscriptions' to move onto the variety of fee-paying porn sites such as 'only fans'. These boys spoke at length about the genre of 'gamer girl' popular at that moment: a girl who is good at games, therefore intriguing to teen boys, but also sells sexual content, and even items, to those who will pay. Such online systems abound on Instagram and Snapchat, which enable you to transfer money to an account to access content behind a subscriptions pay wall; you can become a special category of 'fan' or user who gets access to the content that is only 'teased' in the public profile.

What is critical here is that young people are often being nudged and pushed onto other sites or connectivity that opens up themselves and their data to risks. This is why sociologist Deborah Lupton (2016) calls the online self a 'data self', discussing how children are 'datafied' (Lupton and Williamson, 2017) via participation in technology including social media platforms, given that a range of data with differing values accompanies online identities. Critical for us is that young people require the *support and tools* to understand their data selves and the political economy of the online environment, which is big business. They need to understand that the platforms are targeting them through phishing, nudging, attempting to sell them things (including unwanted content) through legal means and also mining their data, both on the site they are choosing to participate in and if they move to another space, which may be less regulated. Of course, platforms also need to prioritise children's rights (Livingstone & Third, 2017) and do safety by design, as we'll explore in our conclusion.

One by-product of this underlying compulsion to build networks, visibility, traffic and consumption, is using sex and sexuality in various ways to increase the views, hits and engagement with posts. How do young people create themselves as gendered and sexual beings through the cultivation and curation of an online self in these environments? We seek to provide some answers and understandings, noting that sex and gender are socially constructed and rapidly transforming in intersecting ways with online experiences (Bragg et al., 2018). We will delve closely into each of the seven schooling environments we researched to show how

1 An Introduction to Social Media, Platform Economies ... 19

young people's attitudes to sexual images, and their experiences of sexual content and imagery and digital intimacies online, are shaped by their sociocultural environment and contexts.

As researchers influenced by ethnography and documentary methods, we know that putting the young people's experiences into context is extremely important for the reader to understand the nuances of their experiences and how their environment shapes the social media networks the young people are part of; the types of e-safety and sex education and types of help (or lack thereof) they receive at school; and what types of monitoring and or support they experience from parents and family. The intention is not to directly compare and contrast the school sites, but to show how the resources available and the cultural context mould the young people's normative understandings of the digital sphere and therefore the unique digital sexual cultures that are formed. We will argue, for instance, that elite independent schools offer more digital literacy and protection, but this certainly does not mean that young people in these schools are not experiencing or enacting image-based sexual harassment and abuse; on the contrary, the teens' ways of hiding this in these environments may simply be more developed. We also show dramatically different levels of maturity and development within age groups across school sites. So for example, whereas one group of 13-year-old girls debate whether it would be safer to send nudes when you are married, another friend group of 13-year-olds has already experienced a girl in their digital network posting fellatio videos, and their major concern is to find out from us at what age they should have a boyfriend, since they wonder if these types of digital performances are what you must undertake in order to be in a relationship with a boy. These huge differences mean that sex education needs to be responsive to varying contexts and vulnerabilities, and we will show just how lacking and inadequate most of the sex education provision in schools is in dealing with these areas of concern.

We understand that what we are discussing may come as jolting to readers who are not part of these social media eco-spheres. Indeed, our intention is to denormalise this shock. With this book, we seek to offer knowledge about how young people have experienced these issues *from their perspectives*. We seek to empower parents and educators, as well as young people themselves, with information and tools to be thinking critically about our engagements with the online world. But we must start by simply listening. The stories we will tell are offered with the intention of better understanding gender, power and inequality as they relate to social media images, and finding practical solutions to support young people to reduce and ultimately prevent image-based sexual harassment and abuse.

References

Adams, R., & Crerar, P. (2024). Sex education in English schools set to be banned before children are nine, May 14. *The Guardian*. https://www.the guardian.com/education/article/2024/may/14/sex-education-in-english-sch ools-set-to-be-banned-before-children-are-nine

Albury, K., & Crawford, K. (2012). Sexting, consent and young people's ethics: Beyond Megan's Story. *Continuum, 26*(3), 463–473.

Association of School and College Leaders. (2021). *Resources: Understanding and Combatting Youth Experiences of Image-Based Sexual Harassment and Abuse*. https://www.ascl.org.uk/Microsites/IBSHA/Resources

Barrett, N. (2024). How have social media algorithms changed the way we interact? *BBC*. https://www.bbc.co.uk/news/articles/cp8e4p4z97eo

BBC. (2024). *The Instagram Effect*. https://www.bbc.co.uk/programmes/m00 149j7

Boyd. (2010). "Social Network Sites as Networked Publics: Affordances, Dynamics, and Implications." In *Networked Self: Identity, Community, and Culture on Social Network Sites* (ed. Zizi Papacharissi), pp. 39–58.

Bragg, S., Renold, E., Ringrose, J., & Jackson, C. (2018). More than Boy, Girl, Male, Female': Exploring Young People's Views on Gender Diversity within and beyond School Contexts. *Sex Education, 18*(4), 420–434.

Bressner, N. (2024). *TikTok's addictive algorithm: 17% of kids scroll app "almost constantly"*. https://www.axios.com/2024/03/22/tiktok-youtube-kids-scroll-time-data

Campbell, M., & Edwards, E. (2024). *We looked at all the recent evidence on mobile phone bans in schools – this is what we found*. https://blogs.lse.ac.uk/parenting4digitalfuture/2024/04/10/phone-bans/

Department of Science, Innovation and Technology. (2024). *Sharing nudes and semi-nudes: advice for education settings working with children and young people* (updated March 2024). https://www.gov.uk/government/publicati ons/sharing-nudes-and-semi-nudes-advice-for-education-settings-working-with-children-and-young-people. Accessed September 15.

De Ridder, S. (2017). Social media and young people's sexualities: Values, norms, and battlegrounds. *Social Media +Society, 3*(4). https://doi.org/10. 1177/2056305117738992

Döring, N. (2014). Consensual sexting among adolescents: Risk prevention through abstinence education or safer sexting? *Cyberpsychology: Journal of Psychosocial Research on Cyberspace, 8*(1). https://cyberpsychology.eu/article/ view/4303

Gov.UK. (2022). Press release: 'Cyberflashing' to become a criminal offence. https://www.gov.uk/government/news/cyberflashing-to-become-a-criminal-offence. Accessed August 1, 2024.

Hasinoff, A. A. (2015). *Sexting panic: Rethinking criminalization, privacy, and consent*. University of Illinois Press.

Henry, N., McGlynn, C., Flynn, A., Johnson, K., Powell, A., & Scott, A. J. (2020). *Image-based sexual abuse: A study on the causes and consequences of non-consensual nude or sexual imagery* (1st ed.). Routledge. https://doi.org/ 10.4324/9781351135153

Jørgensen, C. R., Weckesser, A., Turner, J., & Wade, A. (2019). Young people's views on sexting education and support needs: Findings and recommendations from a UK-based study. *Sex Education, 19*(1), 25–40.

Kleine, D., Pearson, G., & Poveda, S. (2016). *Participatory methods: Engaging children's voices and experiences in research*. Global Kids Online. Available from: www.globalkidsonline.net/participatory-research

Krieger, M. A. (2017). 'Unpacking 'sexting': A systematic review of noncon-sensual sexting in legal, educational, and psychological literatures. *Trauma, Violence and Abuse, 18*(5), 593–601.

Lapowsky, I. (2024). How Platforms Skirted the Spotlight—and Stumbled—in the 2024 Election. https://www.techpolicy.press/how-platforms-skirted-the-spotlight-and-stumbled-in-the-2024-election/. Accessed August 1, 2024.

Lapowsky, I. (4 Feb. 2025). 15 Moments that Defined Facebook's First 15 Years. *Wired*. https://www.wired.com/story/facebook-15-defining-mom ents/. Accessed August 27, 2024.

Livingstone, S., & Third, A. (2017). Children and young people's rights in the digital age: An emerging agenda. *New Media and Society, 19*(5), 657–670. https://doi.org/10.1177/1461444816686318

Livingstone, S. & Pothong, K. (2021). *Playful by design: A vision of free play in a digital world*. Digital futures commission, 5Rights Foundation. https://digitalfuturescommission.org.uk/wp-content/uploads/2021/11/A-Vision-of-Free-Play-in-a-Digital-World.pdf

Lupton, D. (2016). *The quantified self: A sociology of self-tracking*. Polity Press.

Lupton, D., & Williamson, B. (2017). The datafied child: The dataveillance of children and implications for their rights. *New Media and Society, 19*(5), 780–794. https://doi.org/10.1177/1461444816686328

McGlynn, C., Rackley, E., & Houghton, R. (2017). Beyond 'revenge porn': The continuum of image-based sexual abuse. *Feminist Legal Studies, 25*(1), 25–46.

McGlynn, C., & Johnson, K. (2021). *Cyberflashing: Recognising harms, reforming law*. Bristol University Press.

Rahman-Jones, I. (2024). *Snapchat most-used app for grooming, says NSPCC*. https://www.bbc.co.uk/news/articles/cze3p1j710ko. Accessed June 13, 2024.

Ringrose, J. (2010). Sluts, whores, fat slags and Playboy bunnies: Teen girls' negotiations of 'sexy' on social networking sites and at school. In C. Jackson, C. Paechter, & E. Renold (Eds.), *Girls and education 3–16: Continuing concerns, new agendas*. Open University Press.

Ringrose, J., & Eriksson Barajas, K. (2011). Gendered risks and opportunities? Exploring teen girls' digital sexual identity in postfeminist media contexts. *International Journal of Media and Cultural Politics, 7*(2), 121–138.

Ringrose, J., Gill, R., Livingstone, S., & Harvey, L. (2012). *A qualitative study of children, young people and 'sexting': A report prepared for the NSPCC*. National Society for the Prevention of Cruelty to Children. https://eprints.lse.ac.uk/44216/. Accessed August 12, 2024.

Ringrose, J., Regehr, K., & Milne, B. (2021). *Understanding and combatting youth experiences of image based sexual harassment and abuse*. School of Sexuality Education and Association of School and College Leaders. https://www.ascl.org.uk/ibsha. Accessed August 12, 2024.

Robinson, A. (2020). *Revenge porn pandemic: Rise in reports shows no sign of slowing even as lockdown eases*. https://saferinternet.org.uk/blog/revenge-porn-pandemic-rise-in-reports-shows-no-sign-of-slowing-even-as-lockdown-eases

Salter, M. (2016). Privates in the online public: Sex(ting) and reputation on social media. *New Media and Society, 18*(11), 2723–2739. https://doi.org/10.1177/1461444815604133

Setty, E. (2021). Sex and consent in contemporary youth sexual culture: The 'Ideals' and the 'Realities.' *Sex Education, 21*(3), 331–346. https://doi.org/10.1080/14681811.2020.1802242

Snap Inc. (2024). *Snap Newsroom*. https://newsroom.snap.com/en-GB/uk-mau-21million. Accessed August 15, 2024.

Tiidenberg, K. (2018). *Selfies: Why we love (and hate) them*. Emerald Publishing.

Tolman, D. M. (2002). *Teenage girls talk about sexuality*. Harvard University Press.

UNCRC. (1990). *United Nations conventions on the rights of the child*. https://www.unicef.org.uk/wp-content/uploads/2016/08/unicef-convention-rights-child-uncrc.pdf

UK.Gov. (2024). *How we promote and teach online safety in schools?* https://educationhub.blog.gov.uk/2023/02/how-we-promote-and-teach-online-safety-in-schools/. Accessed September 15, 2024.

Walker, K., & Sleath, E. (2017). A systematic review of the current knowledge regarding revenge pornography and non-consensual sharing of sexually explicit media. *Aggression and Violent Behavior, 36*, 9–24.

Open Access This chapter is licensed under the terms of the Creative Commons Attribution-NonCommercial-NoDerivatives 4.0 International License (http://creativecommons.org/licenses/by-nc-nd/4.0/), which permits any noncommercial use, sharing, distribution and reproduction in any medium or format, as long as you give appropriate credit to the original author(s) and the source, provide a link to the Creative Commons license and indicate if you modified the licensed material. You do not have permission under this license to share adapted material derived from this chapter or parts of it.

The images or other third party material in this chapter are included in the chapter's Creative Commons license, unless indicated otherwise in a credit line to the material. If material is not included in the chapter's Creative Commons license and your intended use is not permitted by statutory regulation or exceeds the permitted use, you will need to obtain permission directly from the copyright holder.

2

South East Community College: Youth Social Media 'Produsers' and the Apps Opening the Floodgates to Non-consensual Sexual Images

South East Community College was the first school we visited in this research project. It was a sunny spring day when the research team arrived at the school. The team included Jessica, a research assistant and two facilitators (one woman and a man) from the sex education charity supporting our research. Jessica was both nervous and excited, because she had worked in this school nearly 10 years previously in 2011, at the point when social networking sites, as they were called in academic parlance at the time, were taking off. At that time, smart phones with social media apps did not exist, and the main mobile technology used by the young people was the now defunct Blackberry.

We were now in an entirely different era of platform applications used primarily through smart phones. We were eager to try out the participatory methodology that we had developed, which included visual prompts to discuss images, looking at young people's phone apps together, and introducing the social media drawing templates we had created (Fig. 2.2) to enable young people to 'show and tell' us about their experiences of how social media worked in practice—what went into and out of their phones.

© The Author(s) 2025
J. Ringrose and K. Regehr, *Teens, Social Media, and Image Based Abuse*,
https://doi.org/10.1007/978-3-031-92322-7_2

In this chapter we want to explain how young people are consuming social media, but are both users and producers of content, making their own images via a new web 2.0—a dynamic that Axel Bruns (2006) termed 'produsage' (to combine production and usage into one word). Young people perform their selves on social media, self-producing images (and sometimes sexual images) that are then circulated, often widely, beyond their control. We will explore how gendered and sexualised power dynamics shape how images of girls' and boys' bodies are produced and consumed differently, and the different sorts of risks that girls and boys navigate as they learn how to manage their social media experiences.

As we will be exploring throughout our school chapters, context is highly important to our study and to understanding youth digital experiences, which are part and parcel of their everyday lives in their homes, neighbourhoods and in the schools they attend. Our study is school based and locates the young people in their everyday sociocultural environment, which is often not the case where internet use is studied in a disembodied way that neglects the relationship between real life (IRL) and the virtual world (URL). As with any research, our project went through a lengthy ethical review process. All the research encounters were set up through support from the outset in dialogue with the management of the schools. Parental consent was gained for all participants 16 and under; and written consent was obtained from every participant in the study, through a process of signing a form at the start of the interview process; all participants were anonymized (given fake names) and any identifying features of the individuals or the schools have been removed. We have stayed close to how the young people spoke in the quotes used throughout this book.

We start our research journey in this chapter with South East Community College (SECC).[1] SECC is a mixed 'sex' (but we would say mixed gender) comprehensive state school or college in a highly deprived area of East London. The borough is amongst the 20 most ethnically diverse, and amongst the top 5% of most densely populated local authorities

---

[1] As noted, our study received approval from our university research ethics committee. We follow strict ethical protocols around anonymity and confidentiality of our data using pseudonyms for the names of the schools, teachers and students as well as altering some elements of the school demographics and information so they are not identifiable.

in England. At the time of the research, 45% of the children were eligible for free school meals, the main marker of social deprivation in English schools, nearly double the national average. The school was also in special measures and needing improvement on every one of the Ofsted measures.[2] Indeed, Ofsted had visited the day before the first research visit and teachers were still feeling stressed and harried as a result. Despite these challenges, however, the commitment and devotion of our teacher contact at this school meant that there was a strong climate of respect and a sense that young people felt safe and supported to discuss issues there. Our teacher contact, Mrs. Keating, was very invested in the research, having worked extensively with the sex education charity which was supporting it, pushing for school investment into better sex education, and making space for us to come into the school and work with her students despite a range of constraints. Mrs. Keating supported the research diligently despite the challenges faced in this environment, including not even having rooms to host all the interviews. During the first visit, the rooms were not available and when we returned the following month to conduct further interviews the same problem occurred, and Mrs. Keating hastily re-located two focus groups together in the school library. We want to bring our strong supportive dynamic with the teachers in all of our research schools into sharp relief at the start of our school chapters. None of our research encounters would have been possible without their support and teachers often contributed to discussions, sat in on the interviews, as happened in this school with the younger groups and facilitated our process of gaining parents' consent for their children to take part throughout. Not only did a committed woman teacher strongly support the research in this school; one of the strongest youth feminist voices in this research came from Janelle, aged 15, who we'll meet shortly, who explained the ins and outs of posting selfies, the risks girls faced around their images, and called for better sex education to cover issues of sexual assault and harassment, as she reminded us that feminists have been speaking up for women and needed to continue to do so.

---

[2] Ofsted is the UK government Office for Standards in Education, Children's Services and Skills who inspect services providing education and skills for learners of all ages in the UK. Ofsted inspectors evaluate schools' 'overall effectiveness' acting as an audit.

Gendered Rules of Body Images

As was our standard practice, on this first visit working with the year 10 groups, the young people self-selected into friendship groups to participate in the research. These tended to be gender segregated and the two groups were comprised of 7 girls and 6 boys. Each researcher was paired with a facilitator from the sex education charity to carry out the interviewers. After signing their consent forms the group interviews started by showing the young people visual prompts of everyday media including advertisements and selfies. In Fig. 2.1 we can see some of the prompts spread out across a table in the science lab, amongst seven fifteen-year-old (year 10) girls.

Discussing a popular recent advertising campaign in London for a fast fashion brand, they noted men were in full dress suits or baggy track suits, whereas women were either in body suits or skintight Lycra leggings. The girls noted immediately that the women were wearing less clothing. They also commented that the images were photoshopped and fake. Using visual prompts, we also asked young people to think about the differences, or social perceptions of differences, between professionally produced images and privately produced images, showing women and men doing mirror selfies, the woman in bra and underwear and the man with his shirt off in a pair of jeans.

We wanted students' opinions on gendered pressures and how they apply such rules to their own images and those they encounter on social media platforms. The girls discussed how the professional model in a bodysuit is acceptable because someone else is taking the photo in a paid capacity, but taking an image of one's own breasts or butt was something that made the person seem like they wanted attention. The girls spelt out some of the social norms and conventions that demarcate the production of 'sexy selfies' and the ways adults judge such images of young people's bodies, with Calli noting, 'showing the body, like if an adult or a parent saw that, like, it's inappropriate.' They also discuss whether or not a girl taking this type of photo is doing it because they 'crave attention'. They pose this as a dilemma—while one may want to gain attention through images of one's body, there is shame and judgement attached to this, so that girls must tread carefully.

Fig. 2.1 Group of seven fifteen year old girls engaging with the creative research methodologies and visual prompts of advertising images, drawing on the social media app templates

We also asked students to think about images of male bodies in advertising and male selfies including topless mirror selfies. Young people generally agreed, however, that body image pressures seemed to have more direct effect on girls than boys in their peer groups:

> Alisha: Because for a girl if their body is not a certain way it's like they get more hate for it, if that makes sense, but with a boy it doesn't really matter what their body is, no-one really cares about it.

The girls also pointed out, however, that there was more pressure on boys to buy designer clothing and to show their value through displays of wealth, in brands like the designer jeans being photographed in the headless torso selfie; so it is not that boys do not have pressure but the form it takes is very different and with different sexual implications than for girls:

> Alisha: Because girls… like, for example her, like girls we are meant to respect our bodies, we are not meant to be showing, well girls obviously can, it's not wrong if we want to, but if you post that on Snapchat boys are gonna be like, they're gonna cuss you for it, where if a boy done something like that it wouldn't be as bad.

> Diamond: Yeah, I feel like even with clothing, and your parents, if you've got something that's too low cut, or too revealing, that your mum will tell you to cover up, whereas if a boy wanted to go and play football and take his top off there wouldn't be a problem with that. But we could wear a top that had like a little bit of cleavage and like there'd be an issue with it, with parents.

The group were aware of sexual double standards around what they can wear and how they can represent themselves online, and pointed out how contradictory and even hypocritical it was to tell girls not to use their bodies in these ways, when these types of (seminude) images are everywhere:

> Janelle: I think, oh yeah, in the media they show like girls that promote underwear brands, and then like online if a normal person, who is not like a model, or like an Instagram promoter, if they done that it would be shown as wrong, and people tell them it's wrong, but then they see it on the media, and like other girls are doing it. So I think it's really hard to tell a child you shouldn't be sending nudes, when they'll go on Instagram and they'll see girls with millions of likes, because they posted a photo in their underwear.

They were also very aware of the sexual double standards around girls' nudes which they felt from parents, noting boys have more 'freedom':

Calli: If your parents was to find out a girl was sending nudes, you'd get in so much trouble for it, but if it was like a boy they would get in a little bit of trouble, but they don't really care that much, so boys probably feel like they can do it, but girls are like forced not to do it. Boys just have a lot more freedom with stuff like that.

As Diamond went on to tell us, her mum treated her and her brother entirely differently in relation to sexuality and relationships both online and offline, in ways that she says are 'not fair':

Diamond: So I have an older brother … If I was to talk to boys on social media, and my mum would say there would be a problem. If my brother did it … there would be no problem. My brother, he has his girlfriend coming over the house, mum said I will *never ever* be allowed to have a boy in the house, but like I've said to her before that's not fair… but she said it is different for me and she doesn't want to encourage me having boys over the house, if she does that it's encouraging me more to like do sexual activities and to do stuff. But then I said why is that alright for my brother? She said because he's a boy and it's different, but I didn't really argue with her, I just left it.

Creating and Posting Images

To look deeper into this process of navigating norms of self-representation, we turned next to how images worked in social media apps on their phones. It's important to understand how these technological elements work and shape young people's experiences online. So rather than going in and directly asking young people what was risky, exploring the app usage with them in depth revealed where and how the apps were opening them up to risk in ways they often didn't realise or pay any attention to. These technological features are the affordances of social media applications that shape, facilitate and limit user experiences.

Given some schools' policies of Wi-Fi restriction, and also issues of deprivation, a few young people did not have phones, and many did not have access to data. In this school 2 boys related not having phones in the focus group.

Given young people would not necessarily be able to or want to share their digital images, we also used participatory and arts-based methodologies, asking young people to draw their social media experiences using social media drawing templates we prepared (Fig. 2.2).

Using the social media templates was very important and novel in *recreating* some typical content that they received, particularly if it was disappearing content from Snapchat that they no longer had access to. The opportunity to create and share visual data provided a mechanism for the participants to draw and quite literally, '*show* and tell' their experiences of receiving and sharing images, in ways that offered up different understandings than interview talk. The drawing methodology enabled us to explore the specificity of content shared and received, as well as

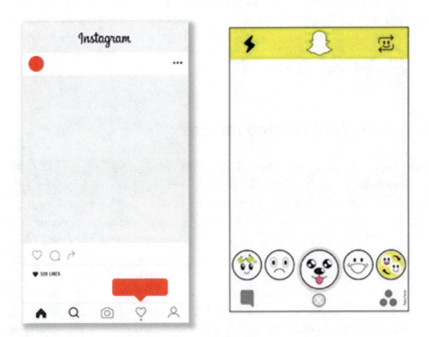

Fig. 2.2 Templates for participants to use in drawing social media images

capture disappearing media like Snapchat images (which disappear after 10 seconds).

What we found was that all the girls in this group used Snapchat and Instagram with some of them avid users, but the way that they used the platforms differed. On Instagram, they noted using caution:

> Calli: Because I feel like when you post something online it's going to be on there for like a very long time, like even with Instagram accounts, when we was in primary school you know how many like different ones you had.

> Diamond: I remember when I could search my name on Google and I found all my pictures from Instagram on there.

Instagram, seen as more of an archive, is treated with more care, and one girl notes that she had not posted anything on there for over two years. Unfortunately, one of the main messages of this book is that platforms operate differently and therefore create different risks. So whereas Instagram, as a permanent visual display app with carefully cultivated feeds, was treated with caution in this school, the girls had very different attitudes to their main communication platform, Snapchat, as we explore in depth below.

Connectivity: Quick Adds, Snapscores and Shoutouts

We found that on Snapchat, young people often add unknown users by assuming they are friends of friends and they do so in order to increase their Snapchat scores because of the game-like functions of the platform. Young people told us there was a lot of emphasis on generating higher scores through amassing more followers on Snapchat. This was one of the first things discussed in this group around their online networks and relationships, as they discussed the ways that their peers would try to generate more contacts and followers on Snapchat through a process called 'Shoutouts'. Shout-for-shout-out (SFS) was a process of sharing one another's Snapcodes to help their friends gain more connections on Snapchat. One girl, Alisha, excitedly discussed getting more views, adds and contacts through shout outs, while another girl, Janelle, was more cautious and said: 'I don't really open shout out messages, because I don't shout people out.'

Sensing something significant and trying to get to the bottom of their strong feelings about Shoutouts, the interviewer asked if they could share a Shoutout, at which they collectively agreed to share several of Alisha's images. Alisha's phone, typical of teen girls, has bunny ears phone cover, and the first shout out image she shares is of her face in her school uniform with tie and blazer. Pink hearts were superimposed on it and her 'snapcode' identifier is visible on the image. Another was of herself in designer jeans, Timberlake boots and a crop top to show her life outside of school.

Young people do Shoutouts because the more connections you have the higher your Snapscore (Snapchat's user engagement metric), a score which can be connected to visible popularity. Snapchat has a quick add feature. Users appear in a quick add list if they share a mutual friend or 'another connection' and can be added based on the supposed connections they share. So if the young person doesn't know the quick add, they are merely a suggestion to increase their network based on who other children have added already. This feature allows users to create virtual connections with large networks of known, unknown and semi-known users. Young people described how they frequently received requests from unknown users, and also commonly accepted those requests. The quick adds promote speed of accepting contacts and therefore reduce the ability to monitor and control who is adding you, and we see how young people accept unknown contacts, who can turn out to be 'full grown adults' in the words of the students. As the Year 10 girls say, even if an account is on private, with quick add someone can be added who is a friend of a friend.

An Open Gateway for Adult Predators

Next, the girls turned to explaining some of the immediate responses they had gotten to shout out posts and quick ads. After having her photo shouted out Alisha told us:

> Alisha: Somebody sent me messages like saying wanna trade? And at first I didn't know what trading meant, and they was like send each other things. I just blocked them.

In another case a girl noted getting sent penis streaks (streak is a video sent on Snapchat) after being shouted out:

> Calli: So I was opening like streaks and I just saw it, I didn't know what it was at first because it was unclear, so I replayed the video and the person must have thought that I liked it or something, because he kept texting me after that, then I was thinking what are you doing? Because it was a grown man. And then I just blocked him afterwards because I was disgusted.

> Interviewer: And what was in the video?

> Calli...He was sending pictures of his...dick I think, I couldn't think of the word for it, yeah, and then he showed his face in the video as well.

They went on to explain that Snapchat had two types of streaks: a still image and a video:

> Patrice: Yeah, when you tap it they send nudes, for example if it's a picture they'll send just the dick but if it's purple they'll probably send them masturbating.

Immediately following shout outs on Snapchat, girls are receiving unwanted sexual images of penises or videos of masturbating and having to field this content and learn strategies to deal with it, including in the case above blocking the sender. Going around the room we learned that seven out of seven of the girls had received this type of unwanted content from 'randoms.' Importantly the shout out images clearly identify the girls as teenagers, with one of them dressed in a school uniform. The technical process involved is that once you open a streak, then the person can see that it has been opened, which can be viewed as an acceptance and encourage further material being sent. Calli recounts having to deal with the same sender multiple times:

> Calli: And then, so when that happens I tell them to stop sending them to me, because I haven't added them back, so I tell them to stop sending it to me, and for example one time I told them to stop sending them to me and they asked me why, and I said because I don't want to see it, and then he was like you don't like it, and I was like no. And then the conversation stopped, but then he sent it the next day, so I blocked him. Yeah, that happens.

Here, Calli explains a process where she has to patiently explain why she doesn't want to be sent images of penises and masturbation videos. Diamond continued:

> Diamond: they'll pop up and they'll put like heart eyes or something like that, or like the aubergine emoji, stuff like that, and then they will start sending you nudes and stuff like that, and saying do you like it, or stuff like that.
>
> Calli: They would ask you to rate them sometimes.
>
> Diamond: Rate them. The dick basically.

Here the girls relate a tactic of sometimes being asked to rate the sender's penis, which relates to normalised porn dynamics of men comparing the size of their penises.

Bearing in mind that this was the very first research interview in our study, the researchers were a bit taken aback by what was being described and the sense of matter of fact-ness in the interview – of these processes being completely ordinary and girls having to manage these types of encounters regularly, so we asked next about frequency:

Interviewer: Can you give me any idea of how common this is?

Diamond: Quite common.

Janelle: Very common.

Alisha: It's mostly when you do shout for shout outs, for me.

Patrice: Yeah, that's when a lot of people add you.

Diamond: But it's not intended for them to send it, you just do it to get more views, like that. On Snapchat as well you add people back all the time.

Alisha: We don't really concentrate.

Diamond: Don't think about all that.

Alisha: Especially when you just see names, like a lot of people on my Snapchat are friends of friends as well as my friends.

The affordances of Snapchat create the conditions through which girls receive a range of unwanted sexual content. Shoutouts are a practice to build your network and get more followers and a higher score point and more streaks. Quick adds are accepted without checking because of assumptions about knowing individuals' 'friends of friends' or 'mutuals'. These processes happen organically as part of participating in the platform culture of Snapchat; the girls say they 'don't concentrate', 'don't think about it', 'I just add them'. That is, until they are faced with being harassed and having to remove the harasser from their contacts.

Turning to the focus group with boys, which was happening down the hall; they gave similar types of accounts of posting selfies. They had discussions about choosing images to post because they liked the light in the photo or it showed them with a new 'trim' (hair cut), or stylish clothes. They also explained doing Shoutouts on Snapchat and they similarly did get sexual content sent to them across Snapchat but also through Instagram messages and on Playstation 4 (PS4) gaming sites.

38   J. Ringrose and K. Regehr

However, the sexual content that the boys are receiving is different: it is links for them to go to another site to buy services. The images are sent as a titillation and hook to get them to engage with the account, therefore a precursor to sextortion. It is also significant that none of the boys, as we went on to discover through the project, had fallen victim to this or clicked onto these group chats or links; perhaps due to a shared understanding of the risks. As we found in this first set of interviews, this phishing was treated as a joke by the boys.

> Troy: When you go on PS4 people go on there yeah, some random hack, and PS4 Girl, eighteen or something, and then they'll text you and it'll be can you call me, and they'll send you a link to a website and you need to use your credit card to facetime them.

> Will: Fraudsters.

> Interviewer: Is that something you've seen on PS4 as well?

> Troy: Happened like six times. (Year 10, boys).

The boys laughed about receiving this 'fraudster' content, stating that it was clear that they were bots and not real people. The boys also reported blocking porn push content more quickly and readily than the girls were able to block unwanted sexual images and messages, which were experienced as more harassing.

15-year-old girls faced a different dynamic as they are often sent the material right away, whether this is the erect penis or the man masturbating. The difference between the partial nude sent to the boy meant to push him to buy sex services, and a masturbation video sent to a girl, is significant. The image/video is not sent to the girl with the goal of getting her to sign up for sex services. Rather it is sent with several possible motivations, one of which is as a form of assault experienced by the receiver. There is sense that the penis is being weaponized through these interactions.

> Diamond: there was this one man and he was texting me for months, like just texting, and I was ignoring it, like I'd half slide it and then just ignore

it, and then he started sending videos and stuff, so obviously I opened it. It was him like masturbating and doing stuff with his dick …he was like a grown man, he was in his twenties, thirties, but he was from a different country I think.

Alisha: It's most people from America on my phone. (Year 10, girls).

The half slide that Diamond is speaking about is a way to partly open the video but try not to alert the sender to the fact, as they are notified once you watch it, which could be interpreted as a sign of being interested. Rather than block the man right away, which is likely due to gendered behavioural norms like not being aggressive and not wanting to be mean, Diamond does not block the man until months have passed and she has received multiple videos.

The girls say the senders are typically 'grown men' in their 20s and 30s, sometimes from other countries (e.g. if you make contacts in the US there is a greater chance of getting these messages). Diamond surmised that men specifically target younger girls because they are easier to 'take advantage of':

Diamond: Because most of them know who you are, because they added it from a Shoutout, so if they clearly can see you're a child, it's grown men, and they see you're a child, and they're sending these type of images, then they could be trying to take advantage of us. Yeah, like they could be expecting that as we're young they must like be thinking oh they're young, will send it back, or we are gonna respond. Like we're stupid or something. Yeah.

on Snapchat – I've Seen It All!

However, it is also significant that we found the same dynamic with the Year 8 group at this school who were aged 12–13. We carried out this focus group a month later due to shortages on the rooms. Mrs. Keating again had trouble getting us rooms to conduct our research interviews so we ended up putting the girls and boys focus groups together in the school library at the same time as a group were being tutored in Spanish—not ideal for audiotaping an interview but evocative of the lively context of this school. The combined mixed gendered group included twelve 13–14-year-old's (8 girls and 4 boys). They were boisterous and candidly discussed their experiences on social media apps, while Mrs. Keating sat nearby, doing lesson prep, coming over and shushing them occasionally when they became overly rambunctious.

These young people reported sexually explicit content coming up through the Snapstory feed as soon as they started using the app:

Jada…yeah, and they'll swipe up, add you, and you know when you're just tapping through people's story, you'll get onto one where people put it in their story,…They'll play with their pee pee [penis] and it's like a thirty second video.

Chantelle, I must have been surfing through stories, and there was a guy called X, I don't know if it's a girl or boy, but you know them toy dildos? Yeah? A girl, I saw a girl and a dildo and she was going up and down.

Donte: That's mostly pornography

Dionne: I've seen it all.

Bryant: Explicit content.

Dionne: Miss, you know those pages, like actually post things like that, like they post sex videos, or maybe um…

Jada: A girl doing something with a boy.…it's explicit pictures, and it's not like people actually follow it [the Instagram page] to see that content, like they're basically just posting porn.

Bryant: So you're just following a porn account basically.

Dionne: Yeah! (Year 8, Mixed).

2 South East Community College: Youth Social Media ...   41

We can see in this rather chaotic and animated discussion with 12–13-year-olds how the young people are eager to explore some of the ways they have encountered explicit content. As one says, they accept contacts on Snapchat and then recieve content from those new contacts and come across unexpected material on Snapstories like male masturbation videos. They describe it as 'playing with their pee pee' in language that shows their young age. Another one says knowledgeably they've 'seen it all'; another notes some Instagram accounts are 'basically' porn.

The drawing activities undertaken by the group proved very important in documenting some of the experiences they were discussing. We encouraged young people to reflect on the experiences they shared, which they drew and devised advice around, by saying how they responded to the situation or what they thought could be done. For instance, Dionne, aged 12, as she drew her image, described feeling 'scared' and 'uncomfortable' when she received her first unsolicited dick pic from a stranger:

> Dionne: I was at my nan's house, because my nan watches Pointless, and stuff like that, and I can't be arsed to watch Pointless so I was just on my phone. I was scared. My dad was sitting next to me, so I was just like…LAUGHS…my dad was sitting next to me, like I don't want him to see this. I cried
>
> Interviewer: What did you do?
>
> Dionne: I was swearing down the phone, so uncomfortable.
>
> Jada: Word. (Year 8, Mixed).

Another year eight girl (aged 12) recounts her first experience of being contacted by video on Snapchat by a random man (see Fig. 2.3).

> Chantelle: So I was at home, in my room, and I get a video call from a guy, and he was rubbing his belly, but it was a girl account. He just showed me his face. He opened up his top and started rubbing his belly. And he was like do you want me to open my trousers? And I just blocked him.

Interviewer: And what was that through?.. And then also like what you did when you got that, what decisions did you make?

Chantelle: I blocked. He had a hairy stomach, he was not cute at all, or fresh.

Romy: Oh!

Chantelle: I don't get scared, I just think of how demented they must be, and how sad their life must be too. (Year 8, Mixed).

Chantelle goes on to explain that the sender is an 'old man' and refers to the experience as 'pedophilia,' saying the man was using a girl's account. This exemplifies the ways in which Snapchat, as well as other social media platforms, facilitates image-based sexual harassment and abuse by allowing users to create accounts that hide their true identities. Chantelle went on to explain that the man was persistent and contacted her a second time from another account. This time she tells her mum and blocks the second account.

These excerpts and drawings illustrate the common trend of girls initially feeling disturbed and shocked when they first receive this unwanted content; they block, and then seemingly overcome this fear with displays of bravado and self-empowerment. This type of content is also constant, as Chantelle mentions porn being sent to her 'three hours ago'. Blocking is a strategy but awareness of the possibility of reporting to the platform or an adult is not apparent in these drawings.

In their own discussion, the year 10 girls considered people's motives:

Diamond: I think you've got online world and you have real life world, so in the real life world men aren't probably getting as much attention as they would like, or they're lonely, or they don't get enough pleasure …and they go to the online world, so they can, it's more easier to get pleasure and talk to people, it's more like they don't know who you are, so… That's a double life. (SECC, Year 10, Girls).

The girls reason that these men are bored and want attention. They cannot get attention in real life so they turn to the internet. The young

Fig. 2.3 Chantelle's drawing 'He got blocked like the speed of light', 'explicit content 3 hours ago'

people often framed these adult men as predatory to them as children but they had no analysis of how such behaviour is also 'harassing'. The implication is that if they were adults then this type of behaviour would be okay. This issue of age was important, and we wanted to drill down into whether things were different in relation to consent with young people of their same age. Were girls also receiving dick pics from their peers? Did they know them? What did boys have to say about these dynamics?

Peer-to-Peer Images: Trust, Risk and Gendered Sexual Shame

While the above discussions shed light on how the social media platform Snapchat opens young people up to distressing content from adult strangers through a range of features, the main point of the platform from the teens' perspective was to interact with their peers through daily streaks and snaps, amassing score points, and keeping in touch with their network. How then did consent shape these interactions with their peers?

First, we want to emphasise, as we saw above when they excitedly shared the images they created for 'shout outs', that young people are deeply interested in their self images and how they are using these productions to interact with their friend groups. When it came to sharing nude images, both the girls and boys started off discussing how it was a natural part of relationships, which could signal 'closeness'. Indeed, we found almost verbatim the same discussion about nudes in the year 10 girl and boy interviews, which were being held concurrently in different classrooms.

The boys discussed with the researchers that 'sharing pictures' is a normal part of relationships:

Jordon: In a lot of relationships it happens.

Anton: Yeah. If they're secure with each other, and sexual together, they'll send a couple of pictures, but if they've just got together… (SECC, Year 10, Boys).

2 South East Community College: Youth Social Media ...   45

The boys relate that exchanging images is a normal route in relationships and related to trust and intimacy. The girls down the hall, said almost exactly the same thing:

> Interviewer: So that's what I'm also trying to understand, we are, um…when does that become something that one might want to do in their relationship?

> Alisha: When there's enough trust.

> Diamond: When you feel comfortable enough, … (Year 10, Girls).

What quickly became evident, however, is how challenging it was for girls to have trust, given the many cases of girls' images being shared on further without consent. Below are two stories recounted by the year 10 girls:

> Calli: I know this girl, she sent a picture of herself in a bra to these two boys, and said oh it was supposed to be for my cousin, to see if she liked the bra that I was wearing that I bought.

> Janelle: That's stupid.

> Calli: And she ended up moving schools… the person she sent it to told other people, and showed, I think, one or two boys, and they were just saying God she has nothing, and basically making fun of her as well.

> Charlotte: In my sister's year when they were in year eight a girl sent a picture of her boobs like, to this boy and they sent it around their year group and everyone saw it, and now that's what she gets called, a ho, a slut, for sending it. (SECC, Year 10, Girls).

Girls also had sophisticated understandings about why their images would be shared without consent, explaining some of the motivations and impacts of these practices, noting that boys would 'take advantage' of girls to get images and then to 'embarrass them' or 'to blackmail', and boys are rewarded for this abusive behaviour:

Diamond: ...some boys brag to their friends... you see this girl, she sent me nudes, and their friends would be like wow, well done, like they get praised for it basically.

Janelle: The girls get shamed for it.

Calli: Yeah, the girls get shamed

Alisha: While the boys get praised.

Janelle: And then it leaves like the girls, there is a couple, in the school there has been things that's said, and girls get labelled because of stuff like this.

Interviewer: What do they get labelled?

Alisha: Like as hos, as j-bags, as...

Interviewer: A j-bag? What's a j-bag?

Charlotte: It's basically like a ho.

Patrice: Boys have a friendship group, and the girl goes around each and every person of the friendship group, that's when you say a j-bag... (Year 10, Girls).

As we saw earlier in this chapter the girls are acutely aware of sexual double standards that apply to them offline, but also in the online space. They confirm through multiple rapid-fire stories, that although they wish for trusting relationships and for their images to be treated with respect, creating and sending sexual images is always extremely risky for them. Their discussion points to unequal gendered power relations in the wider culture. Images of female and male bodies hold different value and therefore pose different risks. Girls acting sexually and engaging in sending pictures as part of sexual activity is much riskier than for boys. As the girls clearly say, boys are 'praised' if they are seen to be engaging in digital sexual interaction, particularly if they have *proof* through images.

However, they explain that when girls' images are shared without consent it's the girls that are sexually 'shamed'.

Digging into the etymology of J-bag on Urban Dictionary, the J refers to jezzy or jezebel, a well-worn sexual slur, which is also racialized and was used widely in context of slavery in USA (Gilman, 1985). This is refashioned into j-bag, with same intent to sexually shame girls and importantly this is happening in racially specific ways, something highlighted by recent analysis of misogynoir (the combination of racism and misogyny in contemporary culture) (Bailey, 2021). Interestingly, if a girl sends a nude this is discussed as equivalent to a girl 'going around' or sexually engaging with a boy's friendship group. Having multiple partners signals lack of purity and innocence, and the same sexual slur is used against girls who've been exposed as sending nudes. Looking closely at the moral understandings of the teen girls, we can see the girls clearly identify blackmail, intent to embarrass and reputational gain as the motivating factors for boys to share intimate images of girls without consent; their grasp of these dynamics is sophisticated but they are also pointing to the unique racialized slurs operating in their peer groups, which need to be taken into consideration when we are talking about unique challenges facing girls of colour (Lamb et al., 2016).

The year 10 boys were also well aware of these dynamics operating in their local peer networks:

Interviewer: So you all said you have seen a picture that someone's passed around of a girl's body.

Jamie: Yeah.

Interviewer: How frequently, is that like a one-off or has it been a few times, or..?

Jamie: Every day.

Interviewer: Every day, really?

Kwasi: Yeah, and certain, like depends, if you have like thousands of people watching your story that means more people are gonna be sending it in.

Interviewer: So how are those pictures of girls' bodies that are shared without their consent, treated by people?

Kwasi: They just get mocked.

Jamie: Yeah, they get verbally assaulted.

Interviewer: How, what do people say?

Omar: People call them hoes and sluts and stuff. (Year 10, Boys).

In this discussion the boys are discussing sexual images shared with boys that are then reshared without consent onto the boys' Snapstory and then captured and reposted a dynamic that creates a wide spread of non-consensual intimate imagery we will see throughout this book. The boys also talked about an Instagram site called X Hoes (X is the area they live in) where images of women were non-consensually posted, the defining feature was the women were apparently from their local area, which is an attempt to locate and shame them, a classic definition of 'revenge porn' (using intimate images to shame women and girls). At the time of the research, these revenge porn accounts were common and the boys had seen images of girls from the school posted on the page. They were, therefore, aware of sharp differences between girls and boys producing and sharing nude images in their local peer cultures in and around schools, with the risks greater for girls:

Interviewer: Is it different between, um, how often boys would share pictures in that situation, to how often girls share pictures in that situation?

Omar: Usually the girls send them, but certain girls get pressured.

Interviewer: Why do you think usually girls [are asked to] send more?

Omar: Because girls are less horny.

Jamie: Might get pressured.

Interviewer: Why would they send more if they're less horny?

Marcus: Because their man asked them for some.

Omar: They don't really want it that way.

Jamie: They don't want no nudes from the man basically.

Omar: Obviously they'll want it, yeah, but like they don't really, I can't explain.

Interviewer: When you say less horny, are you saying because the men are more horny so they want pictures more?

Omar: Yeah. (Year 10, Boys).

We can see that the boys are aware of girls in their school being pressured; and it is 'certain' girls those who are deemed more likely to respond who become more targeted. The boys discuss being horny which motivates them wanting nudes from girls, but state that the opposite is not true, girls are understood as 'less horny', have lower sex drives, and will not send nude images without being asked. This is the rationale that is used to justify boys asking girls to send nudes which the boys recognise as pressure but also see as normal and legitimate. We can see the baseline of a moral rationality of entitlement that normalises harassing behaviour. While the boys are critical of this behaviour, saying if boys 'send around' an image to 'embarrass' a person it's a 'lack of maturity', it is still presented as a matter of fact and not necessarily something to be challenged.

As we saw above, the boys were also completely aware that girls tend not to ask for or want images of their body parts; and this caused some embarrassment and drawing back of discussion. When the interviewer pressed them to discuss boys sending provocative images such as 'of their belt' as a precursor to a full nude, Jamie started explaining but Omar jumped in cutting him off, saying 'It's recording fam, what the hell!' This shows an important moment where boys are reluctant to discuss these issues for fear of reprisal. The interviewers assured the boys that everything would remain anonymous, and indeed changed tack in line with ethical principles to be youth driven in our explorations. The interruption is an important reminder that young people were wary about sharing some of these issues in what is often a punitive context in school. The realities of them being fearful to speak to adults about these issues remained palpable and is something we want to bring to the reader's attention and to find strategies to address in this book.

Throughout our study, we did encounter moments where some groups of boys would consistently deflect discussion through strategies like the above. We worked on creating a sense of safety and rapport so that they could discuss their views, which we felt was key in understanding contemporary social norms. We paid attention to defensive dynamics of the boys through our analysis, because these norms can legitimate violence, something that needs to be addressed at a wider cultural level.

Indeed we understood and were prepared for masculine defensiveness around discussing these issues, given the ways that schools approach issues of sexuality through shame, and perpetration through silence or punishment. Given this context, we were keen to keep dialogue open, and we were often able to break through silence to productive discussions about these topics.

Returning to the year 10 girls, they were more forthcoming and explained to us that the only reason a boy in their peer network at school would send a nude is that they want to get an image back:

Diamond: But I think boys our age, if they are going to send it to someone they'll probably most likely do it on purpose, yeah, and…

Calli: They expect something back.

Alisha: Yeah, that's exactly what it is.

The girls also discussed having a radically different sense of care around boys' images if they did get sent, when we asked them how they would treat a boy's dick pic:

> Interviewer: OK. So let's say that they had exchanged images, so the girl has an image of the boy's parts, and the boy has the girl's parts, would the girl do anything with the boy's parts?
>
> Janelle: Most likely no.
>
> Alisha: No.
>
> Interviewer: Why is that?
>
> Janelle: Because like say for example if a girl, girls are more like, when girls get in relationships they trust, like they trust more than the boy, like we trust.
>
> Diamond: More than the boys. So where the boys, if you broke up or something the boys would probably expose you, or show their friends, send it to their friends. With the girls they'd keep it to themselves like.
>
> Calli: Or just delete it.
>
> Alisha: Because they still care about them kind of thing, yeah. (SECC, Year 10, Girls).

The girls describe either keeping an image to themselves or deleting it. This differs dramatically from what we saw with the boys' relationship to images of women's bodies, where it was common sense that images would be shared and often with the express attempt to embarrass and shame girls. The girls are modelling a sense of care and trust around images that is common sense to them; they have not been taught this response but it has emerged from their sense of morality as a girl (Brown & Gilligan, 1992). While such an ethics of care might not be universal and

52   J. Ringrose and K. Regehr

we cannot essentialise, the girls' socialisation into heterosexual womanhood is creating more care and respect for images of boys' bodies than they have learned to expect in relation to girls' and women's bodies.

These dynamics of care are further evident if we take a closer look at an episode with a teen boy from their school in some depth. Diamond and Alisha discussed going away on holiday with one of their families to the beach. They discussed how posting your body is OK when you are away on holiday, or at the beach. They say that you should be able to post a bikini because you are at the beach; you are not simply asking for attention, as with the image they discussed earlier of a girl sending some boys a picture in her bra. Shortly after discussing this they mention that a boy in their year sent them a picture of his penis 'by accident' while they were away together:

Interviewer: By accident?

Alisha: Yeah, because straight after he blocked us, because he didn't realise he was sending it.

Interviewer: So who had he intended to send it to?

Diamond: I don't know, he blocked me, so I didn't ask. he sent it to more than one person, so I'm not sure, but then he blocked us afterwards and said it wasn't meant to go to us.

Alisha: I was confused. I didn't know why he sent it.

Diamond: I just asked if anyone received anything from the person

Diamond: If they said yes then I'd ask if they got blocked as well, and I spoke to him about it and he said it wasn't meant to be sent to us.... He was embarrassed. It was unexpected, because I don't really speak to him. (Year 10, Girls).

The girls are both sent a dick pic at the same time when they are on holiday together and shortly afterwards they are blocked from the sender's account. Because the image is sent to them both they ask other girls in their Snapchat network to see if they were also sent one and blocked. The girls say they are confused and discuss the incident later at school, where the boy explains the images were not intended to be sent to them. There is a sense of protecting the boy, of feeling sorry for him. What is important here is the ethics of care that the girls show around an episode of sexting gone wrong. Whereas we heard numerous reports of girls' images being saved and spread, these girls are more concerned about the boy. They approach him and try to discuss it with him. We need to build on the care and respect being modelled by teen girls like Diamond and Alisha. These provide alternatives to a rush to criminalise and punish youthful experimentations, they offer us a way forward as to how schools might also encourage discussion and care in relation to these issues.

The Need for Better Digital Sex Education

In the final section of the chapter, we want to discuss the final portion of the interviews, when young people filled in the social media template drawings to elaborate on the discussions we'd had and illustrate some of the scenarios they'd shared. As we saw earlier, the drawing time enabled the young people to explain further some of the distressing things that they had experienced, including receiving unwanted contacts and content. During these sessions we also asked the young people to explain what their schools were doing to address some of the issues they'd discussed and whether or not they felt that the sex education they had received about these digital issues was sufficient or not. Complaints about the sex education they were receiving were particularly strong in the older groups, who noted they had not gotten sufficient information about digital sex education issues.

Omar: Yeah, sex education is a joke. Whatever.

Jamie: They say people, girls send nudes, like we don't know that. But maybe you could write some advice about how to be safe or like have fun or whatever using the different apps.

54 J. Ringrose and K. Regehr

Kwasi: Common sense.

Omar: Don't send random stuff to people, what the hell, what's the matter with you? (Year 10, Boys).

The year 10 boys tell us sex education is a joke and it appears they are creating messaging for boys not to send random stuff around.

The girls say similarly that they've had school assemblies on 'sexting', about not sending nudes, which wasn't helpful:

Janelle: We have a police officer, that comes into school, and just says that it's illegal to do it, but they don't really explain the consequences or risks of what you're actually doing. They are just saying it's illegal and you shouldn't be doing it, but they are not really helping to understand.

Interviewer: If a nude of you was leaked around would you go to the police, or the school?

Alisha: No.

Patrice: No.

Diamond: Because they said it's illegal so you'll feel like you're doing something wrong as well, so you wouldn't really go for help, even though that could help, you'll be scared.

Janelle: The policeman in our school doesn't help with anything. (Year 10, Girls).

The girls explain here how the abstinence approach isn't helping them to understand, and it also creates fear and a sense of doing something wrong which means they are left feeling unsupported. They also noted that the mass assembly format was a problem:

Alisha: Yeah, so it'll be like everyone's there, not really small groups, so lots of people will be laughing about it and making jokes, not really taking it serious, as it would be in a small group. (Year 10, Girls).

2 South East Community College: Youth Social Media ... 55

We will see in further chapters that this approach to discussing issues of digital sexuality in large groups can be counterproductive.

In addition to aiming to prevent image-based sexual harassment and abuse through education, focus groups discussed lowering the age at which they learn topics related to digital sex education. According to year 10 girls, digital sex education should start at Year 5 because the age of sexting is dropping. They expressed concern about a younger sibling managing these social media contexts, which we will also pick up in subsequent chapters.

Diamond: To be honest I think it's going down, like the age is going down.

Patrice: Yeah, younger.

Charlotte: Because I see like year sevens show off their bodies.

Tiffany: My sister, she come home one day and she told me a story of a boy like he had took a picture, and they're only in year six [11 years old]. she said it was going around the WhatsApp group, and like she thought it was funny and stuff... but I was like whoa, a year six boy knows stuff like that. When I was in year six I didn't know to do stuff like that.

Interviewer: So it was of his parts, the picture.

Tiffany: Yeah.

Alisha: Feel like when you're younger as well you don't really understand the consequences of what you're doing.

Interviewer: So when do you think that schools should start educating young people?

Diamond: Year five and six.

Interviewer: Year five and six?

56   J. Ringrose and K. Regehr

Janelle: Yeah, because in my primary school we did sex education and everything but we didn't really talk about the importance of social media, and to be honest all we talked about was hormones, basically and puberty.

Calli: When we was in primary school it wasn't that deep.

Charlotte: We never really used social media that much when we was in primary, it wasn't that popular, but it's got more popular now. (Year 10, Girls).

In the above passage we see how private message groups like WhatsApp are used to screenshot and share images of young people more widely than original senders, in this case an 11-year-old boy's nude of 'his parts'. The girls are clear that these issues are happening earlier and earlier and that the best way to deal with this would be to educate younger people earlier.

The girls discuss needing to include social media in sex education in Year 5, which is under 10 years old. Janelle continued, adamant that education needed to start younger so teens would know their rights:

Janelle: I don't think that most teenagers know what a sexual assault can be, so they'll be like, they're thinking that oh, say a boy touched them inappropriately and they didn't enjoy it, they felt uncomfortable, but they are thinking they can't do anything...about it because...

Callie: They think it's normal.

Janelle: Yeah, it's normal, or they didn't do anything, and that is sexual assault, but most teenagers don't know that, so they don't do anything about it, and they just leave it. And they're feeling bad. I don't know what every single sexual assault is, I don't know what you could define it as.

Interviewer: OK, and this is really interesting, and it's not unrelated, because do you think that some of the things that happen online are a form of online sexual harassment?

Janelle: Yes. (Year 10, Girls).

In this excerpt, Janelle contends that most people her age do not have awareness around what online sexual harassment and abuse are because of lack of education on these topics. She went on to draw the following mind map about how schools need to address online sexual assault in sex education.

In Janelle's (year 10) Online Sexual Assault and Sex Education Mind Map (Fig. 2.4) she spells out that what is needed is better sex education which covers what happens online, including: sending unwanted pictures, wanting parents to talk more to kids about this and having police tell them what to do in situations, rather than simply scare young people. The mind map is called Online Sexual Assault, which shows a shift to understanding that these processes can constitute abuse, as she and her classmates demonstrated in great depth in their interview.

Conclusion: Now There are Feminists

This chapter started with the Year 10 girls critically interacting with everyday visual images of women's and men's bodies, identifying the types of sexual double standards that exist in society and how their bodies as girls were treated differently than those of their male peers and siblings. As Diamond pointed out early on: 'it's not fair'.

We also found that these unequal sexualised dynamics in society put the girls at greater risk online. We learned about the everyday encounters of receiving unwanted sexual content on the platform Snapchat. Platform affordances like Snapchat Shoutouts enabled adult predators to find and harass teens. Snapchat's game-like features encourage high interaction with the platform through repeated streaks to gain a high 'snapscore'; and we saw young people opening themselves up to harm by turning off privacy settings and default modes on the apps to enable quick adds. Even though the young people demonstrated high digital literacy about their images on posting platforms like Instagram, the apparently ephemeral nature of Snapchat lulled them into practices which created contexts they had to swiftly learn to manage.

Despite the type of bravado and messages like 'Be careful' 'Be cautious' (Fig. 2.5) in their drawings, where they gave tips on blocking and

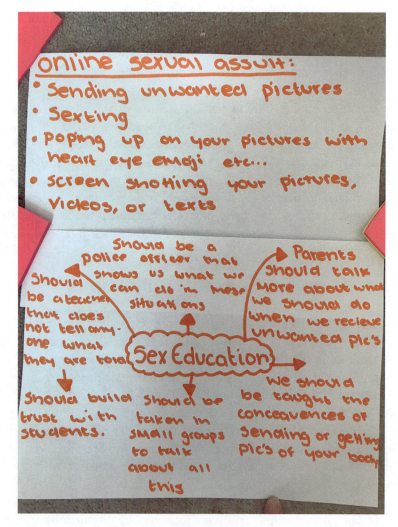

Fig. 2.4 Janelle's mind map for better sex education

reporting this content, we found through in-depth discussions that young people often struggled to block these predators, sometimes waiting months and rarely if ever reporting these episodes, as was confirmed in our survey findings about the shockingly low rates of reporting harm and abuse online.

Fig. 2.5 Examples of warnings drawn on the templates

When it came to peer-to-peer dynamics, we saw sexual double standards in full swing. Girls and boys acknowledged very different gendered dynamics emerging around the treatment of girls' nudes by boys and boys' nudes by girls. Whereas boys called non-consensual sharing of girls' images 'immature', they were witnessing 'revenge porn' sites in their digital media networks, including a site called X Hoes based on their local area. We start to see how the physical neighbourhood and online network converge in ways that can create specific digital realities for youth, depending on where they live and go to school. Boys did not challenge such practices amongst one another, despite recognising to an extent that they were abusive.

Girls demonstrated a markedly different ethics of care around nude images of boys. The girls explained that they would keep to themselves (not share) or delete boys' nudes, because as they put it, girls cared more in their relationships. This became evident when Alisha and Diamond related an episode of an 'accidental' dick pic sent by a male peer at school. Rather than shame him, they approached the boy to discuss it with him at school despite the boy having blocked them on social media after it happened. We saw a responsible, ethical and caring approach from these 15-year-old girls which we suggest should be modelled and promoted in schools in relation to consent, as we'll discuss in the conclusion to this book.

Indeed, one of the main messages we would like to emphasise in relationship to this school is that despite technically failing and being in an area of high deprivation, the commitment of the teaching staff to create a space of safety and respect for discussion, with their supervision was notable. The dynamics of caring and respect modelled by the staff followed through to the teens, particularly the girls, and as we were leaving Janelle told us:

> I don't think in our generation it will ever be fair. I think everyone in this generation is basing stuff from the past, history, because you see how women were portrayed as a sex toy, or patriarchy where men controlled women, and how women were kind of a lower, like men were more superior basically, so people are more judging of a girl. But now there are like feminists and people who speak up for women and their rights.

As we saw earlier, Janelle explained passionately that teenagers needed a better understanding of online sexual assault, to know how to respond, and as we left the interview, she reminded us about feminism and women's rights. Despite her sense that things will 'never be fair', Janelle gave us hope as researchers that young people are finding their way through these inequitable conditions of 'patriarchy' in their online worlds, at school and at home. We will return to these issues of gender equity and youth empowerment throughout this book.

References

Bailey, M. (2021). *Misogynoir transformed. Black women's digital resistance.* NYU Press.

Brown, L. M., & Gilligan, C. (1992). *Meeting at the crossroads: Women's psychology and girls' development*. Harvard University Press.

Bruns, A. (2006). Towards produsage: Futures for user-led content production. In *Proceeding of the 5th International Conference on Cultural Attitudes towards Technology and Communication*. School of Information Technology, Australia, pp. 275–284.

Gilman, S. L. (1985). Black bodies, white bodies: Toward an iconography of female sexuality in late nineteenth-century art, medicine, and literature. *Critical Inquiry, 12*(1), 204–242. http://www.jstor.org/stable/1343468

Gilman, S. (1986). Black bodies, white bodies: Toward an iconography of female sexuality in late nineteenth century art, medicine, and literature. In H. L. Jr. Gates (Ed.), *Race, writing, and difference* (pp. 223–261). University of Chicago Press.

Lamb, S., Roberts, T., & Plocha, A. (2016). *Girls of color, sexuality, and sex education*. Palgrave.

Open Access This chapter is licensed under the terms of the Creative Commons Attribution-NonCommercial-NoDerivatives 4.0 International License (http://creativecommons.org/licenses/by-nc-nd/4.0/), which permits any noncommercial use, sharing, distribution and reproduction in any medium or format, as long as you give appropriate credit to the original author(s) and the source, provide a link to the Creative Commons license and indicate if you modified the licensed material. You do not have permission under this license to share adapted material derived from this chapter or parts of it.

The images or other third party material in this chapter are included in the chapter's Creative Commons license, unless indicated otherwise in a credit line to the material. If material is not included in the chapter's Creative Commons license and your intended use is not permitted by statutory regulation or exceeds the permitted use, you will need to obtain permission directly from the copyright holder.

3

Lion's Co-educational Independent Boarding School: How Highly Selective School Status Shapes Digital Sexual Cultures and Identities

Lion's Independent School is a highly selective day and boarding secondary school. London-based celebrities send their children here as do some global elites, with those young people using the boarding option. Just outside of London in a neighbouring county, accessible via car and public transport, the school is far enough into the rural countryside to boast an impressive campus with a mix of Georgian stately architecture and state of the art new buildings. Altogether we were a team of 4, with Kaitlyn and Jessica joined by a man and woman facilitator from the sex education charity, with some of us driving to the campus and others arriving by train.

Driving in to the car park, the huge scale of the campus was evident, with buildings here and there connected by paths and surrounded by trees and green space. Having parked we were unclear where to go and asked some passing students, who directed us to an art installation across the campus as a marker for finding the reception building. We started walking but since it was taking a long time we asked for directions again and were told to keep going. We were amazed by the extensive manicured grounds, almost on the scale of a university campus. As we neared the

© The Author(s) 2025
J. Ringrose and K. Regehr, *Teens, Social Media, and Image Based Abuse*,
https://doi.org/10.1007/978-3-031-92322-7_3

64   J. Ringrose and K. Regehr

reception, we encountered two sixth form boys boisterously driving a kit car on the walking paths.

The green and open space of the campus, with students free to roam the grounds, was certainly an exceptional sight to encounter, entirely different from many of the state schools we were researching, as will be seen. Entering the school lobby, we were instructed to wait in a separate guest sitting room with glass bottles of water and snacks, complete with its own toilet renovated to high specification and fitted with bespoke luxury branded soap and hand lotion like an elite airline lounge. In the independent sector the foyer and toilets need to be impressive, as this is where prospective parents visit and form an impression of the school and whether to commit their considerable funds or not.

Our teacher host, Mrs. Pound, who oversaw personal and social health in year 8 at the school, graciously took us to lunch before we started the workshops. We were taken to an impressive dining hall, where we were given a delicious gourmet meal from the well-stocked canteen. Mrs. Pound regaled us with stories about the boarding students' elite overseas families and the celebrity parents shuttling their children to and from the campus. Later, we were given a complete campus tour that included viewing the brand-new multi-storey science and technology building, which had been sponsored by private and corporate donors. We were told this was where the boys had built the kit car we'd seen racing around the campus earlier. Overall, the school was extremely well resourced and the level of privilege we felt was acute.

Steps to Sexting: Avoidance through Humour

We interviewed two groups of year 8 students that the teacher had put into single gender groupings of girls and boys, with the male facilitator paired with Kaitlyn to conduct the interview with the boys. All the young people were 12–13 years of age. In the interviews with the boys, the interviewers found they were scathingly critical of selfie production as a feminine, 'girls" preoccupation. Some boys reported reluctance to post images of themselves altogether, telling us they didn't see any 'sense' in taking selfies. As Hugo explained, 'I would never willingly take a selfie.'

3 Lion's Co-educational Independent Boarding School ... 65

After explaining their aversion to selfies, the group continued by saying they would definitely not 'sext' or post explicit imagery online. Hugo, whose friends joked that he aspired to be prime minister, was convinced that he needed to protect his future identity as potentially a CEO of a major company.

> Hugo: Well there are, in the future, more recently, jobs are, people, like CEOs of companies…when people are coming to get jobs they'll look them up on social media and are trying to find positive things that will back their um, points, hire them into the company, but if they go on social media and they find like nudes on the internet, then the chances are the company won't hire them…there's always things get leaked through the internet in different ways, for example an Instagram post... if you look up the user name you can find them on the internet…Also I don't really see much point in it, because if you're gonna go that far and want to show off parts of your body I don't think it should be over social media, it's like I don't see the sense in it. (Lions, Year 8, Boys).

Here Hugo explains that from his position it doesn't make sense to put yourself on the internet or show your body. We can see this as a very privileged position where he sees no sense in using his body for such purposes because he has so many other options available to him. It's also obvious that the boys have received some e-safety awareness training about protecting their identities online. Hugo also appeared to produce the 'right answers' for the adults in the room, creating a careful mask through laughter and distraction to avoid saying anything about his own body or desires or likes at any point. Indeed, when the discussion of selfies turned to nudes he proclaimed:

> Hugo: uh a nude could probably be a sign of being sexually promiscuous in general public. For example nudes could always be classified as a sext, but not all sexts could be classified as nudes.

> Interviewer: OK, do you all agree with that?

> William: No.

Hugo: I think the point to get across is the kind of thing where all Kings are men, but not all men are Kings

Kyle: What are you on about?

Hugo: Or it could be considered like squares and rectangles, squares are always rectangles but rectangles are not squares.

LAUGHTER

Kyle: It just doesn't work. You cannot compare this to geometric shapes!!

David: No, no!!

LOUD LAUGHTER

William: Poor guy, it's not helping.

David: So I think he's trying to say, like I don't personally believe this, I think he's trying to say that all nudes are sexts, but not all sexts are nudes. (Lions, Year 8, Boys).

The conversation was interrupted by continuous laughter as the facilitators got the impression that the boys had never been asked to discuss this issue in any way that related to them personally. Hugo kept trying to move the discussion into the realm of formal logic on generalisations, eliciting laughter over his absurdity, that made the discussion difficult. Hugo also declared that anyone who sexts 'feels that it's necessary to be sexualised to be accepted in society' and the interviewers got the impression they were listening to an anti-sexting assembly being parroted back to them.

The interviewer persisted in trying to think get the boys to think about what could be happening in their day-to-day peer networks and to try to engage them about their perspectives on sexting:

Interviewer: So is sexting ever OK? Or you guys don't think it's OK?

3 Lion's Co-educational Independent Boarding School ... 67

Hugo: I don't think it's…

Wei: No.

Rohan: No.

Hugo: I think it's bad, it should be abolished

Interviewer: Abolished! The only way to abolish it is for someone to be constantly monitoring it, but how would you feel if someone was monitoring all your messages?

Hugo: That would be fine.

Interviewer: OK, so everyone in this room thinks that sexting should be abolished?

William: No.

Kyle: No

David: No.

Hugo: Yeah. (Lions, Year 8, Boys).

After Hugo declares a motion that nudes should be abolished and says he doesn't mind if all of his social media is monitored, we can see a very strong disagreement emerges between the boys, which is important to highlight. The facilitators felt they were dealing with vastly differing levels of maturity and comfort levels. Hugo was intent on shutting down the conversation, while other boys became keen on discussing what to do if they received unwanted sexual messages, which had happened to one of them:

William: I think it would be just quite confusing, I think I'd just like not reply for a bit and see what they say. Also you don't want to reply in case you say the wrong thing.

68   J. Ringrose and K. Regehr

Dave: Exactly

William: Not like you're a terrible person.

Rohan: No, just do the classic ... Sorry, my mum just called me, got to go, bye.

Kyle: My mum's called me!

David: This is falling to chaos!

Wei: Yeah. (Lions, Year 8, Boys).

At this point, sensing the boys' discomfort with having this conversation with a woman present, and the descent 'into chaos' described by David, Kaitlyn excused herself from the room for a comfort break. It was notable that after she left the boys opened up almost immediately with a more honest refrain with the male facilitator who asked the boys to reflect on their earlier comments about sexting and if they thought that they may change their mind about how they use social media when they are a bit older, to which they candidly replied:

William: Yes! Everybody gets more horny!

LAUGHTER

Kyle: Straight up, that is the answer.

Albert: It really is the answer.

David: Ninety nine percent of the changes...

Rohan: It's called hormones! (Lions, Year 8, Boys).

Having perhaps gotten their laughter and embarrassment out of their system, the boys went on to discuss their views more calmly:

3 Lion's Co-educational Independent Boarding School ...   69

William: I guess because the age of consent is sixteen certain people feel it's not right to do it before then, but also if people aren't in a relationship, because I, like I think, yeah, pretty much everyone in our year hasn't been in a relationship... like when you're thirteen it's not...

Albert: Actually, I think that like a lot of it comes from the younger age, if you make good friends with someone and you get comfortable about them, and then you like speak to them a lot. I think then you like sort of come to the idea of like I like to spend time with this person, I think it would make sense if I um be, making it like official, and then it carries on like that. (Lions, Year 8, Boys).

Whereas one boy frankly discusses the age of consent and being too young to sext; the other presents the idea that sexting could be a part of stages in a relationship, something they went on to debate further; noting that sexting and nudes should happen in the right context and not out of the blue:

William: If you were talking to someone in real life they wouldn't suddenly get undressed.

Albert Because it's not in context.

William: Almost slightly disturbing.

David: ...it's like going from step one to step seven.

Albert': What's step seven?

William: Sex.

Albert: What's step six?

David: I dunno. You think.

Albert: So what's step three?

Kyle: Yeah, what's step four?

Albert: Be like well I'm at step three.

David: Step three, find a girlfriend. Step two... (Lions, Year 8, Boys).

We see that with some careful negotiation the boys can more rationally discuss steps in relationships, and how and when sexting might happen and how they might react, noting that sexting could be a respectful and normal part of a relationships but it didn't have to be. The boys are also firm that they would want images to be sent with consent and with a mutual understanding.

Putting your Best Foot Forward: Elite Femininity, Consumption/Status Selfies and Nudes

It is notable that we found a dramatically different scenario with the girls. First of all the girls were keen to discuss their selfies. They were avid selfie takers and they showed selfies they'd taken around the school grounds as well as images of their pets and their leisure activities including holidays. Offering a very different set of leisure activities than the teens from poorer contexts, we saw a series of images of these girls aged 12–13 out shopping, taking a group mirror selfie at a party, sitting on a park bench and one shared a portrait of their dog. They also discussed using Snapchat filters for images (see Fig. 3.1) One notable selfie was shared by Tilly, which was a picture of her feet in pale blue converse trainers overlooking hills in Switzerland, taken while she was paragliding. Julie, similarly, drew her experience of posting herself surfing (see Fig. 3.1).

For girls like Tilly and Julia social media posts are already a way to convey wealth and luxury lifestyle (Cohen et al., 2022; Liu et al., 2019). It was also notable that Tilly had amassed 256 likes on her Instagram image of her paragliding, and that this 'status update' was shared as a relatively unremarkable element of her lifestyle amongst this group (Marwick, 2013). Unlike boys like Hugo, therefore, who proclaimed they would 'never knowingly take a selfie', these 13 year-old girls have public profiles, they are on display and as we went on to discover, their

3 Lion's Co-educational Independent Boarding School … 71

Fig. 3.1 Julia's drawing of posting surfing experience, using Snapchat filters and 'mug shot' on her private account with just friends

higher user engagement on sites like Snapchat and Instagram meant they were also receiving much more unexpected and unwanted sexual content.

When we turned to discussion of sexual images they had received, we also had a starkly different conversation to that with the boys. Right away three out of the eight girls in year 8 at this selective boarding school had already received dick pics from unknown senders on Snapchat. One girl also told us that she had been pressured by a peer to send nudes:

Tilly: I feel if it's anything I'd feel more girls [send nudes]

Georgia: Yeah, but I think it's more like for boys to ask for girls to send them though.

Julia: No, I feel like boys have to have that attitude where they're like a bit too...like a bit too cocky and stuff, and it's like not a big deal to them.

Tilly: But like for girls it could be like personal to them. You know?

Julia: I feel like a boy would send one and then ask, be like can you send one back? And then that's when a girl would send one back. (Lions, Year 8, Girls).

In contrast to the boys, the girls are operating Instagram and Snapchat accounts and already receiving unsolicited dick pics and some are also already being pressured to send nudes. The girls also note the sexual double standards we discussed in the previous chapter, noting that genital images are not as big of a deal for a boy and that dick pics in peer groups are primarily used as a proposition to 'get one back.' The transactional dick pics that we will see again and again throughout this study is where a genital image is sent with the aim of soliciting a nude back from a girl. We argue that transactional dick pics are a doubled form of harassment when they are sent without being asked for and are unwanted but also used to pressure girls to send an image back. This often puts girls in highly challenging situations, particularly if this happens amongst the known peer group, as we'll see later in this book.

3 Lion's Co-educational Independent Boarding School ... 73

Julia, who had experienced pressure to send a nude of herself, said she went to her sister for help. This is significant across our data, where we find that in the absence of adult support either at school or at home, many consult with older siblings or family members who are not yet adults but in a liminal space of being an older young person, who is seen as offering more understanding and support around issues of digital technology, in the face of the dramatic and often disproportionate responses which young people feel they get from adults.

When we asked these girls about the risk of sending photos of themselves they were also very concerned about getting caught, because their parents were monitoring their social media. As one of them put it, 'My parents would freak.' The girls in particular in this school were aware that their parents and siblings would be monitoring their accounts. They complained about this and had developed strategies to try and get around parental monitoring.

Georgia: She [her mum] says people only send pictures of themselves having a good time, that's why they think it's a nice picture.

Julia: Yeah, people are saying social media is all bad, you know, it's all fake, no-one posts anything genuine, but the thing is it's not all, OK it is a bit like that, but it's not all like that, because, you know, for me I just want to post stuff, because, I don't know, they're [photos] just nice...

Georgia...and it's a good way to share it with people I know.

Charlotte: But that's what you can get a private account for, and post like...

Georgia: Random photos.

Tilly: For your friends, even when you're like this, you know if you look really bad in it, I still post them because it's funny.

Interviewer: And would you call that your spam account?

Tilly: I have one.

Georgia: I have one.

Julia: You've got two.

Interviewer: Having double spam accounts?

Charlotte: I have two accounts. (Lions, Year 8, Girls).

In these discussions we can see the girls are devising a range of strategies to secure privacy online away from their parents to hide their social media engagements, including having spam accounts under different names. These types of strategies are something that is very worrisome for parents, but is in fact created by harsh regimes of surveillance and monitoring which leave young people feeling trapped. From a child's rights perspective it is important to enable spaces for young people to discuss and explore these issues in a safe and supported way. This is why parental understanding and support around sexual content is so important, so that girls in particular do not feel they have to have hidden accounts that lack security functions and potentially open them up to hacking, scams and unwanted sexual content that they then feel unable to ever report for fear of being punished for having secret accounts in the first place.

The girls went on to have a sophisticated conversations about sexting and the stigma and judgement it could potentially bring upon them, indicating to us that they had internalised the types of moral judgements that were pronounced by boys like Hugo who was scathing about people 'sexualising' themselves and 'promiscuity':

Tilly: Yeah, I feel like you would just be judged and I wouldn't trust, if I were to send one, I probably wouldn't, but I would do it to like someone like a hundred percent I knew wasn't gonna send it on, or do anything with it, or just delete it after or something.

Georgia: If you wanted to have a serious relationship you wouldn't send something like that.

3 Lion's Co-educational Independent Boarding School ... 75

Charlotte: If I was with someone oh yeah we are serious now I wouldn't send them that because I just find it childish to be honest.

Julia: If you're just looking for like...

Georgia: A fling.

Julia: a one-night stand or something then maybe.

Georgia: If you're looking for a proper relationship, that you're gonna like marry someone...

Charlotte: That's like if you have a relationship that isn't gonna last. (Lions, Year 8, Girls).

Here after Tilly starts to admit that she may well like to send a nude if she were not going to be judged or placed at risk the other girls come down upon this idea as 'childish' They assert that nudes will likely 'downgrade' a relationship:

Georgia: I feel like if you sent that [nude] to someone it would downgrade it [the relationship].

Charlotte: If I ever did, I wouldn't, but if I ever did send someone something like that, it would be a signal that I don't want something serious.

Julia: But if you didn't want something serious, why would you send such a picture?

Tilly: People do!

Georgia: I just feel like there are some people who could be at a point where, this will sound weird, but all they're really interested in is sex.

Charlotte: It would kind of be like hey, come around tonight or something like that. (Lions, Year 8, Girls).

76   J. Ringrose and K. Regehr

The girls suggest sending images could not be a part of a serious relationship and explicitly argue that the only reason you would send such an image is sex. Tilly tries to reason that people do this, but the others continue to challenge her. Sending images is pathologised as part of casual sex – like a one-night stand. The girls see nudes as tied to the wrong type of sexual image, and all but Tilly are anxious to position themselves as not that type of girl. A few of the girls find it impossible to imagine a scenario where sexting could be ok, one even goes on to suggest that one should be married before they sext, which generated laughter and joshing from the group:

> Julia: If I were married to that person then maybe I'd send something, but otherwise then it would be locked.
>
> Charlotte: That's so weird.
>
> LAUGHTER
>
> Julia: If you had like kids and…
>
> Georgia: Married!
>
> LAUGHTER
>
> Tilly: I feel like I don't get…Why would they need to send nudes if they're married?
>
> LAUGHTER
>
> Julia: It would be how much I would trust that person. (Lions, Year 8, Girls).

The girls have an impassioned debate over whether or not they could ever trust someone with their images, with Julia declaring she would have to be married for sexting to be OK! A mirror image to Hugo above who felt it was better to abolish sexting, we can see just how risky their naked bodies are to these elite girls, and yet despite this risk they are receiving requests for images online, pressures they have to navigate amidst a highly conservative schooling environment.

Reflections on their Digital Sex Ed

Finally, then, turning to the issue of how to better address these issues in this type of schooling context, the girls were adamant they couldn't turn to their teachers:

Tilly: I would never go up to a teacher and be like what do I do?

Charlotte: Yeah, because all the teachers say you can talk to us about this sort of thing...

Georgia: But I would literally never actually feel comfortable doing it.

They all agreed that it would feel embarrassing because teachers are 'old' and wouldn't be able to understand or give them any 'relevant' information. They continued:

Georgia: Yeah, they always say that they educate us on everything fully, but they never tell us... stuff, stuff that we actually need to know...everything is like...hormones, and then they don't actually show us or like teach us anything.

Charlotte: We don't do internet stuff.

Julia: Well...passwords... Cyberbully...

Georgia: If we keep doing it every year we already know it, there's not really much point just doing it, if you know.

Tilly: Yeah, I think I watched the same video this year that I watched in year five about cyberbullying. (Lions, Year 8, Girls).

The girls say that while the issues of 'hormones' is the focus of sex ed, and passwords and cyberbullying is covered in online safety, the school is not teaching them what they really need know about 'internet stuff', including how to actually deal with abusive content online like unwanted dick pics. They also are given the same videos to see over and over; a common trend reported amongst the young people in this study. As other sex education researchers have found, many young people simply find the content so out of date and 'boring' they do not engage.

The boys confirmed the same things, noting that their sex education was not only inadequate but happened too late:

William: Yeah, when you go into secondary school a lot of us are getting phones and the obvious thing to do is get some form of social media to talk to your friends, and the obvious one was Instagram.

Albert: And immediately, because you aren't being taught about the dangers you aren't fully aware of them, so I think before you go into secondary school you should be taught about them.

William: I think for sex education we got taught in like year seven, and they say they teach it from there because that's when you start to get your phone, but you want to have it before, because you can already have done things, or received things that could be really like quite embarrassing or that you don't want happening. So I think you should be taught in at least year five or something like that.

Hugo: no. It's too early, they don't process the information.

William: I think it's in Sweden they get taught from like a really young age. Because they are super open about it. I think they should teach these exact same things they teach us but at a younger age, because I think if you're restricting what they're allowed to know... I think that's not fair, because they could come across it, and then they will be completely confused about it, so it's only fair on their side to teach them about everything, because that's just how it should be. (Lions, Year 8, Boys).

Right till the end, Hugo disagrees with the others. He challenges some of the boys' desire for more education earlier to prepare them for things happening on social media that could be embarrassing and difficult. You can see the internalisation of fear and anxiety from Hugo, as he wants to shut down discussion that makes him uncomfortable. His classmate William, however, patiently continues to explain that other countries have more up to date and earlier sex education, and that since young people get a mobile phone in Year 7 they need space and support before that to start learning about what they may encounter online. There is also the implication that the education they are receiving from parents around these issues at home is largely inadequate and they need more understanding in order to manage these issues. As researchers we found it fascinating to see the back and forth on political views about age-appropriate sex education between Year 8 boys at this elite school and were heartened to see teen boys like William challenging the 'restrictive' attitudes and environment and calling for better, more inclusive sex education.

Conclusion

In this chapter, we've delved into an elite, selective boarding school environment. Parental influences in this elite school and the others we studied were important drivers on e-safety, shaping both the school's attention to these issues but also the young people's awareness of the need to keep their profile and identity safe from fraud, phishing and hacking, given what could be at risk with their family's status and money. The main messaging in this school has been around cyberbullying, password protection and privacy—securing one's digital footprint. Hugo translates this into certitude that he must never put his reputation at risk because he could jeopardise a future as a 'CEO'.

We also saw in this context that boys and girls are having vastly different experiences of social media apps like Snapchat and Instagram. Even within a heavily protected environment, the girls are already displaying their wealth through their status updates and images. They were also already getting unwanted dick pics on Snapchat social media feeds, as well as transactional dick pic requests and pressure to send nudes back. The girls are navigating this context with little support and highly judgemental attitudes at school and in their peer groups and families. They described surveillance on social media from their parents, particularly mothers, and not being able to discuss issues of concern around sexual experiences online at their school. They comment upon the outdated nature of their educational 'cyberbullying' resources which don't even touch upon issues to do with tech facilitated sexual harassment. In the absence of adult support, older siblings and friends are often the guides called in for advice. This peer support, however helpful, is problematic given these young people may also not have the correct knowledge around harassment and abuse, and therefore are failing to report such experiences.

Indeed, these girls have already internalised an acceptance of cyber-flashing as the norm. They have also internalised shame attached to feminine sexual bodies, which they note make it easier for boys to send nudes than for them to do so, since they would face reputational risk. This is a point made several times by Tilly, a girl in the group who is shut down for expressing her curiosity about sexual images. Indeed, it is important to note that the girls' concern about sexy and/or nude or nearly nude selfies is not because they necessarily all oppose these practices, but rather they already know that they will suffer grave consequences and sexual double standards should their nudes fall into the wrong hands. The girls are aware that there are much harsher consequences for girls and women in society than for boys and men should their images be shared non-consensually. For them as upper middle class elite girls, these risks are understood in relation to social class—the wrong sexual practices, whether online or in person, could mark them out as low class and would downgrade the relationship and potentially impact their chances of a proper heterosexual relationship and ultimately marriage. This is already foremost on their minds, with Julia going so far as to say she would not sext till she was married. Responding to judgemental attitudes like those expressed by Hugo, for the girls, being responsible, not appearing promiscuous and protecting their sexual reputation is necessary in order to be desirable to the boys in their elite peer group. Nudes could mark them out as irresponsible, ruining their reputation and the possibility of a genuine relationship.

Both the girls and boys were also; however, highly reflective about the limitations of the digital sex education they were receiving. The girls noted that they saw the same repeated content yearly, never being taught 'what they actually need to know'. Boys agreed and added that they felt that they should be learning about these issues much earlier. Despite the loud contestation from young Hugo, who repeatedly asserted that they were children and were too young to learn about these things, most of the boys persisted in their desire to have more insight into what they were experiencing in order for them to understand and better manage their use of mobile phones. As we continue, we will look at how important it is to create support strategies based on empowering all young people across such different school/life/technological eco-systems so they can garner greater knowledge of themselves and others. The alternative is to blinker them off into contained silos of privilege but also ignorance, where one's own digital identity is perhaps protected but at the expense of understanding, compassion or empathy with others.

References

Cohen, S., Liu, H., Hanna, P., Hopkins, D., Higham, J., & Gössling, S. (2022). The rich kids of instagram: Luxury travel, transport modes, and desire. *Journal of Travel Research, 61*(7), 1479–1494. https://doi.org/10.1177/00472875211037748

Liu, H., Wu, L., & Li, X. (Robert). (2019). Social media envy: how experience sharing on social networking sites drives millennials' aspirational tourism consumption. *Journal of Travel Research, 58*(3), 355-369. https://doi.org/10.1177/0047287518761615

Marwick, A. (2013). *Status update: Celebrity, publicity, and branding in the social media age*. Yale University Press.

Open Access This chapter is licensed under the terms of the Creative Commons Attribution-NonCommercial-NoDerivatives 4.0 International License (http://creativecommons.org/licenses/by-nc-nd/4.0/), which permits any noncommercial use, sharing, distribution and reproduction in any medium or format, as long as you give appropriate credit to the original author(s) and the source, provide a link to the Creative Commons license and indicate if you modified the licensed material. You do not have permission under this license to share adapted material derived from this chapter or parts of it.

The images or other third party material in this chapter are included in the chapter's Creative Commons license, unless indicated otherwise in a credit line to the material. If material is not included in the chapter's Creative Commons license and your intended use is not permitted by statutory regulation or exceeds the permitted use, you will need to obtain permission directly from the copyright holder.

4

Outer North Academy: Geolocational Risk and Tech Facilitated Violence: Responding to Cyberbullying, Racism and Child Sexual Exploitation at School and in Neighbourhoods

Situated in a highly ethnically diverse area in the outskirts of North London, Outer North Academy (ONA) serves one of the most economically challenged wards in the city. Within a suburban area of very high deprivation and crime, it falls in the bottom 10% for social deprivation of all wards in the country. While the school sites in this study have all been anonymised, the high crime rates in this area play a significant role in the discussions with the young people.

Academy schools, like ONA, are no longer run by the local councils, they have been taken over by academy trusts typically because they were failing, and they can be sponsored by private donors or in some cases are contracted out to private management companies (Ball, 2009). Academies do not have to follow all the state mandated curriculum and policies, apparently to enable more freedom, but in reality, they are often more punitive, with news reports finding students in academies are suspended 30 times more than state schools (Fazacerly & Savage, 2023). This is important for this chapter as we find that issues with mobile phones have been dealt with by phones being taken away at school and home. We also heard of an episode of punishment for harmful digital

© The Author(s) 2025
J. Ringrose and K. Regehr, *Teens, Social Media, and Image Based Abuse*,
https://doi.org/10.1007/978-3-031-92322-7_4

sexual behaviour in which a student was put in an isolation room, which engenders protest from the other boys.

Upon arriving at the school, we found that, like other schools in greater London, it was enclosed by high fences with barbed wire and a secure entry point for visitors, not unlike a prison. We entered through a remote-controlled gate in the chain-linked fence. Making our way to reception in the main building, we passed a lot of portacabins, once temporary, now permanent classrooms. As was recently seen in the scandal over Britain's crumbling schools, spending on school buildings in the public sector is inadequate. Portacabins are a cheap option to expand school buildings. Unfortunately, they are often retained far beyond expiration date, as in this case. This, like the other state schools we visited, illustrates the huge discrepancy between state and private schools in terms of lack of investment in the buildings and the grounds, as well as other indicators such as the quality of food provided.

At ONA we worked with 18 young people aged 11–15 in the year groups 7, 8, 9 and 10. Our discussion starts at Year 7 and we make our way up to the Year 10 group charting some changes in how the young people use technology. We look at how the context and geography of the neighbourhood interacts with technology and the Snapchat app in particular, creating an intensification and normalisation of risk and violence for these young people. We highlight the need for an intersectional lens when looking at how teenagers interact with technology in their everyday lives and communities. The young people in this school are often vulnerable and marginalised due to the deprivation in their area; this creates additional layers of risk that come into play when they are using technology like Snapchat. This is not a license to pathologise these young people, who are savvy tech users and who at various points call out issues of racism, sexism and homophobia in our discussions. However, as we outline, the technological vulnerabilities created by Snapchat intersect with issues impacting the young people in often, as they note, 'dangerous' ways that urgently need to be addressed. We also, however, address the techniques of punishment at the academy asking questions about how to facilitate genuine behavioural changes.

Year 7s: Snapchat's Bitmoji Avatars, Snapmap and Snapstories —"Its actually so dangerous|"

In ONA, as mentioned above, we were able to discuss issues of social media and images across the ages of 11–15. The Year 7s were a mixed gender group (6 girls and 1 boy), who were between 11–12 years old, and included two gender and sexuality diverse young people (one identifying as gender fluid and the other as bisexual) who explained how important countering LGBTQ hate online was to them as we expand upon later.

While the age verification of Snapchat is 13, it's noteworthy that all the Year 7s used the app, many of whom said they had started years before, some at age 9. Snapchat uses many fun and gamelike features, but also Bitmoji avatars as profile pictures. The avatars are a cartoon-like face and so may have no resemblance at all to the actual user. Through the anonymity and Bitmoji gamification of Snapchat, predators are able to create and use fake accounts to engage in online sexual harassment. For example, participants said that some people make up Bitmojis (i.e. cartoon avatars) to look like younger children, in order to manipulate young people into talking to them.

> Selin: Yeah, it's actually, if you're on the internet you have to be safe, because there are some people on the internet that say oh I'm 16 years old, but little do you know they're probably 30 or…
>
> Maira: Or 50.
>
> Fera: Like a 40-year-old grandad.
>
> Maira: And they're just like saying oh send me a pic of what you're wearing right now send me a pic of where you live. (Year 7, mixed)

These Year 7 students demonstrate their ability to detect unknown people who are attempting to contact them or access information about them when pretending to be someone else.

Selin: Yeah, like sometimes, say like, because some of us use social media just to communicate with our friends, and if like somebody is like, adds us on Snapchat, and I add them back and ask them who are you, do I know you? And they're like I'm your best friend, because it happened to me once.

Interviewer: Yeah?

Selin: They said they went to my school, it was like they went to my primary school, and they asked me what school do I go to now, and I was like really it's none of your business, and I'm not going to tell you, unless you prove that I know you. And then they sent a picture of one of my friends, because I think they have her on Snap as well, and then yeah, I asked her is this you, and then she was like no, it's not. And then I blocked them.

Selin: But I didn't report them or anything because I didn't think of that.

Fera: I think like it's not OK for older people to start adding us on Snapchat... (Year 7, mixed)

Selin describes an unknown contact posing as a friend, and how she blocked them. She relates not reporting them, however, because she 'didn't think of that.' This illustrates that reporting functions are rarely used on Snapchat, because, according to the young people, they didn't think of it or they felt they wouldn't work. Despite not understanding reporting on the app, the young people claim with a lot of bravado that they are smart and mature, and well aware of things like the Snapmap:

Selin: Yeah, but we're smart, because like we're in secondary school we are more mature, and in primary school they were teaching us in workshops on online safety and stuff, and like we know, and like we're mature, so we know like when someone's lying about who they are, or trying to like know your location and stuff. On Snapchat ... people on the map can see your location. Yeah.

Fera: Always turn it off, put it on ghost mode so nobody knows like where you live or where you are.

4 Outer North Academy: Geolocational Risk and Tech ...

Jyoti: What I do, if I've just added someone, I immediately block my location from that specific person...

Fera: Yeah.

Jyoti:...because I don't mind my friends knowing where I am because I might want to like meet up with them or something, and also like I don't count like showing your age as personal information, because like I know they're not gonna know, there's millions of twelve-year-olds on this planet...

Naza: And eleven-year-olds! (Year 7, mixed)

Geolocation is a worrying affordance found on Snapchat and other apps with location tracker functions such as running apps, as we discovered through the students showing us how they used this app as in the following exchange:

Interviewer: So that's something that you're thinking about when you're using your social media, because you said you were turning on the ghost mode?

Selin: Yeah, ghost mode. So people that are following you, if you do that, you know, they can't see your location. Some people are actually so dumb on Snapchat they keep their location on. Now when I've gone to the map, because I have ghost mode, I've gone to the map and I've seen where everyone is, and I've texted those people and said put your location, your ghost mode.

Interviewer: Can you bring up your map now?

Selin: Yeah.

Interviewer 1: Can I see it?

Interviewer 2: Because a couple of you also said that you would want to keep your location on so your friends know where you are.

88   J. Ringrose and K. Regehr

Selin: Probably like if, most people have their phones turned off right now.

Fera: You can see where people are, like this is my friend N, she's on X Street!

INDISTINCT REMARKS

Jyoti: It's actually so dangerous! (Year 7, mixed)

The young people in the study showed us their different Snapmaps on their Smartphones (which we cannot show images of due to copyright). We saw a dense Snapmap of the Year 9, 13–14-year-old girls at ONA school (showing many friends with Snapmap on) and a less dense map from the Year 7s (11–12 years old), (with privacy settings on). Cartoon like characters appear on the map which are the Bitmoji avatars that 'represent' the user on Snapchat (according to the platform guidelines). The Year 7 students' Snapmap has very few contacts on the map, compared to the more populated map we found with the Year 9 students (discussed later in this chapter). This type of exchange where the young people could explain some of the features on the app in live time, in this case demonstrating how the map works and pointing out where their friends are on the map, was very valuable for our research. The young people also went on to draw their experiences with messages of warning about not putting your location on social media, see Fig. 4.1.

The mass popularity of Snapchat across Britain and other contexts, means this phenomenon of youth using Snapmap is not unique to London. However, when the Year 7 students discuss ghost mode, which prevents people from seeing their Snapmap and declare the tracking function 'so dangerous', this could be in response to some difficult situations that have arisen in the school. A geolocation and tracking app is more risky depending on who one's contacts are and where one lives. All of the young people at this school discussed the area's violence, gang activity, knife crime and feeling unsafe in their neighbourhood. The Year 7 group say their area is 'dangerous' and has:

Fig. 4.1 Year 7 drawing of a home and warning not to put images with identifiable location on social media

Fera: Stabbings and stuff.

Selin: Yeah, there's been 50 people killed in like, well not 50, 30 I think, last year.

Naza: Oh yeah.

Fera: A lot of people are dying.

Maira: Yeah.

Fera: Yeah, and most of it's like random stabbings, like just to prove yourself, like gangs and stuff, like knife crime, they are just trying to prove how cool they are, but it's not really that cool.

Selin: Because anything in the world is actually a weapon. Like if it's a really sharp pen...or fork. (Year 7, mixed)

The group went on to recount stories of siblings in gangs, a violent hold-up at knife point and other recent incidents in their neighbourhood.

Maira: A lot of the stabbings they happened around my flat, and there were all roads blocked off, and people were late to school, and some of them didn't come because their parents were scared that something was going to happen. And there's the stabbings that happened a few months ago, my mum didn't let me come to school because she was scared that something was gonna happen, so the day after my dad had to drop me off and pick me up every day, and I wasn't allowed to go home by myself.

Fera: I'm not allowed to walk to school, …there's this park near my house and I'm not allowed to walk through it, because there's always like these shady men there. So I have to either take the long way around or I get a bus.

Selin: Shady men, …men there just sitting down, and they look like a little sketchy, because there are these people in my road, like opposite of my house, they're really weird, every time me and my cousins or my friends, they come around my road, and we start playing with our bikes and like we go to the park and stuff... I see these men that come out of the house opposite and they're always like looking at us like this, like staring at us, and I just turn around, because I'm really brave, I turn around and I'm like is there a problem here, like why are you looking at us? (Year 7, mixed)

4 Outer North Academy: Geolocational Risk and Tech ...

As well as the 'shady men' who may be encountered in the environment of the school, the young people are acutely aware that people can use online affordances to locate you in real time and space.

> Maira: ...if like you put stuff on your story they can find your location by like specific landmarks, because what some people do they like take a video outside of our school and then they put it on like Instagram or Snap, and then like you can see the sign of the school or the actual building of the school. And like they put their uniform and everything. (Year 7, mixed).

The young people demonstrate detailed awareness of how to avoid giving clues that could show where you live or go to school. Despite all of these precautions, however, they still have to deal with contacts posing as friends and as children of their same age. Talia explained she has been asked for nudes by contacts pretending to be 12 years old:

> Talia: I've been asked for a picture...I was on Instagram and there's this guy that I knew that oh he wasn't 12, by the way he was speaking to me, so he started saying oh send a pic, and like send nudes and stuff, and I said no thank you! (Year 7, mixed)

Three of the girls in the Year 7 group had been sent unsolicited penis images: one of these episodes is recounted by Talia below:

> Talia: Basically he just randomly added me [on Snapchat] um, like he's like he had the, he didn't even have a Bitmoji, it was a boy I think, and he was like send me a pic and I'll send you one, and then I'm like I don't know you! (Year 7, mixed)

In addition, the young people are targeted with the promise of earning money by becoming brand ambassadors:

> Selin: A few months ago there was this um thing on Instagram, it was like a Nike ambassadors thing, and you had to repost to get a chance to be a child model for like Nike clothing. I found out immediately how

92   J. Ringrose and K. Regehr

fake it was, because they said oh just DM your private information, and your phone number, and your address.

Jyoti: That's a lie.

Fera: Another company, they said oh um, can we just use like, like body parts of you, so we can put it on an advert? And I'm like no? And they said we need a name too if you want to sign up. And I was like I don't want to sign, one, and two, you don't just go around random people asking them to show their body parts, and they said I know but we are doing it for an advert, and we need your address and email, and like I said I'm not gonna do it. And they said OK then, um, bad luck that you're not gonna join because it's gonna get lots of money and then I gave an answer, something like I don't want to and I don't give a crap about money, and they said OK then… (Year 7, mixed)

While the Year 7s put up a brave front, saying that they are smart and mature and know how to handle such interactions, both by random strangers posing as contacts the same age as them, but also by contacts posing as companies phishing for images and location information, the range of such encounters which they relate shows just how vulnerable these younger children are.

Year 8s: "Snapchat is Both Helpful and Harmful at the Same Time" Live Location Sharing and Snapstory Spread

Increasing Snapscores by Adding Random People

In the Year 8 focus group, we spoke to three 13-year-old girls: Venus who was Congolese, Irina of Romanian descent (who complained she hated when people called her a 'gypsy'), and Naza who is Kurdish. Recall our discussion with the Year 7 young people who noted that you had to purposely cover up your uniform and school crest to avoid location identification from the photo. The Year 8 girls are either unaware of this or have thrown caution to the wind, they showed us a photo of their friend group posted on social media in front of the barbed wire fence at school, in their uniforms with school crests clearly visible on their blazers. The social media photo had multiple markers that would make them identifiable. We found that as some of our participants got older, they paid less attention to the security features on social media in a bid to up their Snapscores (the amount of interactions on Snapchat) and increase their contacts to widen their popularity. The Year 8 girls discuss Snapscores, with Irina and Naza noting how important these scores are to Venus:

> Interviewer: So how important are these Snapchat scores?
>
> Irina: I don't care about them.
>
> Venus: Yeah, I don't really care about them.
>
> Irina: Oh no, she cares the most.
>
> Venus: What do you mean, I care the most? Go on then?
>
> Naza: She does loads of stuff to do it.
>
> Irina: Because you send it to people [Shout-out] and it goes up and up. But I don't do it.
>
> Venus: I do it. (Year 8, Girls)

As seen in Chapter 2, one of the main mechanisms to increase your Snapscore and followers is through the Shoutouts. The girls discuss how Venus does Shoutouts, and she admits at the end that she does this and draws an image of her 'shout outs' later in the session (Fig. 4.2). The Snapscore is portrayed prominently in Snapchat profile and when the Snapcode is generated to do a shout out. The girls discuss Venus wanting a high score and they shared her Snapscore status at around 50,000.

Fig. 4.2 Venus's drawing of 'Shouting out yourself'

Venus went on to explain that after the Snapchat Shoutouts she was repeatedly approached and sent unwanted sexual content by unknown contacts:

Venus: Basically I was on Snapchat once and there's always these people, I don't know their names, but they're always popping up to me, they text me, and I don't even know who, they add me, and then they start sending nudes, like pictures of their private parts and stuff, and I just block them straightaway. (Year 8, Girls)

We can see clearly how the 'quick add' function allows a vast number of people Venus doesn't know to send her messages. When we ask her how the senders find her, Venus claims she is not aware of the privacy settings; noting she needs to fix them and learn the settings. The complexity of the peer group's interactions with each other and with the urban environment starts to become clear when we ask what they do to protect themselves:

> Irina: I would like block and report them, because like I'd report them for like inappropriate stuff, and like they won't send it again.

> Venus: I don't know the people that are doing it. But last time there was a rumour going around on Snapchat around this boy, he asks for girls' pictures, like nudes, and he wants the nudes, yeah, and then apparently this girl got raped and then after the man, the exact man that apparently raped the girl, texted me, and I texted him back and then afterwards he was like oh do you want to meet up? And I was like no. And then I blocked him straightaway. (Year 8, Girls).

While Irina discusses blocking and reporting, Venus only blocks the senders, and also claims a man who may be a rapist has contacted her asking to meet up.

Geolocational Enabled Violence

Shortly after, it emerges that Venus has had her phone taken away by her parents on advice from the school. This happened after she made contact with a boy from primary school on Snapchat seemingly striking up a romantic connection, but then the boy stopped responding to her messages and calls. Then one Saturday out with her friends, Venus posted her location on her Snapchat story. The boy asked her to meet him in a McDonald's parking lot, but he did not arrive, rather his cousin and several girls turned up and 'beat up' Venus:

Venus: Basically I posted on my story that we were there, and it had my location, you know how Snapchat, when you slide, it has your location of where you are. I posted that on my story and he called and said meet me at McDonald's, like when I got there they were there, I didn't know they were, yeah, I didn't know they were there, they all got outside there. And I'm talking so fast... you know like near the McDonald's. On Monday when there was this gang fight in McDonald's and knife stabbings and stuff... that's the one where I got beat up. It was in McDonald's.

Interviewer: What happened?

Venus: They went what have you got to say for yourself? And I said sorry. And they pulled my hair, and I ran away.

Naza: There was girls.

Interviewer: How many girls?

Venus: Five. But I don't know like what school they go to, but it's the boy's cousin...(Year 8, Girls)

After this incident Venus and Naza were added to a group chat by the boy's cousin and were being further threatened:

Interviewer: So have these girls stopped harassing you?

Naza: Well after the incident in January they kept asking me for money and stuff, like oh we won't beat you up if you give me money, and then I was like but I can't give you money. Because they made that kind of group chat with me, the cousin, and the girls in it, because they added me on Snapchat, and then yeah they were saying stuff like ah, because they basically know a girl called X in Year 9, and they were like oh X could tell us where you are and stuff, we could beat you up, we could get her and me and stuff. And then that's when, that was the last time we spoke.

Naza: Yeah, I think about, one of them I feel like I saw them the other day, when I was walking near, and she was looking at me on the bus.

4 Outer North Academy: Geolocational Risk and Tech ... 97

Venus: I was scared to even go with my sister over to the shop. I couldn't even go …

Naza: Because my heart was beating, I couldn't sleep, I didn't want to come to school, because I couldn't sleep at night and I wasn't waking up in the morning properly. Oh I'm gonna start crying. And I couldn't hold it in, and I went to the hospital because I thought it was something wrong with my heart, and they were like no, nothing's wrong. And then after we talked about anxiety and mental health, I was like oh my word I have anxiety because of them, and then I went to tell Miss [form tutor] in the end. And I don't have it anymore. (Year 8 Girls)

Additional girls from the school became involved as Venus and Naza were added to a group chat claiming that Venus had done something wrong by being in Snap contact with the boy. The attackers were also blackmailing Venus, asking for money, and threatening to beat her up again, and threatening that one of their peers at Venus's school could tell them where Venus and Naza were located while they were on school premises. Naza experienced extreme anxiety about the Snapmap tracking, nearly breaking down during the interview, explaining that after going to hospital for anxiety, she ended up telling her parents who then alerted the school. The boys' cousin threatened further to expose Venus's home address (doxing or sharing personal information) through this group chat:

Venus: She was blaming it on me and she was gonna tell my information, so people know where I lived. But she didn't…

Interviewer: OK, so you've got yourself out of that group?

Venus: Yeah, just left the group. I've blocked them. But he still, the other day I checked, and he liked my picture, which is a bit weird, I don't know why he was going through my stuff.

Interviewer: The boy?

Venus: Yeah, I don't know why he was looking on my Instagram. (Year 8, Girls)

Venus has blocked all of the attackers and the boy on Snapchat but the boy is still following her on Instagram, and he has since gone through her public Instagram photos (liking some of them) to make sure she knows that he is watching her. She also shows us an extensive blocked folder on Snapchat; that she has made of people that she doesn't know trying to add her on Snapchat. The significant thing is the blocked folder is still there and she looks at these contacts. This is a cautionary tale of physical harm, blackmail, stalking and threatened doxing all via Snapchat, and all of which are forms of tech facilitated violence (Powell & Henry, 2017).

Snapchat Circulation of Racism

Venus relates more Snapchat related problems: a classmate, a girl with the user name 'sexymotherfucker' used the website Urban Dictionary to make a post about a new term: 'Congolese Bitches': 'This Congolese B Word always wants to get rated, and no-one rates her.' The girls explained that girls get rated by 'their looks and how funny they are, and do they 'fit in the group' and whether someone will be friends with them, so it's a crucial ranking related to being an accepted part of the peer group. Urban Dictionary has been researched as contributing massively to the growth of hate online (Ging et al., 2020). While not explicitly naming Venus on the website the girls then screen captured their entry and reposted it on Snapchat identifying Venus:

Venus: Some people, they sent it to Snapchat, and reposted the…

Irina: They do everything with that, if there's beef someone has to post it onto Snapchat, loads of things that happens on there.

Venus: Without Snapchat no-one would have found out. Because Snapchat is harmful and helpful - at the same time. (Year 8, Girls)

4 Outer North Academy: Geolocational Risk and Tech … 99

In this example racism and sexism intersect as the student uses the online interface where anyone can login and 'define a word' ('Congolese Bitches'). The Urban Dictionary post is then screen captured and re-posted on Snapchat tagging Venus in a post that calls "Venus the B-word with no ratings" (unliked). This malicious post is then further circulated around via Snapchat. Venus took this example to the Head Teacher as she was so upset and the teachers told her you can't report this type of thing to the police. Venus seemed very deflated by this, and realising that little can be done about racist content, saying the school doesn't do "enough" and the police can't do anything, they cannot stop people saying hateful things online.

Snapstory Enabled Child Exploitation Material

Nearing the end of the interview we ask what schools could do better to address these types of online hate and digital violence, and we ask the young people if they have any questions for us. Venus stops, then quietly ventures: 'I want to know at what age do you think you should have a boyfriend?' The group then confer about whether they should tell us about a story about a girl, Nicky, from a neighbouring school.

> Venus: Miss, basically this girl from [Neighbouring school] on Snapchat she posted a picture, a video, of her sucking, [dick] yeah, that.
>
> Naza: Her boyfriend.
>
> Interviewer: So where did she post that?
>
> Naza: On Snapchat. She posted it on her story!
>
> Interviewer: How old is she?
>
> Irina: She's in our year as well, Year 8.
>
> Venus: She has bare [a lot of] followers. Oh my God, I need adds on Snapchat!

Naza: How could she do that?

Venus: I don't know, she has a boyfriend, and...maybe wants to show off on like...but probably her mum knows, how can her mum let her do that?

Irina: Yeah.

Venus: I'm scared, when I'm older...

Interviewer: Scared?

Venus: I'm scared to do it when I'm older, you know... I'm scared. (Year 8, Girls)

Here, the girls describe a girl Nicky, who is their age in their Snapchat network who has posted a video of herself performing fellatio on her 'older' boyfriend on her Snapstory. Venus reasons she did it to attract more Snapchat adds (followers). Naza asks 'how could she do that?' Venus responds it's about 'showing off', wondering how her mum could let her do that, indicating she thinks all parents are following their children's accounts. Venus then explains that she is 'scared' that she'll have to do the same when she is older. While performing fellatio as competitive proof of sexual mastery and achievement between teen girls is not a new phenomenon (Fava & Bay-Cheng, 2012), what has changed is the imperative to share proof of sexual acts through social media apps. Legally this content is considered child sexual exploitation where a minor is producing 'indencent' sexual imagery. Consent is not clear in the scenario, which the girls discuss, appearing both disgusted and fascinated by the video. When we ask what young people should do when they see this type of video, Irina confidently replies that you should report the person and block them, to which Venus says:

Venus: Yeah, but she's my friend, so why should I block her? there's nothing I can do about that, we can't just not be friends because she done that thing.

4 Outer North Academy: Geolocational Risk and Tech ... 101

Naza: But apparently people bullied her at school.

Venus: Not everyone's gonna do it, but when you're older you are obviously gonna do it.

Interviewer: Why have people bullied her at school for it?

Irina: It's just the age, she shouldn't have done it.

Naza: She shouldn't have posted it.

Venus: I think she could do it but it's just age, and if her parents know about it then she should...

Irina: Yeah, but she shouldn't post that on Snapchat because...

Venus: No, but people say you should have it when you're 16 and plus but there's loads of people at this young age who are doing it. (Year 8, Girls).

Here we can see Venus repeatedly defending Nicky who's been bullied at her school; positioning such videos as normal when you are 16. The age of consensual sexual images being legal is 18 not 16, demonstrating the young people have no understanding of the law. Nonetheless while she tries to defend Nicky, Venus also feels she is 'too young'. We can see a tense emotional landscape where Venus is both shocked and scared by the video but wants to protect her friend. To dig deeper we next tried to investigate their views on the motivations:

Interviewer: OK, let's talk about it a little bit more. What do you think motivated her to want to share it?

Venus: She wanted to show off that she's...

Naza: Maybe she was like, oh you can't do this and stuff, I don't know.

Irina: Maybe someone dared her.

Naza: Or he forced her.

Venus: Why would she even do that in the first, why would she even record it?

Irina: Maybe he recorded it.

Venus: No, she recorded it.

Naza: How do you know?

Venus: Because I could see on the video.

Irina: EWWW! you watched it?

LOUD VOICES

Interviewer: So you must have a feeling that she wanted people to see that. Right?

Venus: She can do what [other] people can't. (Year 8, Girls).

In discussing Nicky's motivation, Venus maintains it is to show off, Irina thinks it was a dare, Naza suggests she could have been forced. Venus strongly, insisting Nicky recorded it herself, arguing that Nicky wanted to do what others cannot do at her age. This raises the question of Nicky's agency. As noted, from a legal perspective the video is child sexual abuse or exploitation material (formerly child produced pornography), but for the girls the motivations and Nicky's agency to produce the video are important issues they are grappling with. In cases like this we need to hold the conversation open. What do we make of the fact that Nicky is held up and possibly admired because of her audacity? What do we make of the fact that 'bullying' of the girl who has shared her sexual practice is considered normal and discussion of the 'older' boy is minimal? What conversations do we need to be having with young people to help them manage the commodification of sex, and its performance online, which is increasingly common in an age of social media subscription porn, as we'll find out further as we proceed in this book. What is significant is how the smartphone and social media apps like Snapchat have dramatically changed the visibility of sexual images and videos, amplifying the spreadability, permanence and searchability of this content with long lasting implications.

In spite of or perhaps because of all the 'drama' disclosed in this discussion Venus is desperate to regain her phone, which has been taken away by her parents in the wake of these episodes. As Venus told us poignantly above, 'Snapchat is harmful and helpful at the same time.' As we will argue throughout this book, an abstinence approach of taking away young people's phones will never offer a long-term strategy. It will not help them to manage these digital relationship contexts; it won't support them with learning the skills needed to navigate a complex technologically mediated world.

Year 9: "Hey beautiful send nudes" Snapchat predation and sexual shaming

Moving onto our interviews with the next age up in year 9, we quickly saw how issues with Snapchat persisted. Recall the Year 7 Snapmaps—the 14-year-olds had a densely packed Snapmap filled with Snapchat contacts, explaining to the interviewer:

Mila: All these people I can see exactly where they are!

Destiny: I can zoom in to this person and I can see exactly where she is…you can literally go to her.

Zara: I can literally see that she's on X street!

Mila: Yeah, but I know all of them so they know I'm not going to like start stalking them or something. (Year 9, Girls)

Rather than declaring the Snapmap dangerous as the Year 7s did, the Year 9s knowingly joke that they will not 'stalk' any of their contacts on Snapmap. However, the girls went on to recount stories about the physical dangers of the tracking element.

> Mila: …Because they saw that someone followed her and then they saw, I think he was like 16 or something and I think this girl is only like 13 and they obviously followed her. They'd seen where they are, they know that she goes to this specific school on that road. They obviously know there's a school on that road. So I think a couple days after that she saw this guy following her or something and then she, she like she kept thinking about how could he follow me and stuff. And then she realised she didn't put herself on ghost mode. So then she put it on and just blocked him. And then I think, I think she told the school or something cause the school kind of dealt with it. (Year 9, Girls)

Mila explains the Snapmap is risky, explaining how a friend of hers is followed on her way home from school via Snapmap. She also notes that the school has since cautioned them around not using the tracking element of Snapchat. We think this is a really important area for digital literacy about tracking apps.

In addition, however, we also found that the Year 9 girls were increasingly navigating issues of unwanted sexual content on the Snapchat app. These included more pointed experiences than the younger groups of being sent more dick pics as well as repeatedly being asked to send back nudes. Expanding upon the issues of adults posing as children which we saw in Year 7, the Year 9s explain in more detail how the Bitmoji works, making the age of the Snapchat user unidentifiable:

> Mila: Because on Snapchat you can make your own like kind of character in a way:

> Zara: Bitmoji.

> Mila: Yeah and like how old are they like 35 like olds

> Amber: And they add girls.

Destiny: And then the thing looks younger than they actually are. So then they'll be like hey, and they'll call you beautiful and stuff.

Zara: Yeah hey beautiful.

Amber: Send me nudes and stuff. Then they'll send you a dick pic expecting a nude back or something then it just escalates a bit too quickly.

Mila: They basically groom you.

Amber: Yeah they're like, they're using you for stuff they want. (Year 9, Girls)

It's becoming clearer how the game-like elements of Snapchat can be used to conceal identity, and offer opportunities to predators like the Bitmoji avatar like profile picture. Predators can also find young people's QR Snapcodes that share their details, when they participate in Shout Outs:

Interviewer: How do they find your profiles?

Amber: They can literally just type in like Mila and someone will come up and they'll be like add them.

Zara: Or someone else has them on someone else's story. Like they tag them and they can add you from there and they can message you from there.

Destiny: It could escalate so quickly. Like, it's, it's quite dangerous like in a way. (Year 9, Girls)

Acknowledging the dangerous elements of how fast one's contact details travel through Shoutouts, the girls try to manage the Snapchat quick adds using the decline feature, but also describe negotiating a murky territory of 'mutuals' or friends of friends and not being sure if they should decline people or how to differentiate random men from semi-known boys:

Mila: I mean sometimes it's like older men, but most of the times it's like boys from different schools. Like I like the look of you or something like that and then they'll be like, let me just add her and stuff.

Zara: Yeah and then the boys from different schools.

Destiny: Or like your friend knows them.

Interviewer: Like a friend of a friend of a friend.

Mila: Yeah. Like you just have them on Snapchat. (Year 9, Girls)

The girls quick add mutuals or 'friends of friends', creating a context of followers who they don't actually know but only 'have on Snapchat'. This sets up an easy context for non-consensual encounters.

Mila: Well, the boy added me, so I added him back thinking he was our age. So I was like okay it's a boy from another school it's alright and then he suddenly just sent me a dick pic, I didn't even text him, and I saw it then I blocked him straight away...No.

Zara: He could be like hey beautiful and then he'll send a dick pic straight after then, be like, let me see your body or something. (Year 9, Girls)

Mila adds a boy back who suddenly sends a dick pick. Zara says this can be used as a proposition: 'let me see your body'. The girls reason that dick pics are sent with the intention of getting nudes back and they describe the motivation behind a transactional dick pic:

Mila: Boys they want to look big in a way.

Amber: They want to be like oh this girl's sending me nudes. Oh my god look at me I'm so popular I'm big and stuff, my friend's with me.

Zara: They've got three parts.

Mila: Because boys are like I want to see that more.

Amber: Girls have got three parts boys have got one.

Interviewer: What are the parts?

Mila: [inaudible] So I think a boy has like one, the girls have three parts vagina, boobs bum, it's like a lot on show.

Zara: Especially if they, they think they have a big bum. It's like, let me show this off.

Mila: Like I have the boobs I have the bum. Let me just show it off let me just impress loads of people. But then like someone could screenshot and then it would go wrong. (Year 9 Girls)

The girls discuss boys wanting girls' nudes because it will make them look popular. They also describe girls putting their parts on show to impress people, but warn that images can be screenshotted and spread, recounting this type of behaviour from boys.

Interviewer: Um, do you think there is pressure for people to send nudes?

Mila: Yeah. Hundred percent.

Interviewer: Where does the pressure come from?

Zara: Boys.

Mila: From wanting the other person to like you, wanting to impress them …just like the boy wants them and is not pressuring but like oh my god please send them like you look really good.

Amber: Well it is pressure, like please send them your body is really pretty. Or it will be like I won't screenshot it, please. (Year 9, Girls).

Here the girls debate whether something is 'pressure' or not, with Mila saying it's not pressure and Amber saying it is. They go on to say if girls do engage sexually online they get called 'freaky'.

Mila: I remember when someone asked me if I was a freak there was this boy on Instagram. Oh my God. I didn't know him he texted me saying, oh my God, I like you so much are you a freak [inaudible].

Zara: I'll send them something and then it just goes wrong.

Amber: Yeah like, yeah, really wrong.

Destiny: They get what they want and then they call her a slut too.

Mila: They like sweeten the girls up to get what they want then screen shot the nudes. And when they put on their story, they're like, oh look what this girl just sent me she's such a sket. I never even asked for it urgh and stuff like that because like they [the girls] don't save chats the girl has nothing to prove against

Destiny: And then plus she sent the nudes as well so she's in the wrong then. (Year 9, Girls)

Mila recounts a boy giving her a compliment 'you're a freak' and how this sets up a situation to send a nude, whereupon she is 'slut shamed' called a slut or the British slang 'sket'. While Mila was careful not to implicate herself in the telling of this story, it seemed obvious that she was describing her own experience. The girls are aware of how women and girls are shamed for sending the images even though they were pressured, and how girls are not believed (Banet-Weiser & Higgens, 2023) about the pressuring dynamics in ways that replicate wider rape culture in society. This relates also to how girls are not ready to use the information against boys, such as the chats to 'prove' what lead to the image exchange:

Mila: And then a girl sending nudes no one's going to really listen to her they're gonna be like urgh why did you do that. They're not going to believe her side of the story.

Interviewer: Why is that?

4 Outer North Academy: Geolocational Risk and Tech ... 109

Zara: Yeah, because they think the girl's dirty and stuff.

Destiny: They look down to her for doing that

Amber: Even if they asked for it.

Mila: Even if they do sort of the same thing that they just think, okay, like she sent nudes so she's bad.

Destiny: It's the boy that's the victim he didn't even ask for them. [inaudible] (Year 9, Girls)

The girls have a complex debate here about male victimisation, arguing people argue boys are the victim if they have nudes because a girl sent them, noting how unfair this is:

Interviewer: What do you, what do you think about that? About the way girls are treated in that situation?

Mila: Horrible.

Amber: It's disgusting.

Mila: Because it's like the boys that are like trying to get the girl to do something and then the girls are looked down upon for doing what the boys got them to do.

Zara: But at the same time the girl's the one who sent it and she knows that she shouldn't, she shouldn't send.

Destiny: It's bad.

Mila: But then if you, if people actually listened to the girl they would be like okay, like she did get pressured to do it.

Zara: If it's threatening then it's in a different way. [inaudible]. I feel like that's maybe a different aspect of things but like if it was just like, oh send me nudes, I love you so much then like they should just block them.

110   J. Ringrose and K. Regehr

Destiny: Girls need to learn that like there are boys out there that are going to be like oh I really like you. Like you're really pretty but they don't like them. They literally just want nudes and like some girls don't understand that and then they fall for their trap and they send nudes and then it's like they can't do anything about it once it's out there, it's out there. So like in a way it is disgusting how boys treat girls but like they are the ones that send the nudes in the first place. (Year 9, Girls)

Some of the girls are clear that this dilemma girls are in is horrible and disgusting, but Zara argues girls know they 'shouldn't send'. Mila argues people should listen to girls and Zara feels that pressure has to mean threats and girls need to block boys and not fall for 'I love you so much', which Destiny agrees with expressing deep cynicism about boys and masculinity as putting girls in a 'trap.' As has been shown in much research, girls have a no-win situation. If they send images that are shared without consent, they have no recourse; the boy is able to turn the gaze away from their non-consensual behaviour onto the girl as at fault for creating and sending a nude in the first place. This relates to the sexist anti-sexting messaging which we looked at in the introduction to the book. Girls' nudes rather than pressuring and harassing behaviour and non-consenusal sharing of image, are what considered 'dirty' and looked down upon because of age old double standards and sexual shaming of women and girls.

The girls go on to describe the pressure amongst boys to act this way.

Destiny: Cause they like, they feel happy that they got them or like, cause they're like, oh my God, I'm so big I got a nude. [inaudible].

Mila: Look how pretty she is it's like in a way baited her out or something.

Zara: Like look I'm bad cause I baited someone out for their nudes. Everyone's going to look up to me now because I baited someone's nudes....

Mila: [inaudible] if you're popular at school, like one of the popular boys, then maybe it's a bit like if someone found out you had, a girl sent you nudes and you didn't share them, it'd be a bit like, why don't you share

4 Outer North Academy: Geolocational Risk and Tech ... 111

them? Like it's kind of what you're meant to do. Like even though it's not, but like....

Destiny: It's like if you see if you see your friends, do it you think, okay, that's like a normal thing to do that share your nudes and like you see, you see your friends are sharing other people's nudes and you think, oh my God, I should do the same things.

Mila: Say you're like I'm not gonna pressure her and bait her out. Then all the boys are gonna be like, oh, why didn't you bait her out and stuff … its pressure for them to like send it on as well. (Year 9, Girls)

The girls discuss how the boys have pressure not only to demonstrate that they have gotten a nude, but to show that they have 'baited out' the girl—(baiting refers to enticing someone to do something for you—a show of power and manipulation). In this case they have enticed a girl to given them something valuable (a nude) which they then non-consensually share with the male peer group. This is quintessential male homosocial bonding strategy, where the relationship with the same gender group trumps any other form of intimacy. The bonding occurs because you have gotten something valuable and used your power to manipulate the situation for your own ends—display mastery. This is discussed matter of factly: 'it's what your meant to do' as a boy—share the nude as a trophy—'look how pretty she is'. The girls realise that from an early age, boys are valued not only for the fact of being able to display the high-capital nude image but for their capacity to trick and manipulate girls into doing it for 'love'. Despite the girls protesting this behaviour as horrible and disgusting, they understand these are the social norms that girls need to grasp and expect in their heterosexual courtship rituals. The girls accept there is no way for girls to act sexual or share images without a high risk of being judged and shamed through sexual double standards.

Year 10: "Look What I've Got" Masculinity and the Normalisation of Homosocial Misogyny

In the final interview at this school, with the oldest teens in a Year 10 mixed gender group of two girls and three boys, the young people were reticent with the interviewers. In her field notes the interviewer says: 'They were a very quiet and awkward group—lots of pauses and encouragement of discussion needed especially in the first half of the session.' The girls barely spoke. The interviewer speculated this may have been because the girls did not want to discuss some of the issues in front of the boys who were outnumbering them and were demonstrating highly sexist perspectives. One boy in particular expressed judgement and casual sexism, saying for instance, that he made fun of his mate for playing video games with girls. In this interview, we discovered the level of fully entrenched misogyny and sexual double standards normalised in the peer culture of the school, as curiously another episode of a blowjob being filmed and circulated (further child sexual exploitation material) was discussed; this time the episode came to the attention of the school and more of the focus of the discussion was on the experiences of the boy who had in this case filmed and circulated the video:

Kamal: This person gave that person who's two years older than her a blow job. That's the rumour that came out.

Ahmed: The person that gave it is in our year.

Kamal: Yeah we won't mention her name.

Interviewer: Who recorded that?

Rashid: I think it was the guy.

Interviewer: Then what? Sent that to other people? showed it to other people?

4 Outer North Academy: Geolocational Risk and Tech ... 113

Ahmed: Probably sent it to his friends. (Year 10, mixed)

In this scenario the boys describe a 14-year-old girl who had a sexual video filmed and distributed by a 16-year-old boy who sent the video to his friends. The boys went on to very carefully distance themselves from having seen the video:

Interviewer: Did any of you see this video?

Kamal: So, no one saw the video, but there was rumors that there was a video, right?

Interviewer: Do you know of anyone who claims to have seen the video?

Ahmed: Yes.

Interviewer: Do you believe them?

Kamal: Yes, because they seem to know the details of it. That's why.

Interviewer: What did they say?

Rashid: It was, or should I say what he said, ah, that was, it was, it looked nice but weird at the same time. (Year 10, mixed)

In this exchange it's clear that Rashid has seen the video but corrects himself to the third person, explaining 'his friend' thought the blowjob video was 'nice and weird at the same time'. The interviewer then tries to understand the outcome of the situation:

Interviewer: Okay. And what did you say happened to the boy?

Kamal: He was, I don't know, he was bullied almost.

Rashid: He got penalised somehow....everyone was going around shouting his name free this person, free this person as like a joke.

Interviewer: So people were kind of supportive of him?

Rashid: Supportive in a jokey, basically there's this thing if someone's in like an exclusion room or something like that and you're like that friend or something, you just shout their name say free this person randomly through the halls for no reason whatsoever.

Interviewer: So that boy had been punished in school by going to that place?

Kamal: I don't think he was punished in school.

Interviewer: Do you mean legally?

Rashid: Yeah legally he's over the age of consent, whereas she's not. (Year 10, mixed)

The school's response to this episode is to put the boy into an 'isolation room' or exclusion room which research has shown is prison like and dehumanising (Sealy et al., 2021). These forms of punishment have been questioned as lacking support structures or strategies for behaviour change. Indeed, there is a culture in the school of protest against these jail-like processes, and some of his peers take it upon themselves to wander the halls yelling out 'free him'. This school behaviour shows homosocial banter and defending mates against punishment, but more significantly the way the issue is addressed fails to challenge the behaviour in a meaningful way, which could support behaviour change.

The boys have a high level of understanding of the legal technicalities, noting that the girl was under the age of consent, and yet they have no awareness of an image-based abuse happening with a sexual video being shared without consent. This is where the focus on child pornography becomes problematic because the element of sexual abuse of sharing images and videos *without consent* is neglected, and the focus is solely on the legal age of consent for physical sex and sharing images. The modes of punishment are also ineffective, leaving the sentiment in the school that this boy has been *unfairly penalised,* (feeding into male

4 Outer North Academy: Geolocational Risk and Tech ... 115

victim mentality) hence the response of his peers shouting 'free him' from the exclusion unit.

We also saw in this group consistent blame being placed upon the creator of nude images with no understanding of image-based sexual harassment or abuse when images are shared without consent and little empathy for the victims:

> Interviewer: So in terms of sharing pictures and stuff, you said it's more common to see pictures of girls that have been shared around. Um, so why do you think people share those pictures? Not why does the person in the picture share it, but why would someone receive it then show it to others?

> Kamal: they might see it as sort of a joke as like so funny. They just don't rate that person or they want to be rude.

> Ahmed: Yeah. Ruins their reputation basically.

> Interviewer: Any other reasons why someone might show a nude of someone? Other than as a joke?

> Rashid: Maybe out of pride like they might think, oh, look at this look what I've got and then they might send it to their friends or maybe pressure from their friends to send it to them.

> Ahmed: I don't feel that it's right to send it in the first place, but if you receive it then you shouldn't send it to someone else, it's that person.

> Kamal: They want attention.

> Interviewer (to Simone): Do you have something you want to say?

> Simone: Maybe they just want to show social media who they really are. Look at me. Get some more attention.

> Interviewer: Are you talking about a person who sends nudes themself or a person who shares a nude of other people?

116   J. Ringrose and K. Regehr

Simone: A person who sends it of themself.

Interviewer: What about if someone shares it around with other people when the person in the image isn't OK with that?

Rashid: When I say they shouldn't have been taken in the first place it's more for their own safety more than anything. Because once you've done it, it's out there you can't turn back. (Year 10, mixed)

In this exchange the interviewer tries to get the young people to think about issues of consent by raising questions about when the receiver of an image shares it with others without permission, but the group stead-fastly argue that it is the sender of nudes (the girl) who is 'wrong in the first place'. One of the girls, Simone, who barely spoke in the interview, is pressed by the interviewer to share her views, and agrees with Kamal that a girl sending nudes is simply asking for attention. The group main-tains a victim blaming stance, indeed turning the boy into the victim, something driven by the isolation room culture at the school. The lack of understanding of consent in this Year 10 group, who cite the main moti-vation for sharing images non-consensually as a 'joke', was disheartening and something that must be addressed in critical digital sex education to make clear what constitutes image-based sexual abuse.

Conclusions and ways forward for critical Snapchat education

In this school, we have seen some of the dynamics of Snapchat in peer groups in an economically deprived area with high crime rates, and how the platform raised serious issues of safety for young people. We saw how the Snapmap and Snapstory location feature enable physical violence to occur off screen in real life. The Bitmoji avatar element of the app means that identities are concealed, and ages are concealed—they appear 'younger'—hence requests from adults posing as young people may be accepted. The quick adds option without privacy settings opens the door to adults posing as children (friends) and creates opportunities for phishing and hacking. In relation to sexually explicit content and consent on the app; the Snapchat app renders young people, especially girls, vulnerable to quick add barrages through the Shoutout Snapcode circulation. Girls were also accepting requests from a nebulous category of 'mutuals' who seem to be known from the neighbourhood, but online abusers use these possibilities to harass girls.

In our discussions, the young people felt that greater awareness of Snapchat would be really helpful, with the Year 7s telling us they are 'smart' and 'mature' but also noting they needed help in navigating these issues. As in other settings, we found the school did not have high quality sex education that addresses the digital issues in play, nor adequate support in understanding and addressing sexual violence as part of a wider landscape of crime and violence and policing in their neighbourhood. As such there was a lack of response to how these issues play out through youth mobile phone social networks.

For instance, Venus and her friends told us they didn't receive enough pertinent information in Personal, Social, Health and Economic Education (PSHE). They had e-safety films on cyberbullying and sexting but were left to figure out on their own and with friends how to address the everyday nitty gritty details of what was happening in their peer groups:

Venus: I figured out most by myself. Yeah, because loads of people say things, like different words, and I'm like I don't know what this means.

Naza: Like different types of sex and stuff.

Irina: They never tell us.

Venus: I work it out myself.

Naza: Yeah. Or like oral sex or something.

Irina: They don't tell us. They say that they cover everything but they really don't.

Venus: It's not really the sort of thing you just ask, like what does this mean? Because you are kind of like just expected to know it, and then you kind of just go along with not understanding what people are talking about. (Year 8 Girls).

The group created mind maps, lists and diagrams about what they wanted to see differently in their sex education to address these gaps:

In Venus's top tips list (Fig. 4.3) she again asks to be taught at what age you should have a boyfriend, and presumably what that would entail; and she also wanted to learn more about racism and LGBTQ issues, to be covered in their sex education. She discussed needing help to 'understand' these issues so they were not left working everything out amongst themselves. Like the girls in Chapter 2, we see Venus navigating racism and sexism combined in her everyday life, such as being called a Congolese Bitch, and lacking adequate support for addressing these complex interconnected racialised and sexualised dynamics at school (Lamb et al., 2016).

Similarly, the Year 7 group also said they needed better sex education including how to stop LGBTQ harassment online:

Selin: Whenever I'm on Snapchat looking at someone's stories there's always a drama going on.

Jyoti: That's the thing I hate other than when people are like making people of LGBT.

Fera: Yeah, I don't like it.

Selin: Yeah.

Selin: It's very …oh LGBT's disgusting.

Fera: Yeah, they start making fun, because you know some of the boys, they start saying to people, they start saying to other people as a joke oh you're so gay.

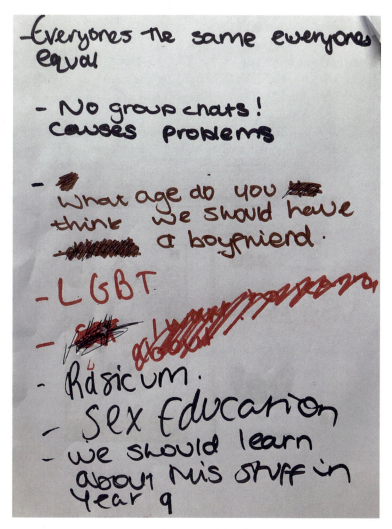

Fig. 4.3 Venus's Better Sex Education List—Everyone is equal, no group chats! causes problems, What age you think we should have a boyfriend, LGBT, Racism

Selin: Oh you're so bisexual. It is actually really offensive to gay people in general, and others like lesbians and bisexuals and that.

Jyoti: It's more offensive to me because I'm actually a part of it.

120 **J. Ringrose and K. Regehr**

(Year 7, mixed)

While we felt some despair at the Year 10 groups' blatant misogyny, we left the school incredibly impressed by the youngest students, who passionately defended LGTBQ rights and education on these issues:

> Jyoti: ...Never be afraid to express your sexuality, because you can be who you want to be, and nobody should like make fun of because of your gender or something like that...And no matter what you do you should always ask people for help if someone's trying to blackmail you or something, or try to like harm you or something like that, and never joke about genders and sexuality.

> Fera: I think children should learn about how LGBT people should be accepted, and how to stay safe online, turn the accounts into private, and turn off your locations. If you do get cyberbullied you should tell somebody who you trust and then they can help you. And some people, they're LGBT, and they are part of the LGBT community, and um, some Muslims aren't really allowed to be part of the LGBT, so if you are then you should do something about it. (Year 7, mixed)

Fera says children should learn that LGBT people should be accepted, pointing out that if religious beliefs are exclusionary they should be challenged.

Overall, ONA school highlights the need for an intersectional approach to digital literacy that takes account of how racism, sexism and sexual exploitation can play out in tandem. Vulnerabilities around tracking features, spreadability of profile information, mass acceptance of contacts, all elements enabled and promoted on Snapchat, create an intensification of risk for more marginalised young people who are attending schools in areas of high deprivation. Real material in-person risks such as physical violence from peers enabled through a technological platform like Snapchat increases in these contexts. The answer is not to take away young people's phones, depriving youth of their agency and literacy around managing digital technology as we found happened to Venus. Nor is it simply to place vulnerable youth into isolation units rather than address ethics and consent around relationship cultures and digital images. We firmly believe it is up to adults and wider society, from big tech companies to government and educators in schools, to address these issues with much better supports for young people and develop context specific resources and approaches that explain both the legal harms in full and youth rights, as we will outline in the conclusion to this book.

References

Ball, S. J. (2009). Academies in context: Politics, business and philanthropy and heterarchical governance. *Management in Education, 23*(3), 100–103. https://doi.org/10.1177/0892020609105801

Banet-Weiser, S., & Higgins, K, C. (2023) *Believability: Sexual violence, media, and the politics of doubt*. Polity.

Fava, N. M., & Bay-Cheng, L. Y. (2012). Young women's adolescent experiences of oral sex: Relation of age of initiation to sexual motivation, sexual coercion, and psychological functioning. *Journal of Adolescence, 35*(5).

Fazackerly, A., & Savage, M. (2023). Strictest academy schools in England suspend 30 times more pupils than the national average. *The Guardian.* https://www.theguardian.com/education/2023/dec/16/strictest-academy-schools-in-england-suspend-30-times-more-pupils-than-the-national-average

Ging, D., Lynn, T., & Rosati, P. (2020). Neologising misogyny: Urban Dictionary's folksonomies of sexual abuse. *New Media & Society, 22*(5), 838–856. https://doi.org/10.1177/1461444819870306

Lamb, S., Roberts, T., & Plocha, A. (2016). *Girls of color, sexuality, and sex education*. Pagrave McMillan.

Powell, A., & Henry, N. (2017). *Sexual violence in a digital age*. Palgrave.

Sealy, J., Abrams, E. J., & Cockburn, T. (2021). Students' experience of isolation room punishment in UK mainstream education. 'I can't put into words what you felt like, almost a dog in a cage.' *International Journal of Inclusive Education, 27*(12), 1336–1350. https://doi.org/10.1080/13603116.2021.1889052

Open Access This chapter is licensed under the terms of the Creative Commons Attribution-NonCommercial-NoDerivatives 4.0 International License (http://creativecommons.org/licenses/by-nc-nd/4.0/), which permits any noncommercial use, sharing, distribution and reproduction in any medium or format, as long as you give appropriate credit to the original author(s) and the source, provide a link to the Creative Commons license and indicate if you modified the licensed material. You do not have permission under this license to share adapted material derived from this chapter or parts of it.

The images or other third party material in this chapter are included in the chapter's Creative Commons license, unless indicated otherwise in a credit line to the material. If material is not included in the chapter's Creative Commons license and your intended use is not permitted by statutory regulation or exceeds the permitted use, you will need to obtain permission directly from the copyright holder.

5

Central Comprehensive: Religion, Honour, Digital Sexual Double Standards and Victim Shaming and Blaming

Central Comprehensive is a mixed gender inner-city state comprehensive school located between wealthy suburban boroughs and the city centre. It is the most deprived school we worked in for this study. It has a very high percentage (nearly 70%) of speakers of English as a second language, meaning there are many newcomers, migrant and vulnerable populations living in the catchment area of the school. Many families were receiving housing benefit and living in council housing (state-owned low rent housing allocated on the basis of vulnerability). It follows that the school also has an extremely high percentage (nearly 65%) of students who are eligible for free school meals (the marker of social deprivation in English schools as we've explained previously). This is nearly double the percentage in some of the other state schools we researched.

Demographically, many Bangladeshi Muslim students attend the school, so while not technically a faith school a large majority of the girls and women teachers at the school were wearing hijab dress including Mrs. Kareem, the teacher who coordinated school access for the research. Mrs. Kareem discussed her concerns over the lack of sex education that the students had received to date at the school in part due to the religious make up, which is why she was working with our research charitable

© The Author(s) 2025

J. Ringrose and K. Regehr, *Teens, Social Media, and Image Based Abuse*,

https://doi.org/10.1007/978-3-031-92322-7_5

partner, the sex education organisation, which was being brought in to deliver sessions for the first time the following school year.

There has been very little research on sexting amongst Muslim teens. One study of Muslim Moroccan youth found that young people held high rates of 'sexting-phobic views' and consequently 'rate those who engage in sexting comparatively worse' (Soriano-Ayala et al., 2020: p. 9). We found similar trends in Central Comprehensive, judgements which we explore from the perspective of cultural gender norms and sexual double standards. While we touched upon sexual double standards in Chapters 2, and 4, we delve into them in much more depth here.

Sexual double standards (SDS) is a concept that refers to evaluating men and women differently when participating in the same sexual acts and activities (Bordini & Sperb, 2013). Scholars also discuss gender specific 'sexual scripts' or normative patterns that are adopted and played out around sexual consent (Ruvalcaba & Eaton, 2019). Cis gendered heterosexual men gain status for engaging in sexual activities which mark them as competitive in the heterosexual matrix (Kreager & Staff, 2009).

(Hetero)Sexual scripts condition men and boys to initiate sexual activity and focus on their own sexual pleasure, whereas women and girls are meant to be passive objects for male sexual attention and conquest. Boys and men are rewarded for being 'players' and for achieving sexual 'conquests', whereas girls are sexaully shamed for the same activity. The sexual double standard creates a binary around the female virgin and the whore. When women and girls violate these codes they lose status or economic benefit because they are viewed as damaging their currency of virginity, innocence, sexual propriety and self-respect (a term we will hear a great deal in this chapter). This then leads to sexual shaming or 'slut-shaming', or attacking women and girls for sexual activity and calling them derogatory names (Van Royen et al., 2018).

These are the cultural and historical roots of the dynamics of sexual double standards that are transferred into online spaces, and which shape the reception of digital sexual imagery, and why female nudes are treated very differently from male nudes as we will see in this chapter. Men and boys also benefit from demonstrating sexual prowess online. They also, however, receive social benefits from sharing sexual images without consent (image-based sexual abuse). Heterosexual males are rewarded for displaying an active masculine (hetero)sexuality that successfully 'conquers' female targets and in the digital space this is demonstrated by obtaining sexual images from girls (Ringrose et al., 2013). Boys must demonstrate proof of their 'trophies' by displaying them. They must 'show and tell' to their male peer group (typically) in a familiar locker room dynamic, but this tends to happen in semi-private online spaces like WhatsApp chat groups. This helps explain why boys are more likely to pressure girls for nudes and then to show other boys so they can get social kudos, as we have already seen in previous chapters. Sexual double standards also, however, lead to digital slut shaming and victim blaming. Women are shamed as sluts for making sexual images, even when they are distributed without their consent (Herriot & Hiseler, 2015). As we've explained, through this logic those sharing the images (typically boys and men) without consent (image-based abuse) are actually rewarded for this activity, and it is not recognised as abuse (Henry & Beard, 2024).

Sexual double standards both online and offline remain prevalent in British society in general, and come into every chapter in this book, but in this school, characterised by a strong religious background grounded in patriarchal morality, the issue of sexual shaming of girls derived from sexual double standards was intensified. Specific gender norms around female sexuality and honour come together through honour based violence, and we look at how this is enabled through technology and specific social media practices. We will look at how the girls we interviewed accepted the reproduction of beliefs that condone honour based violence (Brookfield et al., 2024), which we consider as a form of culturally specific internalised misogyny. That is, we will see ways that girls identify with the sexual aggressor over and above solidarity with other girls and women, because they are invested in the patriarchal and honour based norms that ground sexual double standards. We also, however, discuss how one black British girl resists these trends in ways that show a battle for gender equality in these schooling contexts. Finally, we show how some boys in this school demonstrate empathy and concern for girls and women, but also feel resigned about the status quo.

Hijab and Social Media Representation

It was a sticky, hot July morning when we visited the school shortly before they were breaking up for the summer holidays. While most of the research team was at the school already, Kaitlyn was late. As she fought her way through the bustle of a central high street, men in suits were carrying Pret-A-Manger paper cups and vendors peddling Union Jack tat were calling out to passing tourists. She turned a corner, and just like that, the noise and suited men seem to fade away and were replaced by hijab wearing girls, who floated down the warm pavement towards a starkly modern building.

Inside the school, Kaitlyn pulled out her phone: 9:02. She texted to let the rest of the research team know she was downstairs, but the woman at the front desk chastised her sternly, 'This is a no phone environment.' This first interaction offers an important glimpse into the disciplinary nature of the school and its orientation towards mobile technology, taking a banning approach and with minimal digital literacy supports. Kaitlyn was issued a guest pass and waited for Mrs Kareem to collect her to show her to the research rooms. Mrs. Kareem, by contrast, was warm and welcoming. She had been eager for the research team to come in and conduct this project, as she noted the school was behind on sex education programming, particularly issues to do with digital technology. Mrs Kareem was concerned that the school would struggle to implement the new compulsory sex education curriculum which was becoming mandatory in the coming year.

The research team conducted four focus groups with 13 young people, eight girls and five boys across Years 9 and 10. Amongst the eight girls, seven wore a headscarf. The one girl who did not wear a headscarf identified as Black British. As with all our research interviews, we started by talking about the practices of making selfies. Having anticipated that we would be working with a range of culturally and faith diverse young people, we included a Snapchat image of a girl in a hijab in our visual prompts at the beginning of all the focus groups. These prompts proved very useful in this schooling context, generating interesting discussions about social media images in relation to wearing a hijab:

Anika: I feel like some Muslim boys, because maybe their sister or their mum wears a hijab, I think being around them and seeing how modest they are, they probably understand that some of the girls who do wear the headscarf, they are more modest, so they should like stay away from them, like not ask for anything sexual…

Nadia: But I feel like because like social media is kind of easy to make yourself a new identity sort of.

Raisa: In a way, because you're behind a screen, no-one is talking to you in real life or seeing you in real life, so you can present yourself differently.

Nadia: Also you can make your social media private, so you can choose who will see it.

Anika: Yeah, sometimes with females, because when you wear headscarf females are allowed to see your hair, so I feel like they might only have females, and they are comfortable with females seeing their hair, or like family members.

Shaila: I feel like some people wear the headscarf because of their families…

Raisa: Yeah.

Anika: …so they may post it on social media because their families can't see it, and they feel more comfortable without it.

Interviewer: So do any of you not wear your headscarf on social media?

Nadia: No.

Anika: Sometimes I do, but like it's only girls. (Year 10 girls).

When discussing sexual images, the girls explain that they think that boys understand that girls in hijab are modest (Siraj, 2011), and this extends to the digital realm where boys would not ask girls for anything sexual because of their hijab. They also explain that semi-private spaces in social media provide a where they can have a different identity and be visible without their hijab. They are aware of the privacy settings in order to create boundaries around who sees their hair, a sexualised and sacred attribute according to religious beliefs (Mahmudova & Evolvi, 2021). The girls also drew some of the rules about what you should and should not do when you post images on Instagram and Snapchat, as shown in Fig. 5.1.

The Year 9 group discussed similar issues around selfies and representing themselves online.

Early in their interview, the Year 9 girls said that they knew people who had sent nudes, explaining 'we've seen things'. Indeed, they went

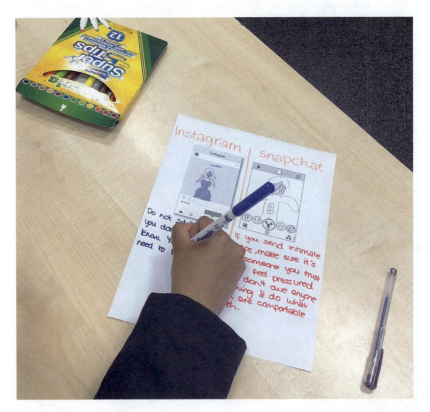

Fig. 5.1 Nadia's drawing—'do not' instructions' about Instagram and Snapchat

5 Central Comprehensive: Religion, Honour, Digital ...   129

on to describe the exact opposite behaviour from Muslim boys than what was discussed by the year 10 girls who said Muslim boys know not to ask Muslim girls for anything sexual. The girls describe a recent situation at the school in their year group (Year 9 aged 13–14) where a boy, Amir, and his cousin sent a fake dick pic to one of the girls in their friendship group, Laila, asking her to send nudes back:

> Fatema: there was this girl who had this crush on a boy in her form group......So she was like kind of staring at him or whatnot and he almost plays her, because he didn't like her......but he started like speaking to her and...Chatting to her.... he was with his cousin at the time. So they just went like oh my God she'll probably do this, let's take advantage of it. ...
>
> Shanaz: apparently he sent a...it was fake, it was fake (penis).
>
> Yasmin: And then she sent a picture of her boobs and her vagina basically to him.
>
> Shanaz: He copied and pasted a picture from Google and sent her that.
>
> Interviewer: Of his penis?
>
> Shanaz: Yeah, it was fake though, which obviously like, you know, kind of... I mean I don't know why she didn't see it because you could literally see the search tag in the thing, but she ended up sending pictures of her actual self to him, and gradually it got out and the whole year knew about it and it was just a very big thing because she kept denying it even though she kept her face in the pictures. (Year 9, Girls).

In this scenario, first, we can see how the technology allows Amir to create a fake dick pic and indeed dick pics are often faceless and anonymous, which means that there is less risk associated with them. (see Fig. 5.2).

The girls talk about the boys 'taking advantage' of Laila liking the boy but they are also judging Laila as in the wrong for not clearly 'seeing' that the image was fake from an apparent search tag in the

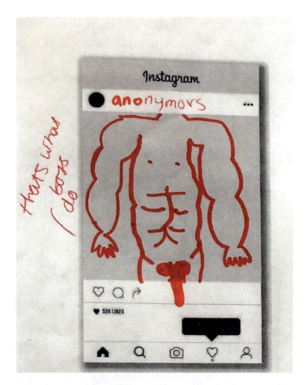

Fig. 5.2 Kaleisha's image of anonymous, faceless dick pics

image; and she is also constructed as at fault for the image having 'got out' to the whole year group since she sent the image in the first place. The main contention in this situation is that Laila was naïve enough to keep her face in her images and that she denies that she sent the image, even though everyone (likely except Laila) has been sent it or seen it on phones. Here we see clear victim blaming logic that has long been discussed as rife in youth digital sexual cultures (Albury & Crawford, 2012; Hasinoff, 2015). The girls continue to discuss how they were shown the image on Amir's phone:

> Fatema: …he (Amir)showed us a picture, but he covered it, because he wanted to show me that it was her face.

5 Central Comprehensive: Religion, Honour, Digital ...   131

Yasmin: Yeah!

Fatema: And that's when I realised it was her (Laila).

Interviewer: Why did he want to show you her face?

Fatema: Because she'd been lying to me about it.

Kaleisha: Oh yeah she (Fatema) was best friends with her (Laila).

Shanaz: We didn't believe that she actually sent it.

Yasmin: He showed us.

Kaleisha: He showed everyone.

Fatema: He sent it to the boys.

Shanaz: He (Amir) took it as a very jokey thing. (Year 9, Girls).

It is notable that when Amir shows the girls the nude he covers her naked body with his hand and shows them Laila's face. The point of showing the image is to 'out' Laila as having sent a nude. Covering the body is a fascinating way to keep the value of the image for oneself while still exposing Laila's identity in order to shame and humiliate her. Laila is framed as deceitful; as Fatema says: 'she'd been lying to me about it'. In contrast, Amir is said to have sent it to the boys and taken the whole situation 'as a very jokey thing'. The behaviour of Amir and his cousin is viewed through a lens of humour rather abuse. The girls go on to explain that they are no longer 'close' to Laila as a result of her behaviour:

Fatema: Yeah, but me being her best friend I literally just told her how I addressed myself, and for me it wasn't even really about the fact that she sent nudes, because yeah it was very like disrespectful to our religion, but it was the fact that she lied to me, because I was her best friend, I was the last one to find out, I like literally defended her throughout the whole week, when she wasn't here.

132   J. Ringrose and K. Regehr

Shanaz: Yeah, she was like no she didn't do it, no she didn't do it.

Fatema: Yeah, literally from the first day someone came up to us and asked us about it I went no, she didn't do it, and even that day she didn't tell me the truth, which is what really like annoyed me, but I didn't want her to do anything stupid, because I know like also it's tough for her as well. But it's just not right.... it's disrespect for the religion as well, and it's also disrespect for her, because it's like now everyone knows her body...

Shanaz: Exactly.

Interviewer: Is she still your best friend?

Fatema: Yeah, but I'm like kind of distanced, like...yeah. I think the fact that she wasn't being honest about it as well. Everyone was more angry about that fact...

Shanaz: That she lied.

Fatema: And I mean she's a hijab right, so she's a Muslim, so for us it was...like...it was all a bigger thing. (Year 9, Girls).

Here we can see that the girls explicitly distance themselves from Laila, who is viewed as disrespecting herself and her religion. Fatema tells us she was Laila's 'best friend' but this relationship is compromised due to the degree of the transgression. Creating and sharing an intimate body image is viewed as incompatible with Islam and in contradiction with the practice of wearing the hijab. Fatema is aware of the probable impact on Laila, also noting 'I didn't want her to do anything stupid', but that is quickly shut down by the judgement of her 'disrespect for the religion' and herself, and her violation of Muslim femininity. The girls use Laila's supposed denial of sending Amir an image as the main reason they are angry, lacking any compassion about why Laila may have acted in this way to protect herself after Amir's betrayal. Fatema goes on to discuss how this could possibly effect Laila:

5 Central Comprehensive: Religion, Honour, Digital ... 133

Fatema: Obviously, personally, I, because, you know, in tutor time they always show us [educational videos] where people become depressed or commit suicide [after experiences with sexting], so, you know, I like kind of took it in a different perspective, said, you know, she did kind of disrespect things that I deeply believe in, however I don't want her to go, and you know...do something to herself because we didn't want to be her friends. So, you know, I said to her, you know, you need to like realise what you've done, I'm not gonna like, not start treating you badly, because I don't want her to do something and then I feel guilty ... (Year 9, Girls).

Fatema explains she understands the possible impact of the girls saying they no longer 'want to be her friends' saying that they've been shown videos and PowerPoints about scenarios where 'people become depressed or commit suicide' after having their nudes leaked. Fatema's religious beliefs about Laila's disrespect are in direct contradiction with concern for Laila, evident as she says she would feel 'guilty' if Laila did something to herself as a result of what's happened.

To recount: in this scenario, Laila is blamed for creating and sending an image to Amir, despite the fact that he is the one who has shared a dick pic first, and gone on to share Laila's image with the entire year group, without consent, in a direct bid to shame Laila. The girls go on to explicitly discuss how the hijab constructs the Muslim feminine 'mentality' that must be upheld for self-respect:

Fatema: Like for example if you think about the hijab, it's like the hijab is, many people think it's the headscarf that we wear, but it's about your whole, your mentality, perhaps the way you dress...or the way you treat people, it's the entire thing. So I think definitely because we've grown up in that, for example us three, and you've (Kaleisha) probably grown up with that in Christianity as well, certain like aspects.

Shanaz: But you're not forced, like even if you're doing it you are not forced to do anything, however...

Fatema: it's your choice.

Shanaz: ...yeah, it's your choice, however...

Fatema: ...if you're gonna like represent something like you believe in, like it has to be...you have to go by it, you have to go by it.

Interviewer: So you think there's more pressure on girls to represent it than boys?

Fatema: I think...yeah. (Year 9, Girls).

Here the girls want to assure us that wearing the hijab is not forced, it's a choice, but by taking up this practice you must embody it completely. Laila is in the wrong because she does not 'represent' her religion and the hijab, she has contradicted her apparent choice. The interviewer also tries to ask about boys in relation to the religion and pressure on girls, to which Fatema replies there is more pressure upon girls.

The girls also went on to explain that the school purposefully did not tell Laila's father about this episode for fear of his reaction (as a Muslim man):

Interviewer: OK so [Laila's] parents were called by the school?

Shanaz: No, not her dad.

Fatema: I think only her mum knows.

Shanaz: Yeah, only her mum knows.

Fatema: And they didn't even say it was a boy, they said it was one of her friends, because number one...

Fatema: Yeah. They said it was a girl even though...

Shanaz: ...with her dad I don't know what would have happened to her if they told her dad.

Interviewer: So what do you mean?

5 Central Comprehensive: Religion, Honour, Digital … 135

Fatema: She would probably like get in trouble, like in big trouble like, she probably would have been sent somewhere or…like that's her family …

The girls relate the school's decision to not tell a Muslim father for fear of his reaction; indicating again the far-reaching consequences for Laila of violating the codes of Muslim femininity, mentioning a fear that she would be 'sent somewhere' because of family. They say the school kept the gender of the boy concealed even to the mother and suggested Laila's image had been shared by a 'friend', explaining the mother's reaction as well.

Interviewer: OK, so what did her mother do?

Fatema: Took her phone.

Shanaz: Literally just took her phone for like three days. Because she has an older sister, who has done… like a similar thing has happened with her.

Fatema: Maybe her sister's a bad role model for her.

Yasmin: But if it was me… I'd rather like get my mum or someone close to me to have a conversation with me so like you understand what you did, to understand why we think it's wrong.

Kaleisha: that's what I think as well, you've made a mistake…

Yasmin: I'd just say just to learn from it.

Kaleisha: Exactly. No, not punished but like…

Yasmin: I'd rather like have a talk, like if I did that…

Kaleisha: Yeah.

Fatema and Shanaz say Laila's sister is a 'bad role model', retrenching shame and blame, while the other girls express wanting a space to discuss

136 J. Ringrose and K. Regehr

mistakes without punishment and being able to learn and talk about it. Kaleisha and Yasmin talk about how much they would like someone supportive to have a conversation with them about 'mistakes' rather than this punitive and judgemental approach to the episode.

We as interviewers wanted to press on to find out how the school had reacted to the boy:

Interviewer: OK. And were the boy's parents called?

Shanaz: No.

Shanaz: I don't think so.

Kaleisha: He [Amir] was called in [at school].

Fatema: At the end of the day is it not a criminal offence though, to have pictures of someone, a minor, on your phone.

Shanaz: Yeah, well, child pornography.

Yasmin: child pornography, you can't keep on your phone…

Shanaz: We have a school police officer, and I think the school police officer…

Yasmin: He spoke to him [Amir], yeah… I don't know what happened, that was a confidential conversation.

Shanaz: Yeah.

Kaleisha: But there was no like legal action taken, and there was no like school system punishment taken.

The girls debate whether what Amir has done is illegal. Fatema declares that it's not illegal for Amir to have images of Laila on his phone, while Shanaz and Yasmin disagree saying it's child pornography. Here we get to the crucial contradiction in the laws around sexting and how this dictates

5 Central Comprehensive: Religion, Honour, Digital ... 137

the way such issues are are taught in schools with detrimental effects. Images of minors are considered child pornography so the image itself is illegal. The messaging has been focused on not producing or sharing intimate images, rather than focusing on teaching children that the sharing of intimate images without consent is also a form of sexual abuse. The messaging to not sext as we've been discussing in this book is an abstinence approach, which means there is less supportive messaging around protecting the victims of image-based sexual abuse, such as Laila. What happens is that Laila is blamed for a criminal act she is the victim of. Police in schools are facing dilemmas daily given their need to protect all the young people involved. In this episode we can see that what happens is a climate of secrecy and silence around the episode, with no evidence of support for Laila whatsoever.

In this example we see the role of 'so called honour based violence' (Brookfield et al., 2024; Richards, 2009). It is 'so called' because it is based on religious and cultural ideals of honour tied to girls and women sexual virtues as protectors of honour, but we challenge what is honourable when it is used to abuse women and girls. In communities where woman and girls are expected to uphold family honour via gender and sexual norms of behaviour (such as dress and modesty etc.) "technology can be utilised to (threaten to) shame them through "distributing or content deemed to be sexualised or intimate" (Douglas et al., 2019). We would advise it is just these types of moral dilemmas created by sexual shaming and victim blaming in cultural contexts like this school that sex education and legal protections should be offering supportive messaging and frameworks to address image-based sexual harassment and abuse, and this must be culturally specific unpacking the nuances of issues like honour based violence.

There was a glimmer of hope towards the end of this focus group. Kaleisha, the black British girl, starts to unpack the implications of blame and shame surrounding Laila and the lack of attention to the behaviour of Amir. She argues the school needs to understand 'both sides', by which she means they should try to look at the pressure Laila received from the boys:

138　　J. Ringrose and K. Regehr

Kaleisha: I think um it was two wrongs in this situation, but I think people very like put it on her, but it was also like you need to understand both sides... And I think she was naïve as well.... It was more pressure put on her because of the boys in our year.

Fatema: I don't really, I think from the situation yeah she's matured about it, but I don't think she's like matured enough in my opinion,

Kaleisha: All the boys completely blinded the fact of what he did. Like just attacked her.... They made it seem as if he (Amir) was the good angel ...

Yasmin: Yeah, exactly.

Fatema: No, but it was like too false.

Kaleisha: Yeah, they were making him seem like the victim.

Yasmin: You know what, if he'd never shown anyone, yeah...

Kaleisha: the fact you are going to people saying oh my God look at this...

Interviewer: How did they make him seem like a victim?

Kaleisha:, because he was even acting like a victim, he said that she sent me nudes, this and that...Because he got it off the internet.

Yasmin: ...oh she sent me these nudes, what do I do? But then he wouldn't say the whole story of the point where he was talking to her for hours up until that point, like to get her trust. (Year 9, Girls).

We can see that Kaleisha, with Yasmin's support, works to move awareness onto the idea that Amir was partly to blame for the situation. She is troubled by the way in which it was 'very like put on' Laila, however, suggesting a need to look at 'both sides' and the types of pressure Laila was put under to send an image. Fatema still criticises Laila as not having matured enough, continuously bringing blame back to Laila's behaviour rather instead of Amir's. Yasmin continues to point to the pressures and how the boys have coaxed Laila to send the image. Overall, it is hard work for Kaleisha and Yasmin to try and shift the blame from the victim of image-based sexual abuse onto the harmful behaviour of sharing without consent and with an intent to humiliate and shame Laila. This demonstrates that the young people had never considered conceptually how to shift analysis from what the girl did to issues of predatory and abusive masculinity, which is what we argue needs to happen as part of schools supporting victims in complex intersectional contexts such as this religious peer group.

'It's Just How Society Is': Religion, Masculinity and the Acceptance of Sexual Double Standards

In the focus groups with the boys, we found the younger boys in this school basically refused to discuss these issues; the researcher noted it was her most difficult interview in the entire project as they were extremely closed down, largely repeating official anti-sexting narratives with single word answers.

Interviewer: How, how would you say images of girls in particular that are leaked are treated?

Nideesh: Oh, uh, most of the time called names, like.

Sanav: bullied.

Pranshul: Yeah. Like, oh, they'll be like disrespected. Yeah.

Interviewer: What about boys? If images of boys' parts were shared?

Pranshul: maybe the same thing, but like less harsh cause like that's just like how this is; how it happened for some reason. (Year 9)

140   J. Ringrose and K. Regehr

As with the girls, the Year 9 boys note that girls whose nudes are leaked will be disrespected. They also note that boys would face 'less harsh' consequences, with Pranshul reasoning 'that's just how this is'. The researcher noted that the Year 10 boys were similarly closed off and they repeatedly asked whether the school would have access to the recording, seemingly very concerned about adults hearing them discuss this topic. Eventually, the older boys did start to open up about the issues and began to discuss a case that appeared to be very similar to Laila's case of a girl who had an intimate video shared online.

> Mo: Yeah, so what happened that girl got exposed and then that was in a couple of weeks, like a couple months after she left the school...she started self-harming and stuff... I saw her a couple times but I never really speak to her, uh, so like she had like, like lines on her wrists and stuff. But then I think right now she's like in a good state. But before she wasn't because like she'd been exposed and stuff. Yeah. (Year 10, Boys).

Here the boys mention a case similar to the one we heard about Laila. Like the girls they are concerned about the 'mental effect' on the girl, acknowledging the impact of how these episodes impact girls and young women in their community noting that boys would be less likely to face shame and humiliation if their nudes were shared without their consent:

> Mo: I think if I was a boy, a boy wouldn't take it to heart. Like they would not want to kill themselves....
>
> Interviewer: Have you, have you come across any situations where boys have shared nudes and they've had kind of negative outcomes?
>
> Rafi: Nah.
>
> Abir: No, I can't think of any to be honest. Unless they've got like something wrong with their thing. (Year 10 boys)

Like the year 9 boys, the year 10 group agrees that boys are less likely to feel shame or be negatively impacted if their nudes are shared, but they also suggest the risk of images being shared is less familiar to them.

5 Central Comprehensive: Religion, Honour, Digital ...   141

What they do suggest is there is risk of their penis being judged. They also discuss how girls would be reluctant to discuss what had happened to them (like Laila) for fear of further reprisal:

> Mo: I think it was, if there's a girl, I think, well they could it could be scared if they say something ...the boy could come to them and hurt them. (Year 10 boys)

> Abir: Girls are more scared because of physical violence. I think maybe but like it's just society how it is. You can't change it. But men it's more often that men are likely yeah to cheat on their partners but also be with multiple people and have like physical contact with others. But women, it's like if they get exposed then it affects them. Not only physically, both mentally, because in the future, who knows when those nudes are gonna come back and maybe if the boyfriend they've had is gonna come back to them and end up him leaving her and that goes into a negative effect. (Year 10, Boys).

Here the boys demonstrate significant capacity to think about the possible dynamics for girls as being far more risky. Girls are at more risk of having their images shared non-consensually, but girls also face barriers to talking about these experiences, reporting them and seeking out help. Mo and Abir note that girls have to worry about boys physically retaliating if a girl reports sexual violence, something that was entirely absent from our discussions with the girls, who simply condemn Laila for not telling them what has happened to her. Abir explicitly acknowledged sexual double standards; men can be with multiple women and cheat on women, but women cannot, something that was also notably absent from the discussion with the girls. Abir discusses how girls have to think about how being digitally exposed will impact them and that in future a boyfriend could find out and leave them. The boys were also frank about why boys act without consent:

> Interviewer: Okay. Why do you think people share pictures of other people then without their consent?

142   **J. Ringrose and K. Regehr**

Mo: They gain something. Like they gain something more people like them they become more popular.

Interviewer: So do you think other people approve of that?

Mo: In this society yeah. I think that's what social media teaches young people. If you're more popular you're more successful. (Year 10, Boys).

The boys express a clear understanding that gaining nudes is an asset for the boys to make them more popular, its part of being a successful (heterosexual) male. They go on to discuss how boys will send an image to one another because it won't 'damage them':

Interviewer: Do you think there is pressure on people to show nudes they receive around?

Mo: Depends who you hang out with. People that are more into relationships and stuff, I think you're gonna feel more pressured. I think there definitely is pressure to share nudes. I think it's like the natural cause like as humans we're growing up like it's really, really, really hard to keep a secret. And if you've got a picture like that and it won't affect you personally, it will affect the person who's sent the nudes, then I think there'll be more pressure to send it because we're, not born, but we're taught that if it's not affecting you, then it shouldn't really damage you and it shouldn't, you shouldn't get yourself involved with it. (Year 10, Boys).

The boys express exceptional understanding here of the different types of peer pressure facing boys which is to achieve status through gaining nudes and by proving and demonstrating this evidence to other boys as part of homosocial ranking. Because of this Mo describes how hard it is to keep the secret of getting nudes from other boys. He emphasises this by saying its 'really, really, really' hard. These Muslim boys clearly understand and articulate that they are free to share nudes because they can gain from it and sharing it won't affect them personally; it will affect the person who has created the image and is in the nude–(e.g. girls like Laila). Mo explains that it won't 'damage' boys, therefore they are not really at risk, and there is the implication that since they will not be impacted by the shaming and victim blaming they should not get involved in challenging these episodes either. What is important about Mo's statement, however, is that he corrects himself from saying that men and boys are 'born' like this to saying 'we're taught' these beliefs. We as researchers find this an incredibly important statement to underscore that such beliefs can also be unlearned and different values and practices can be taught and socialised at school, with sex education offering a prime vehicle for transforming understandings about sexual images and their impacts.

Conclusion

In this chapter, we have explored how religion shapes sexual double standards in the context of the peer groups we interviewed in Central Comprehensive school. We analysed the social restrictions around Muslim femininities and social media images and how sexual double standards lead to a horrifying case of sexual shaming and victim blaming of Laila, who is the target of peer pressure to send a nude via a fake transactional dick pic (which is a form of sexual harassment) and then subjected to image-based sexual abuse (when she shares her own authentic nude with the boy, Amir). This form of image-based sexual harassment and abuse is intermeshed with Muslim religious beliefs and sexual shaming, which has been analysed in previous research as 'honour-based violence'. Laila wears a hijab at school and the sending of a nude image with her face and hair showing is viewed as a violation of her religion and disrespectful to herself and her community. We showed the internalisation of these misogynistic norms by the girls in Laila's friendship, which shapes their behaviour and their subsequent effective ostracization of Laila from their previously close-knit friendship group, In contrast, the boys involved were viewed with sympathy by these same girls, we could explain this as identification with patriarchy and acceptance of men's dominance over women, as theorised by masculinities scholar R.W. Connell (2005) to explain when women chose alliances with men and sexism to ensure harmony in their personal relationships.

We also learned that the school colluded with and created a context for sexual double standards, leading to the legitimation of sexual violence, in the ways they are said to have responded to the situation, compounding the patriarchal power and fear of Laila's father who it is speculated may respond harshly to the perceived sexual shame and lack of respect brought on by Laila's transgression. This again related to the cultural specificity of honour based violence where violations of honour bring extreme shame that condone violence. One of the girls in the focus group, Kaleisha, who was Black British, tried to challenge the sexual shaming of Laila and explore the contradiction and unfairness facing girls through considering 'both sides', with some uptake in the friend group. But this reasoning was met with firm resistance from some of the other girls who remained convinced that Laila made 'poor choices' and disrespected herself and her religion had no one to blame but herself. This narrative aligns strongly with previous research on self-responsibilisation of blame and shame onto girl sexters (Karaian, 2014) but here we see an intersectional nuance of how unredeemable and damning this 'mistake' is viewed in the context of girls' violating the Muslim feminine practice of hijab (Sylwander, 2022).

Finally, we considered Muslim masculinities, and saw how the Muslim boys in the school understood these dynamics of masculine privilege and sexual double standards as normal and 'just how society is'. The boys, however, demonstrated more awareness and empathy for the mental and physical effects of these dynamics upon girls, than some of the girls themselves, acknowledging for instance the threat of male violence if girls report sexual violence, including image-based sexual abuse. Ultimately the discussion of male power reinforced an acceptance of the patriarchal status quo (Connell and Messerschmidt 2005) in this specific honour based community context (Aplin, 2017). Indeed, the boys ended up explaining that until society changed, and boys faced repercussions for sharing images non-consensually, it would simply continue unabated, because boys were never impacted by and therefore would not need to take any responsibility for, the fallout of these episodes.

These dynamics are not exclusive to the Muslim community, but they do show how Muslim girls may be operating within contexts of intensified racialised and religioned sexism in their schooling environments, enabling new manifestations of tech facilitated honour based violence. Drawing insights from these experiences, we argue education that engages with how sexism and patriarchal power inequities play out in relation to varied religious contexts and practices, is sorely needed. The possibility of more equitable values through education was hinted at by Mo, who noted earlier that patriarchal values are taught, not inherent. The year 10 girls also talked about the need for better education to support young people dealing with social media and abuse, given the lack of understanding amongst schools and parents about how social media and apps work:

> Anika: it would be helpful if it was younger people because they understand what we're going through, right? like as in they'll know how certain apps work as well,

> Raisha: Yah they (teachers and parents) are really old...

> Anika: So they can't really understand how we should like go about certain situations if they don't know what the situations are.

> Shaila: And they're like if anything does happen... a teacher we don't even like normally talk to, like you wouldn't be comfortable

> Sadia: I think it would be more useful if they told us the different approaches... online... bad people, ...approach people in different ways, and we might not know all the ways and we might think it's harmless, but if they like explained and like told us more about the different ways that they could like target young people then I think that would be more helpful. It could affect someone more than the cyberbullying assemblies they are doing now. (year 10, girls)

Here the girls are clearly calling for greater awareness of how apps work and how children are being targeted, so that the adults in their lives can understand the dilemmas presented and have more knowledge and foresight into the problems in order to better support youth. The girls articulated that being more in touch with the technology and its impacts

146   J. Ringrose and K. Regehr

would be more effective than the large-scale assemblies the school hosts about 'cyberbullying'. Better understandings of the underlying intersectional power dynamics around honour based violence and how it can be enacted in the peer groups, would be extremely helpful to integrate into relationship and sexuality education that is cultural and context specific. As we explain much more fully in the conclusion to this book, it is only by recognising and addressing these events as various manifestations of image-based sexual harassment abuse that young people will have the support and tools to re-evaluate what is happening and be able to challenge such injustice and violence, as we began to witness with some of the young people in this school.

References

Albury, K., & Crawford, K. (2012). Sexting, consent and young people's ethics: Beyond Megan's Story. *Continuum, 26*(3), 463–473.

Aplin, R. (2017). Exploring the role of mothers in 'honour' based abuse perpetration and the impact on the policing response. *Women's Studies International Forum, 60*, 1–10.

Bordini, G. S., & Sperb, T. M. (2013). Sexual double standard: A review of the literature between 2001 and 2010. *Sexuality and Culture, 17*(4), 686–704.

Brookfield, K., Fyson, R., & Goulden, M. (2024). Technology-facilitated domestic abuse: An under-recognised safeguarding issue? *The British Journal of Social Work, 54*(1), 419–436. https://doi.org/10.1093/bjsw/bcad206

Connell, R. W., & Messerschmidt, J. W. (2005). Hegemonic masculinity: Rethinking the concept. *Gender & Society, 19*(6), 829–859. https://doi.org/10.1177/0891243205278639

Douglas, H., Harris, B., & Dragiewicz, M. (2019). Technology-facilitated domestic and family violence: Women's experiences. *The British Journal of Criminology, 59*(3), 551–570.

Hasinoff, A. A. (2015). *Sexting panic: Rethinking criminalisation, privacy, and consent.* University of Illinois Press.

Henry, N., & Beard, G. (2024). Image-based sexual abuse perpetration: A scoping review. *Trauma, Violence, and Abuse, 0*(0). https://doi.org/10.1177/15248380241266137

Herriot, L., & Hiseler, L. E. (2015). Documentaries on the sexualisation of girls: Examining slut-shaming, victim-blaming and what's being left off-screen. In E. Renold, J. Ringrose, & R. D. Egan (Eds.), *Children, Sexuality and Sexualisation* (pp. 289–304). Palgrave Macmillan UK.

Karaian, L. (2014). Policing 'sexting': Responsibilisation, respectability and sexual subjectivity in child protection/crime prevention responses to teenagers' digital sexual expression. *Theoretical Criminology, 18*(3), 282–299. https://doi.org/10.1177/1362480613504331

Kreager, D. A., & Staff, J. (2009 Jun) The sexual double standard and adolescent peer acceptance. *Social Psychology Quarterly;72*(2), 143–164. https://doi.org/10.1177/019027250907200205. PMID: 25484478; PMCID: PMC4256532.

Mahmudova, L., & Evolvi, G. (2021). Likes, comments, and follow requests: The Instagram user experiences of young Muslim women in the Netherlands. *Journal of Religion, Media and Digital Culture, 10*(1), 50–70. https://doi.org/10.1163/21659214-bja10038

Richards, L. (2009). *Domestic abuse, stalking and harassment and honour based violence risk identification and assessment and management model* [Online]. London, Dash Risk Model.

Ringrose, J., Harvey, L., Gill, R., & Livingstone, S. (2013). Teen girls, sexual double standards and 'sexting': Gendered value in digital image exchange. *Feminist Theory, 14*(3), 305–323. https://doi.org/10.1177/1464700113499853

Ruvalcaba, Y., & Eaton, A. A. (2019). Nonconsensual pornography among US Adults: A sexual scripts frame- work on victimisation, perpetration, and health correlates for women and men. *Psychology of Violence, 10*(1), 68–78. https://doi.org/10.1037/vio0000233

Siraj, A. (2011). Meanings of modesty and the *hijab* amongst Muslim women in Glasgow, Scotland. *Gender, Place & Culture, 18*(6), 716–731. https://doi.org/10.1080/0966369X.2011.617907

Soriano-Ayala, E., Cala, V. C., & Dalouh, R. (2020 Feb 8). Adolescent profiles according to their beliefs and affinity to sexting. a cluster study. *International Journal of Environmental Research and Public Health, 17*(3), 1087. https://doi.org/10.3390/ijerph17031087. PMID: 32046346; PMCID: PMC7037697.

Sylwander, K. R. (2022). 'Fuck Them Walla': Girls' resistance within racialized online assemblages. *Young, 30*(1), 5–21. https://doi.org/10.1177/1103308821997627

Van Royen, K., Poels, K., Vandebosch, H., & Walrave, M. (2018). Slut-Shaming 2.0. In M. Walrave, J. Van Ouytsel, K. Ponnet, & J. R. Temple (Eds.), *Sexting: Motives and risk in online sexual self-presentation* (pp. 81–98). Palgrave Macmillan US.

Open Access This chapter is licensed under the terms of the Creative Commons Attribution-NonCommercial-NoDerivatives 4.0 International License (http://creativecommons.org/licenses/by-nc-nd/4.0/), which permits any noncommercial use, sharing, distribution and reproduction in any medium or format, as long as you give appropriate credit to the original author(s) and the source, provide a link to the Creative Commons license and indicate if you modified the licensed material. You do not have permission under this license to share adapted material derived from this chapter or parts of it.

The images or other third party material in this chapter are included in the chapter's Creative Commons license, unless indicated otherwise in a credit line to the material. If material is not included in the chapter's Creative Commons license and your intended use is not permitted by statutory regulation or exceeds the permitted use, you will need to obtain permission directly from the copyright holder.

6

Stags School for Boys: Elite Masculinities, Nudes as Homosocial Currency and Mastering Your Digital Footprint

All-Boys' Environments and the Performance and Ethos of Privilege

Driving to Stags, a highly selective 'single sex' independent school for boys, our research team ended up at the wrong location. Google maps had led us the nearby partner 'single sex' campus, Doe School for Girls.[1] The proximity, yet physical separation of Stag and Doe schools become increasingly interesting to us as we learned about the digital sexual activity of boys at Stags, which frequently connected them virtually with girls at Does. We learned about several episodes of nude images travelling between the two schools through youth mobile networks, which traversed the land and gate system physically separating the two schools.

At Stags, we worked with 13 boys across Years 9 and 10 through 4 focus group interviews with groups of 3–4 boys. The participants explained some of the key pressure points for boys and digital sexual

---

[1] We put single sex in scare quotes to signify that sex is contested and gender is non-binary, an issue that boys and girls schools are increasingly confronting in the contemporary context internationally (Jackson, 2009).

© The Author(s) 2025
J. Ringrose and K. Regehr, *Teens, Social Media, and Image Based Abuse*,
https://doi.org/10.1007/978-3-031-92322-7_6

149

imagery which we will explore, including discussions of porn, nudes, protecting your digital footprint, and how boys are caught up in the sexual double standards of youth digital intimacies that we have been discussing in this book.

After we found Stags campus, we entered a stern iron gate and made our way to an imposing Georgian building, passing through the main archways to reception to register and wait for our teacher host, Mr. Conway. In the reception area, we encountered a huge, ornate memorial plaque honouring former students. After Mr. Conway collected us, we went up an impressive staircase to the staff lounge area, to wait for our sessions to begin. Making our way to the back of the building to our designated interview rooms, we passed a wall the length of the entire hallway covered in laminated head shots and write ups of prominent men in politics, history, literature and science including Nobel Prize winners. Checking it thoroughly we found it contained *no women*. We therefore called it 'the wall of men', which we felt made a lasting impression about the environment as a whole. Reaching the staff lounge, we noted how well resourced, comfortable, clean and refined this space for staff was with individually wrapped biscuits, and coffee pod machines rather than the instant coffee in state schools, which is often self-funded by the staff, given government cutbacks and budgetary restraints.

How Do You Interact with Girls at an All-Boys School?

One of the main issues that arose early in our conversations with the boys is the difficulty in understanding or relating to girls in the context of an all-boys school. Some of the boys struggled with reference points when discussing gender issues in relation to the visual prompts, often turning to discussions of siblings and family members, in the absence of having girls in their immediate schooling environment. For instance, these Year 9 boys reflected upon their sisters having more pressure or unfair treatment compared to them:

Aiden: I don't think boys are generally as pressured as girls.

6 Stags School for Boys: Elite Masculinities, Nudes ...   151

Francis: I think they're (boys) more generally relaxed.

Damien: Yeah.

Interviewer: Why is that?

Aiden: I'm not sure. I have a sister and she's always like 10 times more stressed than me and we both have exams, but to be fair hers is GCSE. But two years ago, she was still as stressed as she is now and she's always stressful. I just don't care.

Interviewer: What do you think is the main pressure facing boys?

Damien: Being good at video games? [laughter] (Year 9 Group A)

In another group of Year 9 boys one mentioned how his sister was more controlled by his parents around her social media use and posts:

Timothy: My dad got annoyed at my sister for posting on Instagram a picture of her kissing her old boyfriend and it's like, it's not, you wouldn't think that bad, but he just thinks it's like you shouldn't have it on the Internet. (Year 9 Group B)

When asked how they would make contact with girls outside their families, the boys immediately discuss social media and how this has expanded their potential networks:

Tom: There are people that DM over Instagram... we are in a Jewish community bubble. All these people that know each other in like the Jewish community.

Oscar: So that's how people, especially my friends, meet people.

Interviewer: And that would be through Instagram?

James: Instagram or through other friends.

152   J. Ringrose and K. Regehr

> Tom: Snapchat… you can choose who you want to speak to or who you want to see or who you want to see your things. You can choose who you add. (Year 10 Group A)

Here, directly in counterpoint to the girls we've been discussing in other school sites who are often concerned with their Snapscores, Tom notes he carefully chooses who he adds on Snapchat, keeping his contacts limited. Another year 9 boy confirmed Snapchat and Instagram were the main means of communicating and meeting girls:

> Timothy: And nowadays people, if you're trying to find someone, well it sounds weird but like let's say you're talking to a girl or something, you're going to go look at her Instagram. Right? So people on the internet want to look really good because they know that's what people are going to look at to find out stuff about them.

> Hugh: But Snapchat is more like you add your actual friends. I mean not everyone does but like you add your actual friends. So Instagram if you're DMing someone, it's usually cause you don't have their Snapchat. (Year 9 Group B)

> Aiden: I think the first thing you do is request their Instagram and maybe then ask for Snapchat on their Instagram. So you pop up to them and you say, Oh what's your Snapchat? Or something like that. And then they give it to you and then maybe talk a bit in Snapchat, uh, uh, and then you might meet up one time or a few times and then you might want to [send images] (Year 9 Group A)

The boys clarify that they would search for people they don't know on Instagram in order to gain Snapchat access to progress the relationship in a more intimate way than possible on Instagram. Like the boys we encountered in Lion's boarding school, they noted they did not do Shoutouts to up their popularity on Snapchat. They did however still receive a host of unwanted content on platforms like Snapchat:

> Jamie: They're like, they'll send you streaks in their underwear.

6 Stags School for Boys: Elite Masculinities, Nudes ... 153

Interviewer: So what kind of thing would be in one of those underwear streaks?

Jamie: It depends who they are. Sometimes, sometimes they'll put like, like a small corner of a strap or something and some, some girls send whole body (Year 9 Group B)

The Year 10 boys also discuss how these streaks were part of being targeted and sent porn links through Snapchat and Instagram.

Henry: It's like, hey sexy, come and click on this link and get my nudes.

Tom: Yeah it's like a link to some dodgy website.

Henry: Yeah and say the area you live in and say I'll have sex with you.

Tom: Or like a picture like that one. And then it's like click on this to see more. (Year 10 Group A).

The boys share some of the 'girls in their underwear', images for instance a woman pulling her thong panties down her buttocks, later drawing these experiences (see Fig. 6.1). They are aware this is a monetary scheme of some sort. We heard about premium accounts from other boys as well where there is a push for boys to sign up for premium content to pay subscription fees for access to content behind a paywall.

The boys speculate that many of these accounts are 'porn bots'. Tom outlines how bot activities happen: you are sent a message 'do you want to see me naked' or comments on posts. The boys argue you can immediately tell it is a bot because they have few or no followers, noting they are also sent these types of messages on PlayStation.

Not only are they well aware of how they as teen boys are targets for posts to sign up to premium accounts, they also follow 'man influencers' (Roberts & Westcott, 2024) who warn them against this content:

Jamie: An Instagram account he's called Extender. He's just like he does memes but they're like more...

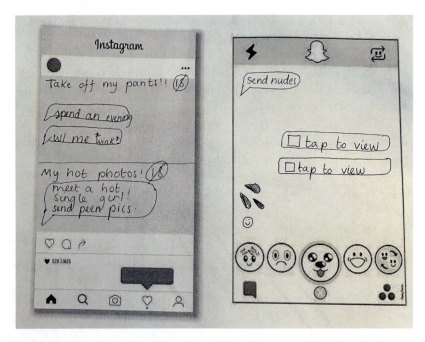

Fig. 6.1 "Take off my pants!!" Instagram DMs from Premium Subscription Accounts

Aiden: Dank.

Jamie: Basically …premium Snapchats …he was just making fun of hoe [whore] girls who do premium Snapchats because I think it's a way of like tax evasion because girls basically just take photos of their body and they get people to pay them through Snapchat and because they pay for it with like Paypal …they (the women) didn't get taxed so it's basically a form of tax evasion. (Year 9 Group B)

Here the boys are discussing an Instagram account that posts 'dank' memes (slang for excellent and weird). The boys enjoy the meme content, some of which is making fun of and criticising sex subscription accounts on Snapchat where girls post taster content (like the thong images in order to draw in customers to buy a premium subscription. The boys have a high degree of knowledge of the economy of premium accounts (as tax evasion!) through Instagrammers warning boys about this content, but the message about the women running these accounts is also sexually shaming as the influencer 'Extender' calls them hoes (whores).

Given the ubiquity of this sexualised teaser content on social media platforms, geared to obtain followers and purchasers of paid-for content, the boys are also adamant that banning porn through age restrictions won't work, as they put it:

Hugh: It's not gonna work!

Jamie: What's going to happen is most boys who don't have ID, will probably just use VPN.

Timothy: Yeah. (Year 9 Group B)

Tom in year 10 agreed:

Tom: they're just encouraging more illegal behaviour by forcing people to get fake IDs, age, date of birth, et cetera for the ban.... (Year 10 Group A).

The boys have candid discussions about the possible impact of the sex subscription content on Instagram and Snapchat calling it porn:

Aiden: I think it normalises nudity and sexual relations.

Damien: Yeah because it's so easily accessible.

Finn: Let's say someone goes on this porn, they see, oh this is quite normal. Maybe I'll try it out then.

Francis: Apparently porn is nothing like real life.

Finn: Obviously not! It's like saying like, mission impossible, like an action film, is the same as your real life. You're not gonna have to be jumping out of planes, things like that. (Year 9 Group A).

According to Damien the mass of sex subscription accounts and messaging on social media is making porn more 'easily accessible'. Francis is also quick to assure us they know that porn is not 'real' and it can shape unrealistic views of sex, with Finn joking porn is like 'mission impossible' stunts. They also told us the 'normal age' when they started getting this content and watching porn was around 11 or 12 and the year10 group shared that the school was concerned about their porn consumption and the PSHE lead had a 'talk with them.'

> James: ... there's a teacher in our school who's taught us, we do this thing called PSHE and what he talked to us about he was like 'look lads I know you all watch it, but just make sure that that does not shape up your idea of what your first time is going to be like. It will be completely different like they're all on steroids or something to make the video as good as it can be. So just make sure that you know that that's not what you're going to be like or that's not what the girl is going to be like.' And so I think we all know that that's not what it's gonna be like.

> Oscar: As well porn's like a job for these people. It's like when you first play football, you're not gonna be, it's not like professional football. I know it's a weird analogy, but it's kind of, it's completely different to playing professionally. And playing like Sunday league. So it's kind of like you know that this isn't what sex is going to be like because it's these people that are being paid to do it and so are following like an exact script in exactly what to do. Exactly. What seemed pleasurable.

> Tom: I need to look exactly like this person because you know you don't really need to because this is their job and you know most of them are probably on performance enhancing drugs and stuff. (Year 10 Group A).

Interestingly, what the boys remember from the conversation with their teacher is the much used trope that 'porn is not reality'. It is significant that their viewing of porn has come before they've had any sexual relationships and the teacher tries to address this tension. They also learn that the actors are likely on 'performance enhancing drugs' (like Viagra for instance); but they do not seem to have learned anything about gender

6 Stags School for Boys: Elite Masculinities, Nudes ...   157

inequality, sexual violence or the issues of consent in relation to pornography; rather, the teacher's advice seemed designed to make the boys not feel inferior about their bodies and sexual performance.

They went on to inform us they think that adults and parents are worrying too much about boys watching porn every day, which they say is not accurate.

> Oscar: if you're kind of addicted you watch it like three times a day. But it can be controlled... using it once a week you watch it.

> James: That's why it's dependent on the person and where you are emotionally. So there's quite a few people will be in relationships with real girls and stuff so it's better to be with that girl rather than just watching porn by yourself. (Year 10 Group A).

The boys discuss the addictive element of porn but also assert that it can be controlled. Interestingly James suggests that one's relationship to porn is dependent on boy's emotional state. He also goes on to suggest its better to be in a real relationship with a "real girl", an interesting notion in the context of the all-boys environment; its also interesting that a real relationship is viewed as a solution to porn addiction, suggesting some of the limitations of this environment, and which also places the burden of boy's healthy sexuality on the other – the girl (Brown & Gilligan, 1992). Importantly, in this section we've explored how boys have sophisticated understandings of porn, including issues of addiction and worries on the part of adults. Boys also explained that they are targeted with porn content on platforms like Instagram and Snapchat as part of a push to sign up for sex subscriptions; meaning it is sent to them without their consent in what is an algorithmic drive to find accounts of their age and gender. The bot accounts prompt boys to subscribe to premium accounts with the economic aim of them buying sex services.

From Porn to Nudes: Homosocial Currency

As we saw above, many of the boys' interaction with girls is limited or, as they put it, 'delayed' in large part due to their schooling environment. They explained they didn't really have opportunities to 'get into relationships', and by this they mean romantic and intimate relationships with girls in real life, until they were invited to parties outside school time, which began for most around Year 9.

> Rafi: Year 9. Because it was [aged] 13, 14.

> Tom: That's when there were more parties and people started getting into a relationship.

> Rafi: it's like when a new toy came out everyone wanted them …

> Oscar: it was like a limited list of people that had actually like got with a girl and it's kind of like you wanted to be on that list. When your friend came in and was like I got with X for the first time yesterday it was really nice. Have you got with one yet? And then you say no, but it's kind of like subconscious pressure to try and get with a girl [inaudible]. (Year 10 Group A).

The boys discuss how parties outside of school time presented an avenue for starting relationships, and Rafi refers to girls as a 'new toy'. Oscar elaborates that it was a 'limited list' of boys who start developing an intimate relationship, explaining that this creates what he calls a 'subconscious pressure' to 'get with a girl'. Tom also explained that their sister school, Doe School for Girls, provided the other best real-life opportunity to meet girls, noting that some of the boys in the school 'have girlfriends in the girls' school'. Rather than having friendships with girls, as is more common in a mixed school setting, girls are less accessible to these boys and are spoken about more like objects of fascination (a new toy). This type of objectification and distance from girls has been found to present a strain for boys in these types of schooling environments (Halpern et al., 2011).

This pressure to get with girls shaped boys' digital interactions as well and they discussed feeling a type of pressure between boys to gain nudes from girls as part of their developing heterosexual masculinity identities:

> Oscar: It's like, um just talking to your friend and he goes, I just got nudes yesterday or something like that. And it just makes you feel like, oh my friend's getting them, I kind of want to get them. Stuff like that. It's not really, they're not forced. They're not saying, oh I can't believe you haven't got nudes or stuff like that. No *actual pressure*. But it's like subconscious pressure of saying, um, I got like explicit images. And have you got any recently, stuff like that. (Year 10 Group A).

> James: Subconsciously rubbing what you've done in somebody else's face (Year 10 Group A).

Oscar and James outline a sort of subconscious pressure felt by boys to obtain images of girls to compete with other boys. Female nudes are positioned as a form of commodity or currency boys feel like they really want, but the main motivator is that you have a competitive edge over your friends (Harvey et al., 2013). Girls' bodies are reduced to objects of exchange between boys in this dynamic. The 'subconscious pressure' is around being able to perform one's heterosexual prowess for other boys. These pressure based on competitive male-to-male relations have been theorised as homosocial bonds between men (Sedgwick, 1985), where boys stake their identities in comparison with one another. Homosocial bonds between the boys are more important than the feelings of the person who has sent the image—the girl (the object, the nude is a commodity with which to gain peer regard).

What also seemed to be happening, however, is that in this environment where the boys have so little real-life contact with girls, the digital platforms become critical for trying to negotiate intimacy with girls, In Year 9 they also commented that girls are pressured to send nudes because boys used the images to masturbate. The single gender environment may be prompting the boys to ask girls for explicit images as part of brokering a relationship in ways that lack any sensitivity or understanding of the girls they are contacting:

Tom: So I was speaking to my friend the other day and then he said since he's got a girlfriend um, he's stopped asking [for nudes]. If you're in a relationship, you shouldn't be asking. It's not right to do it when you're not in a relationship but it's like less wrong to do if you're not in a relationship. (Year 10 Group A).

These dynamics discussed above are interesting in that asking girls' for explicit images before the boy has a relationship with the girl is understood as completely normal. The asking for the images is viewed as part of how one brokers a relationship via the online space. This is problematic because as we have seen already in this book and will explore more in later chapters, many girls view this practice of being asked for explicit images as a form of harassment. Whereas boys in mixed school settings may have the opportunity to learn from girls in their environment that they experience this asking for images as harassing these boys appear to have little concept of thinking about things from the girls' perspective. Tom reports that he has learned from a friend that his girlfriend has explained that asking for nudes from her is 'not respectful'.

These boys are hyper aware of 'subconscious' processes of masculinity where performative (hetero)sexual prowess requires nudes and therefore asking girls they likely barely know is normalised. The boys discussion points to a whole cultural milieux that shapes what it means to be a sexually successful boy and later man is generated in these environments, with new digital practices emerging.

The boys also spoke candidly about how they would share nude photos that were obtained in their peer groups, saying you could '95% of the time' expect that a nude of a girl will be screenshotted, sent to another person or saved without the initial sender's consent.

Tom: People screenshot it and send it and stuff. Cause if you do send a nude it's almost inevitable that it's going to be sent to at least one person.

Oscar: Yeah exactly. But I still think most people would do more on private images to one person than they would put on a story or something.

Tom: Yeah.

6 Stags School for Boys: Elite Masculinities, Nudes ... 161

Oscar: Or they'll like save it. Because if it's, if you're taking a picture from your camera roll, all right, and sending it then it's in the chat and they can save it in the chat without actually like screenshotting it or anything. (Year 10 Group A).

Tom notes that non-consensual sending on of girls' nudes is '*almost inevitable*'. Oscar also lists the platform affordances such as images saving to the camera roll from WhatsApp, which means that they will then have the image saved on their devices, an opportunity ripe for further sharing. When asked what motivates people to non-consensually share an image, they replied with the following:

Oscar: To show off.

Tom: Yeah to seem cool.

Oscar: Like ah look I got nudes from this girl! (Year 10 Group A).

We can see once again that nudes are used as a cool currency amongst boys and as a means to stand out sexually. They went on to say nudes are evidence of the ability to 'pull fit people'. Overall its apparent that boys' concern is not about respecting girls when they ask for nudes, nor keeping the image secure or private when they obtain them, because the main source of value of the nude in their immediate schooling environment is if it can be visibly performed and ownership is proven, something they discuss as subconscious peer pressure. Importantly, however, the boys were concerned about themselves, in relation to the illegality of nudes and whether or not these practices might get them into trouble.

Gaming Crime, Minimising Evidence: Safeguarding Masculine Privilege and a Clean Digital Footprint

We heard numerous stories in this all-boy setting that the boys would show images on their phones rather than send them, so that they wouldn't have an evidence trail. One boy said for instance, nude images 'haven't been sent directly, but I've seen from other people showing me'. What was worrying about this is they did not see this as problematic. Again, the reason they say that these practices are common is due to social pressure between boys:

> Ben: if you told your friends, oh, I just got nudes and then they would be like show us, show us and if you don't show they'll be like, oh, you're lying. You're not going to show me.

> Jake: They're like, oh, you're just lying.

> Max: And then they'll just tell everyone. Because some people just do it for attention. Like we were in history. Someone's nudes came up in a history lesson. (Year 10 Group B).

Not only are the boys are under pressure to get nudes they then must prove the fact through showing the images to their friends. The boys relate how this happens right in the middle of the school day, for instance during a history lesson at school. The boys are actually aware that sending nudes or sharing nudes digitally is a criminal act as they relate a situation from another school:

> Jamie: There's these people in another school, he got sent nudes and he made a group chat and sent it to people and now he's on the sex offenders list.

> Interviewer: Do you think sending nudes sharing nudes of other people can cause harm?

> Jamie: Definitely!

6 Stags School for Boys: Elite Masculinities, Nudes … **163**

Timothy: Like let's say this guy is now on the sex offenders list. That's going to impact you your whole life, there's no escaping that.

Hugh: Yeah. He can't get a job. He's also known for this.

(Year 9 Group B)

Here after the boys express awareness that boys could be legally charged for non-consensually sharing nudes (in a group chat) the interviewer asks about whether such practices can cause harm. Rather than respond with any understanding or compassion for the victims of what has been called revenge porn, but which we call in the book image-based sexual abuse, the boys respond that the harm would be for the boy or man put on the sex offender list since this will impact 'your whole life'.

A similar sentiment cropped up in another group where the boys dismiss any harmful intent of sharing nudes:

Max: Nah.

Jake: It's like a social.

Max: I don't think people actually intend to cause harm.

Interviewer: What are the intentions?

Ronald: Just to show their friends that they received them.

Max: To get gassed. (Year 10 Group B).

Across three of the four focus groups in this school, the boys mentioned concern about 'evidence' that could be found on their phones. In one of the Year 10 groups, they specifically commented that certain practices could protect them from evidence of committing an offence:

Ronald: I think it's like difference between seeing it in real life and sending it. In real life is there's no like record or evidence of it, but social media, you can save it, you can screenshot here, you can do like many things with it.

Max: ....They may keep for themselves but don't electronically snap to someone else who could screenshot it because there's like, but if it was like a girlfriend/boyfriend relationship they may, and there's bitterness between them, then they may, that may result in sending. But if there's like let's say somebody just started talking to you then other way, then you probably won't have anything against them so you probably won't send it to anyone. (Year 10 Group B)

Here Ronald explains the way that social media offers the tools to keep the image and share it, but Max responds that boys will only publicly share an image if something has gone wrong in the relationship. The boys are aware of their privilege and power to be able to either keep the nude for'themselves, share it on their phone, or pass it more widely. It's important to ask ourselves how has it become so normalised for boys to know they can use nudes to harm girls should they choose to do so. Throughout this conversation, both with the admission that they can show photos on their phone screen without being caught, and the possibility that they may send the image on (depending on their relationship with the girl), the entire focus has been upon boys obtaining valuable images of girls' bodies and their homosocial use of them.

While the boys were candid about the ways they would avoid criminal charges by not sharing images digitally, they also seemed to lack understanding of consent around sending of their own intimate images. When asked why men and boys would send dick pics, the Year 9s responded:

Interviewer: What are the reasons for boys to send a nude?

Hugh: Fun. Or they're bored.

Jamie: Let's say they're sending something and they want to get something in return then I guess that's fun. Or if they're bored it's just someone to talk to. Grab the attention of someone.

Timothy Yeah they want attention, exactly.

Hugh: Attention seeking.

Timothy: I have a gay friend, he likes doing this stuff a lot. [laughter]

Interviewer: What do you mean?

Jamie: Because let's say if someone's gay, then they have the same body parts as the person that they're attracted to. So it's less unfamiliar to them. So it's easier for them to go about their business. (Year 9 Group B).

Here the boys suggest that boys will send dick pics because it's fun, they are bored, they want to get something back, or to get attention. They also note it's 'easier' for those who are gay to send 'body parts', apparently because both parties have a penis. Across the entire discussion, any idea of gaining consent to send dick pics is ignored.

Despite a lack of concern over consent around the logistics of boys and men sending dick pics to girls, a few boys were concerned that girls could share their nudes without their consent:

Jamie: if I sent nudes to a girl and she was sharing with her friends. I can imagine them all just like laughing and that would make me feel bad. Think about that. It would just make me feel bad that it's happened. (Year 9 Group B)

The year 10 boys were likewise highly concerned about the possibility of their own images being 'exposed', noting it could potentially 'ruin your life':

Ronald: Imagine every single person having a picture of me. [laughter] It's not even funny, imagine how depressed I would be. At your disposal for my whole life.

Max: That's quite true actually.

Interviewer: Do you think it has the power to ruin someone's life?

Ben: Definitely.

Interviewer : Wow.

Ronald: One of the things is if you don't show your face or don't, there's no way of knowing it's you. Then it's fine. But often if you send a nude, your face, is in it, maybe your house is in it and then it's exposed.

Max: That's why: I think if you're gonna send nudes, you should know who they ...before you actually start sending. Cause that eliminates..., that means it's not a catfish or anything (Year 10 Group B).

Participants clearly feel high levels of anxiety at the prospect of their own nudes being shared and their property and location being 'exposed'. They also bring up the notion of being 'catfished' (drawn in and manipulated; precursor to sextortion) by girls they don't know. Almost verbatim of the concerns of the boys at Lion's elite boarding school, several boys were also extremely worried that a nudes scandal could ruin their future career prospects:

Hugh: Cause let's say you, you want to get a job one day and you've sent one of these pictures and then, but you've only sent it because you haven't been warned about it. Then let's say the person's kept the photo and then it gets leaked, then that's problematic for you.

Timothy: My Dad always says that the like [inaudible] never put anything like, not even necessarily inappropriate, just nothing like dumb on the Internet because it can like come back to bite you. (Year 9 Group B).

Tom went on to explain how the leaking of a gay boy's nude had negatively affected him:

Tom: there was one case that...one boy who's gay, his nudes got leaked. It was really weird this video it got leaked to a lot of schools and now... I know a lot of people who've seen this video and it's just not pleasant.

James: Yeah, it was it was quite bad...

Tom: It got to this school. It's got to loads of schools. (Year 10 Group A).

6 Stags School for Boys: Elite Masculinities, Nudes ... 167

Tom describes as 'unpleasant' how a lot of people have seen a nude video of a gay boy, which was leaked around a lot of schools, getting a 'quite bad' reaction from the boys at Stags. He went on to talk about "unsolicited dick pics" in the LGBT community:

> Tom: there's a lot more images between boys cause there's a few people in a year that are orientated in that way. I'm friends with one of them and I know he gets, like I know that he gets a lot of images from other boys that's kind of unsolicited. I think it's kind of like the way boys, boys are... like its just 50% of UK males have sent an unsolicited dick pic. That's what it's like. That's what at least I think it's like in LGBT community. (Year 10 Group A)

The boys seem to express much more concern and compassion for the boys in their peer group than for girls. They are concerned about boys being criminally charged if they share nudes of girls, but they are also worried about their own images being shared beyond the intended recipient. Oscar even expresses concern about the amount of unwanted dick pics received by his gay friend. It seems probable that the lack contact with girls in their immediate environment creates a barrier to having empathy with girls' experiences, and a lack of self-reflection about how their own practices might be effecting girls, since they do express concern for themselves and their male friends.

Sexual Double Standards of IBSHA

As we noted in our introduction to this chapter, the boys spoke extensively about the adjoining girls' school. We were interested in how digital technology had found a route through the land and gates separating the boys' and girls' schools via the nude sharing practices discussed. Several of the groups at Stags related stories of nudes being swapped between boys at Stags and girls at Does:

> Timothy: There was some Year 8 boy who asked for nudes from a girl.

168   J. Ringrose and K. Regehr

Hugh: And he sent in exchange, like, a nude video of him masturbating.

Jamie: And then I'm pretty sure he got a suspension.

Timothy: His mum found it [the girls' nude] on the phone. Of the girl that sent it.

Hugh: So then she (the mom) reported the girl but then the girl told her school it was also the boy and then I'm pretty sure the boy got suspended.

Jamie: It's been passed around (the masturbation video). Especially it's been passed to the year above. And that's not that common because those years don't really talk. (Year 9 Group B).

In this story, the mother of a Year 8 boy finds a girl's nudes on her son's phone and reports it to the school, but it also transpires that her son has sent a video of him masturbating that the girl has leaked it and it has travelled around both digital peer groups of the girls school and the boys school. It is not clear what happened to the girl in this instance even though it's his video that has been shared without consent, but the boys are concerned because the boy was suspended. The older boys reflected on a similar story where a boys' dick pics were leaked but seemed relatively unconcerned about the impacts upon him:

James: there was a boy, um, who's not in our year that sent um, this girl a picture of his, um, like private areas. And then it got, she basically took a picture of it and then distributed between all of the girls' school and then they found out. So it's kind of, there's also, it kind of depends on the person that you send it to if you actually trust them.

Oscar: He got a bit of stick for it.

Tom: People almost took the mick out of him a bit like ah you did this and it got shared hahaha. (Year 10 Group A).:

James: It didn't have really have an effect on his popularity because what happened was that lots of people would talk to him about it. But it

6 Stags School for Boys: Elite Masculinities, Nudes ... 169

wouldn't be in the way that like how most people would think like ah well done that's so amazing. Like you're so cool and stuff, but everyone actually just basically took the mick out of him …because it's just like a weird thing to do. And especially with the person they did it with. (Year 10).

The boys note that the boy didn't really get negatively impacted by the non-consensual sharing of his image. It was not the image that was the problem according to the boys but the girl that he'd sent it to. These boys discuss the girl as 'constantly' doing stuff, which links to her sexual reputation. They go on to discuss her as 'desperate' for sending the boy nudes in the first place:

Tom: She's really nice, but at that time she was a bit of um, she just.

Oscar: Desperate.

James: Yeah. there was a lot of pressure on her to try and get with a boy because, all of her friends had done it and she felt really left out about it. So she started becoming desperate

Tom: They were like calling her like a virgin and stuff or like a prude and she felt she wanted to try to get with someone.

James: They were at the stage where they'd started texting and stuff. They were gonna meet up but then she couldn't do it in the end. So then, cause it had been like two or three weeks and they hadn't actually met each other properly they decided they didn't really want to be with each other anymore. (Year 10 Group A)

The boys offer a cogent analysis of the motivations behind the girl wanting to 'get with a boy' and the massive challenges in actually being able to physically meet one another, hence the digital image exchange. In the evaluation of what's gone on, however, we see a sexual double standard. First the girl is called a virgin and prude for not being with boys, but then desperate and ruining her reputation when she sends nudes, which are then shared without her consent.

Tom: Yeah I used to be friends with her...she's nice and it definitely changed her. She was really like, she had a bit of being very upset. Um, but then I think she's got a boyfriend at the moment, so she's quite happy at the moment. It's kind of changed what I thought of her. She like completely changed after that she stopped being desperate... started basically knowing her worth and like actually talking to people and stuff before getting involved romantically'.

Interviewer: But the boy, his, he was never seen to be like, um, a slut in the same way?

James: he kind of is like that cause he tries, even though he's not actually like it...everyone kind of took the micky out of him for being that person and trying to cool be by sending sexual photos to people. (Year 10 Group A).

Here Tom finds that the girl having a boyfriend helps him change his opinion of her; she becomes respectable therefore becoming less desperate and knowing her own worth. The boy is never really subjected to the same double standard; others simply 'took the micky out of him' for trying too hard to be cool, noting he's 'not actually like it'. We can see the way that sexual reputation around images works very differently for boys and girls. The girl in this scenario is subject to harsh moral judgement from the boys and urged to 'know her own worth' and not send images despite the earlier admissions that boys are exerting a great deal of pressure upon girls to do so. The boy is never sexually shamed or judge, the boys just 'took the micky out of him' for interacting with a problematic female.

The Year 10 boys are adamant that they would not be able to discuss such cases with teachers and were relieved that this particular example was 'contained'.

Interviewer: Did this come to the attention of the school?

Tom: It was contained.

Oscar: Contained.

James: That's not something you really want to talk to Mr. Acker about.

Oscar: You don't really want to go into the office one day and say 'sir look I received nudes from someone, uh'.

Tom: Like especially if you're quite close with them (the boy who has shared the girls' nudes).

James: And it doesn't affect you. (Year 10, Group A).

Here the homosocial reasoning amongst the boys is crystal clear. They cannot report non-consensual nudes because they do not want to betray the trust of the boys in their peer group who has sent them around. They also note that seeing the nude doesn't affect them, so they don't really need to be bothered by it. What they mean is that they are not personally victimised by the images. Even though they have related a tale of difficult consequences and reputational damage to the girl in particular, that is not their concern. This is the moral reasoning of homosocial comradery and fraternity, which treats women and girls as possessions to be compared and traded amongst boys that urgently needs challenging.

What Should Change in Digital Literacy and Sex Education?

Back in the Year 9 group, the boys explain how inadequate their sex education was and that they learned more about sex education in design and technology when being taught about parts of vacuums than in biology:

Aiden: I mean we, we have watched videos of… like going through puberty and stuff, and for reproduction on our field day; but we haven't really had stuff about sex, actual sex education.

Francis: We learned more about sex education in DT (design and technology) than in biology. Because our teachers always talking about the male and female parts of the vacuums and I'm not quite sure what they call it, but the different dd parts and they got a male part or female part and he always goes on about sex education. (Year 9).

Others noted as well that sex education was missing key elements, including discussions of porn:

Tom: you need sex education at like 11 or 12 before you start like watching porn. So that, you already know what's gonna happen and when you see it happening in porn and you think this is not the norm, this is just, um, this is just people acting and scripted stuff like that (Year 10).

Francis: I think the time when you teach children about sexual education is a time you should tell them about what pornography is and everything.

Finn: With me, [my parents] told me, they told me to ask whatever questions I wanted to ask and they'd answer properly. So I think just teach it whenever people get into it and start wondering. (Year 9 Group A)

Here we can see the boys saying they need education about pornography much earlier. Tom suggests by age 11 or before they start watching porn, and Finn nicely explains a child responsive approach that deals with the issue when young people start wondering and asking questions about pornography.

Another key element missing from sex education was digital issues and consent. For instance, the boys discussed being shown e-safety videos of how to protect themselves from getting on the sex offenders list, rather than image-based abuse, which we saw earlier has significantly influenced how the boys think about this issue:

Timothy: we've seen some like scenarios on like how it could happen. So a company came and for the field day thing. They just gave us just some scenarios. One of them was like girl from another school, had a boyfriend from one other school and then one of them sent a nude image to each other and then the other boy kind of spread it around his school and then after his school got it her school got it as well. Kind of went round like that, Then they told us you would be like say on the sex offenders list, if you did send one and the police found it.

6 Stags School for Boys: Elite Masculinities, Nudes ... 173

Hugh: Yeah that gave them a bit of fear in people really probably cause if they get caught then they go on their permanent record and it wouldn't be good for like their future.

Hugh: So someone sends you (a nude) then you're like the supply to everyone else.

Jamie: I mean it was their choice to give it to you, but then your distributing it, but they didn't know that you were going to send it to everyone else, so you sent it to everyone else without her consent, you will go on the sex offender list and she won't, is that true?

Interviewer: Did they teach you about the law?

Jamie: If you sent one. We know about the sex offender list. But I don't know if we know about any other [laws] yeah.

Timothy: We don't really know.

Interviewer: there are kind of two areas of law here, um, but sharing someone's nudes without their consent is called image-based abuse. Um, and that's a criminal offence like no matter what age you are. So if someone was under the age of 18 and the image was of someone who was under 18, that would be kind of child pornography that they'd be sharing, but they'd also be breaking the law that it would be image-based abuse, which was, which is also against the law. Have you ever heard of that term of image-based abuse before?

Timothy: No. (Year 9, Group B)

We can see that the boys learn about not sending images of themselves and putting themselves at risk. The only mitigating advice they are given however is not to supply a girls' nude to others since they could go on the sex offenders list as a 'distributor' of illegal content. It is notable the language of criminality they are using where nudes become a form of contraband that you need to exert caution over, rather than a primary concern that these practices may be wrong, harmful and abusive. They are also concerned that they, as boys, will go on the sex offender list but say if a girl is caught, she would not, according to what they've been told, which creates a type of male victim narrative where boys are punished but girls are not as if the dynamics of sharing nudes are the same for both genders. The interviewer tries to clarify the issue of consent asking the boys if they've ever been taught about image-based abuse, which they say they've never heard of before. It's clear they have been given no broader education around consent and digital images.

Some did offer thoughtful ideas about peer pressure and what is 'right'. The Year 9 boys acknowledged that girls were experiencing much more pressure to send nudes, whereas boys were being pressured by other boys to attain nudes:

> Aiden: To have images of girls I think there's more pressure for that [for boys]

> Francis: The boys are just like maybe a joke that can go around the school with other boys. Like saying, oh, you're not like you're not man enough if you don't have any pictures.

> Damien: I've seen things like where people do trades like nude for nude.

> Aiden: boys just send it and then they ask girls. Girls don't just send it.

> Finn: I think girls are more sensitive about their body than boys. So like if they don't want to do it, they shouldn't be peer pressured into sending nudes or anything.

> Interviewer: So what would you say to boys?

> Finn: Why are you doing it? I think most boys are actually being pressured by other boys. If you think it's not right then you shouldn't do it. You shouldn't be pressured by friends, to obtain sexual images of people, you should just be okay with who you are. (Year 9 Group A)

Aiden talks again about the pressures boys face to obtain nudes. Through the conversation, the dynamics of non-consent become clear. The pressure to get nudes also pushes boys into further non-consensual acts like 'just sending' a nude to a girl without asking (cyberflashing) and asking girls to send one back (harassment). The boys do not unpack these power dynamics fully, but Finn goes on to suggests boys should talk about this to 'feel okay with who you are' and resist this pressure.

In Year 10, Tom noted that after the 'buzz' of getting the nudes wears off, you realise it's not as important as a real relationship and he offered a powerful reflection on what needs to change in the PSHE in their school for boys:

> Tom: Don't be peer pressured into doing something that you don't want to do and be aware of the laws and consequences that can happen if you send a nude image. Um, there'll always be someone to talk to that can include teachers and parents and in some cases close friends that you know are trustable; and similarly only send images of your body to trustable people or just don't send them all. And the way school can help is that um, they should focus on more than sexual education ... the social issues rather than talking about the biology behind, um, sex. School should talk about what to do if someone sends a nude or any other disturbing images. Cause I don't think people know how to like process it or what to do if someone has sent it. School should also consider making the school counsellor a more prominent figure cause we only get emails about him or her. We don't really know how he or she operates. And like I don't really know where she is, if I do need to talk to her and I think that there should be a lesson dedicated to PSHE that talks about the consequences of social media. Cause we don't really have a PSHE lesson. We just have form time. Well we just talk to a form tutor and I don't think that's really the same. We do have key skills but that kind of rotates every term so we don't focus on it that much. I think social media should be presented in like a light-hearted manner because if it's serious and presented in an assembly, no one would really care cause no one would concentrate. (Year 10 Group A).

Tom makes a plea for a litany of ways to improve the supports in the school, including making a school counsellor prominent, and dedicated PSHE lessons on social media. Other boys in the group confirm that boys need to have more discussions about this but the format would be crucial, given the limitations of 'serious assemblies':

Timothy: I think it's quite awkward when teachers talk to students about sex education especially assemblies because they didn't really feel like a conversation. It just felt like a telling off (Year 9 Group B).

Jake: I think we've, we've had a couple of assemblies on like if you do receive these images, go and speak to people within the school, but I don't think anyone would. (Year 10 Group B).

Rather than large-scale assemblies that feel like 'a telling off', smaller scale discussions like the ones we held with these boys were crucial openings for further awareness. We can see boys possess sophisticated understandings of what they want to discuss and see in their sex education and the effects upon them from not discussing and having dedicated 'PSHE' lessons that deal with issues of sexuality and social media beyond inaccurate assemblies on legal repercussions based in a fear narrative. They also noted that this education should be done earlier and maybe with peers who they could look up to:

Oscar: No one wants to listen to a 50 year old head teacher go like 'Boys sexting is bad.'

Tom: It would have to be someone that they look up to, so like someone that they think, oh, this guy, like he knows what I want to be like in two years...And the person says what they shouldn't do in Year 9 and what you should be like, and especially about, if I come back to the point where it might be like what sex is like, from like a very young age, I think I was like 10 or 11 when my primary school told me about like sex and how it's not like the images that you'll see online and how you shouldn't expect it to be like that. In my life its kind of like drilled into me that you shouldn't believe everything you see online. (Year 10 Group A).

Conclusion: The Missing Discourses of Meaningful Consent

Throughout this chapter we have looked at some of the social impacts in an 'all-boys' selective school in relation to creating a digital sexual self. We saw that norms of homosocial masculinity and pressures to perform sexual bravado to compete with one another in a masculine social hierarchy were pronounced, whereas discussions of digital and sexual consent were almost entirely missing.

The boys offered frank discussions about their reliance upon social media use for social interactions as a main avenue for developing intimacy with girls. The boys' social media accounts were also how they encountered various forms of sexualised media, including being pushed to subscribe to pornified content through algorithmic targeting on Instagram and Snapchat. The PSHE lead at their school had had a talk with them about porn, this consisted of telling the boys that porn wasn't reality and how they should not buy into the performance pressures for men. Issues of consent do not seem to have been covered.

In relation to peer-produced nudes, it is important to raise the question of whether a reliance upon social media for relationships with girls can increase a tendency to dehumanise or objectify girls since these boys have few avenues for connection and friendship with girls. The boys openly admitted that there was a tendency in their peer groups to pressure one another to attain nudes but also to show them to one another as proof of status. While this was happening across the school sites, we've researched for this book the homosocial peer pressure and competition seemed more intense in the all-boys educational setting.

We also saw that the boys have heightened legal awareness of how to protect themselves from digital harm, they mention being careful of the pornbots so they are not 'catfished' (sextorted). They've also had external commentators teach them about not getting onto the sex offenders list if they are caught 'supplying' or 'distributing' nudes, a simplistic focus on keeping the boys' from committing digital crime and keeping their digital footprint clean rather than helping them understand the relational dynamics of consent.

It follows that we also found the boys to be far more sexually judgemental of girls than boys. One Year 10 boy, Tom, led us and his friendship group through a complex discussion of his relationships to masculinity, gay boys getting more dick pics, girls getting shamed and blamed when their nudes are leaked, and frank admissions about how boys protecting their bonds with one another is often more important for them than the feelings of girls. During the discussion, we found boys like Tom were able to break down what is happening in the peer group and offer cogent ideas about what may need to change to challenge masculinity pressures, including what they need for better digital literacy and sex education combined.

However, in concluding this chapter, we think there is a need to question the very fabric of a single sex environment, which needs to be more self-reflective about the forced binary division of gender and its effects on moral reasoning and relationality, and the potential for dehumanising and objectifying feminine sexuality. Are these 'single sex' schooling environments setting up young people to fail at heterosexual relationships by enforcing conservative traditions of gender separation (Halpern et al., 2011)? Why are these single gender environments refusing to address harassing and abusive digital masculinity dynamics? What are the costs of preserving elite male identities in this way? It is incumbent upon such institutions to include explicit masculinity education and discussions of homosociality to tap into discussions of the types of 'subconscious pressure' Oscar discussed, which boys are putting on one another, including digital performances that are harmful to girls. Boys need much more nuanced discussions of digital and sexual consent in order to be able to reflect on male privilege and the abuse of power, which flourishes in all-boys' spaces online and in schools, if such schools are ever to offer these boys a chance to contribute to a more socially just and equitable society.

References

Brown, L. M., & Gilligan, C. (1992). *Meeting at the crossroads: Women's psychology and girls' development*. Harvard University Press.

Halpern, D. F., Eliot, L., Bigler, R. S., Fabes, R. A., Hanish, L. D., Hyde, J., Liben, L. S., & Martin, C. L. (2011). The pseudoscience of single-sex schooling. *Science, 333*(6050), 1706–1707.

Harvey, L., Ringrose, J., & Gill, R. (2013). Swagger, ratings and masculinity: Theorising the circulation of social and cultural value in teenage boys' digital peer networks. *Sociological Research Online, 18*(4).

Jackson, J. (2009). 'Dangerous presumptions': How single-sex schooling reifies false notions of sex, gender, and sexuality. *Gender and Education, 22*(2), 227–238. https://doi.org/10.1080/09540250903359452

Roberts, S., & Westcott, S. (2024). To quell the problem, we must name the problem: The role of social media 'manfluencers' in boys' sexist behaviours in school settings. *Educational and Developmental Psychologist, 41*(2), 125–128. https://doi.org/10.1080/20590776.2024.2329083

Sedgwick, E. K. (1985). *Between men: English literature and male homo-social desire* (p. 92). Columbia University Press.

Open Access This chapter is licensed under the terms of the Creative Commons Attribution-NonCommercial-NoDerivatives 4.0 International License (http://creativecommons.org/licenses/by-nc-nd/4.0/), which permits any noncommercial use, sharing, distribution and reproduction in any medium or format, as long as you give appropriate credit to the original author(s) and the source, provide a link to the Creative Commons license and indicate if you modified the licensed material. You do not have permission under this license to share adapted material derived from this chapter or parts of it.

The images or other third party material in this chapter are included in the chapter's Creative Commons license, unless indicated otherwise in a credit line to the material. If material is not included in the chapter's Creative Commons license and your intended use is not permitted by statutory regulation or exceeds the permitted use, you will need to obtain permission directly from the copyright holder.

7

North West Secondary: Snapscore Micro-Celebrity, WhatsApp Wanking, & Sex Subscriptions Porn Push: Barriers to Platform and School Reporting

Northwest Secondary (NWS) is a state school located in an area just outside the city centre, with extreme polarities of wealth. There are multi-million-pound homes not far from council housing and the school is adjacent to a large council housing estate. Due to the school's location and mixed demographic area, students come from very diverse class and ethnic backgrounds and family income levels. Another significant factor is that there is a 'single sex' girls' former grammar school, now a well-regarded girls' comprehensive, which is often colloquially referred to in the community as a 'postcode private', to denote its primarily middle class demographic. This means that NWS not only has a notable class divide but has a significant gender imbalance. That is, while middle class families often send their daughters to the local 'post code private' girls' school, but for their sons, they are left with a choice of private education (which for most families is not financially viable) or sending them to NWS. The outcome is a three to one ratio of boys to girls in NSW, where the boys come from a wider range of socio-economic backgrounds than the girls. This shapes the experiences in significant ways as we'll explore.

In the school we conducted two focus groups each with boys and girls in Year 7 aged 11–12, and Year 9 aged 13–14. There was a marked

© The Author(s) 2025
J. Ringrose and K. Regehr, *Teens, Social Media, and Image Based Abuse*,
https://doi.org/10.1007/978-3-031-92322-7_7

182   J. Ringrose and K. Regehr

difference between the girls and boys in the interviews, with the girls coming from the council estates, experiencing more social deprivation and elements of 'working class culture' (Walkerdine et al., 2001). We will explore the experiences of one of the girls from the council estate in some depth. Across all the groups, as seen in our previous chapters, what was common was how all the groups were navigating digital spaces of Snapchat and Instagram, with their algorithmically driven cultures of gaining likes and views, and enabling the targeting of youth, which as we've been exploring normalises non-consensual sexual content, with various impacts upon our young participants. Here we continue looking at how Snapchat and Instagram create economies of value and risk for youth—Snapchat by way of its Snapscore affordance and ability to quickly rack up high numbers of unknown followers.

In this chapter we investigate more closely how girls' high Snapscores and numbers of followers shape their peer status, their experiences and feelings of self-worth, and notions of what they should open themselves up to in the attainment of what social media scholars have called a form of 'micro-celebrity' (Marwick, 2018)—that is, public popularity through social media following with potentials to monetise. As we will discuss, some girls in our study, as young as 11, conceptualise receiving dick pics as an indicator of their popularity, with one girl understanding it as part of her micro-celebrity status construction as a nationally ranked dancer. Other girls saw unsolicited videos of masturbation as potentially proof of their desirability or as something they had to get used to and tolerate as part of their experience of 'friendship' with boys. So rather than viewing this unsolicited content as a form of abuse or harassment, the girls position it as a potential self-esteem boost, which we argue shows the normalisation of abuse in digital peer networks. Additionally, we examine boys' experiences of group messaging which pushes pornography on Snapchat and Instagram in an effort to exploit boys financially. We also show how both girls and boys are highly critical of the sex education they are receiving as vastly inadequate in dealing with the nuances of their online experiences.

12-Year-Old Girls: Snapscore Status and the Commodified Self

At NSW school, we worked in a small annex room away from the main building with the girls, while their sex education teacher sat very close by in the cramped space, grading papers. The teacher occasionally joined in with information or to answer a question, interrupting the interview space in a way that was unique to this context. Although teachers were often close to the classrooms or popped in and out or sat adjacent to us, none of the other teachers at the other schools we visited tried to participate in the interview in the way that this teacher did. Her interjections possibly derived from the fact that she was the sex education facilitator at the school and thus highly invested in the topic. Nonetheless, the girls seemed comfortable to speak openly about their experiences, and their conversation turned quickly to Snapchat.

Recall from earlier chapters that Snapchat encourages users to create virtual connections with large networks of known and unknown users through its 'quick add' feature, where contacts appear in other users' 'quick add' list if they share a mutual friend or 'another connection.' This can create very large friend networks of semi-known 'mutuals'. To build these large networks young people have to have their privacy settings off, with a profile that is easily found. This searchability is key in opening up young people to risk.

In our interview with the Year 7 girls, we met Liv, who proudly exclaimed she was going to be turning 12 in two days at the start of the interview. A high social media user, Liv explained the intricacies of Snapchat to us animatedly, including how you could boost your followers through practices such as Shoutouts, which we heard about in Chapters 2 and 5:

> Liv: SFS which means shout for shout out. So you send a picture of yourself, like a face or something, and then you mention that person on your story, and then people add them, and then people add that, and then add, and they keep adding each other. And loads of people post your photo, with your tag, so everyone would add you. Once they add

you then they would be able to text you, and once you do it like they can call you, text your smartphone (Year 7, girls).

As we've seen in earlier chapters 'Shoutouts' refers to the practice of having one's Snapcode (unique identifier code to scan to add a user) circulated to mass followers. Teens tend to do it for each other to boost their Snapscore (the user engagement metric calculated partly on how many snap exchanges the user has had). Often this is done within the context of 'Shoutout for Shoutout (SFS)', where the user will receive a shout out from a friend if you mention them. Here we can see the cumulative force of the Shoutout, with Liv saying people 'add, add and keep adding each other', which we've discussed as a game-like metric on the platform, but which opens the user to being directly 'texted' or messaged via Snapchat.

As in earlier chapters, the quick add function is the main way strangers are added and Liv confirmed she did not know all the quick adds she accepted. Also like teens in other schools, once masses of quick adds were accepted girls were inundated by dick pics as well as requests to trade nudes from 'random people':

Liv: Snapchat, random people just add you and then it says...

Kira: Happens every time.

Sierra: Same.

Liv: Someone, yesterday someone was like to me, someone was like to me, oh you're cute, do you wanna see a picture of me? And I said no, how old are you? They said 15, and they sent a picture and they looked like 49. And then I just blocked them.

Laughter.

Indeed, many of the encounters the girls in this focus group shared with us are extremely predatory in nature, including being sent dick pics with the message 'send one back babe' (Fig. 7.1):

7 North West Secondary: Snapscore Micro-Celebrity ...

Fig. 7.1 Sierra's drawing of 'send one back babes' getting nudes from 'people who add you that you don't know'

The drawing depicts a girl receiving what is referred to as a 'transactional dick pick' meaning a dick pic that is sent without consent but that also requests (pressures/harasses) a girl to send a nude back to them (Salter, 2016). In another instance, Liv explained dick pics as a precurser to sending masturbation videos: 'This was someone who said "wanna see me c-u-m?" (Fig. 7.2) And I just blocked them like' (Fig. 7.2).

Liv and her friends continued to explain why Liv had amassed so many contacts on Snapchat and 1000s of followers on Instagram:

> Liv: If I had data I could show so much like different nudes on my phone.

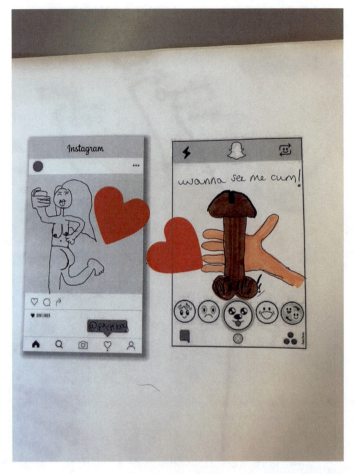

Fig. 7.2 Liv's drawing of woman taking a mirror 'belfie' or butt selfie; and 'wanna see me cum!' an 'older person' sending her a dick pick with the message

Kira: You must get loads.

Liv: Mm, I get so many.

Interviewer: Why must she get loads?

Talia: Because like all of her messages, you can just tell…

7 North West Secondary: Snapscore Micro-Celebrity ...

Sierra: She's a really well-known person, so boys tend to be like oh she's well-known, that means she's.

Interviewer: What do you mean, how are you really well known?

Sierra: Her brother.

Liv:...sort of my brother, because my brother chills around some place and he was a part of a gang but now he left that gang; obviously I look so different right now compared to my photos, when I get home, I put so much makeup on, and I put like some shorts on, like a nice crop top, and sometimes I dress up for fun...(Year 7, girls).

The interviewer asks Liv to tell her what she means by being 'really well known' to which she responds that her brother was in a gang and she also notes using make up, shorts and crop top and 'dressing up' to attain followers. Liz's friends explained in addition to her 'massive snapscore' she had amassed hundreds of followers on Instagram due to her brother's gang associations but her friends go on to explain Liv is a competitively ranked dancer, to which Liv bragged 'I make people follow me' on Instagram. Here we can see that Liv uses elements of her identity (notoriety, appearance, talent) to create a mass following, what Alice Marwick (2018) has called cultivating a 'micro-celebrity' status. In this case, the large Instagram following for an 11-year-old makes her the object of awe and regard from her schoolgirl peers who reason 'you must get loads' of dick pics.

Returning to Snapchat, Liv reasoned that getting dick pics on that platform was part of the trade-off of getting a 'massive' Snapscore (Figs. 7.2, 7.3 and 7.4):

Liv: Basically, obviously, my Snapchat has a massive score, which means loads of people have me as a friend, which means a load of paedophiles can send stuff to me...Yeah....and they just send it when I'm here to do streaks and get a higher score, but they're just doing it the other way because they want that. And I just want streaks, because I...

Interviewer: OK, so what do you think about it when you get them?

Liv: It's disgusting.

Interviewer: Has everyone in this room been sent a dick pic?

Sierra: Yeah.

Kira: Yeah.

Talia: Yeah

Liv: But most of them are videos of people just masturbating in their car. (Year 7, girls).

Liv notes that she has a 'massive' Snapchat score, which is a marker of her peer social status and popularity. She also explains that of course having this many contacts whom she doesn't know means paedophiles will send stuff to her and ask her to send something back 'because they want that' (Figure 7.3 Transactional Dick Pic). She acknowledges accepting these contacts because she wants streaks—this is to up her Snapchat score; and a by-product of this is getting masturbation videos. In particular, they note videos of men masturbating in their car as depicted in Fig. 7.4. The girls went on to explain the videos in more depth:

Liv: Oh my God there's this guy on my Snapchat and he's always sending me this video of…

Kira: In the car, in a car! And you can see the people walking past, and like are you stupid? In the car!

Interviewer: So why do you keep him on your Snapchat?

Liv: I don't, I deleted him, but every time he always finds a way to text me, always makes a new Snapchat and adds me, and makes a new Snapchat….I get about two hundred a day of just dick pic and vaginas..

Interviewer: OK, two hundred a day you think.

Liv: About that.

Interviewer: Honestly? Two hundred a day? (Year 7, girls).

Liv says every time she blocks the user they make a new Snapchat and add her. Here we can see how blocking isn't effective and Liv does not report the user, although if she did so it is not apparent how making new accounts would be halted. Although the interviewer is incredulous and questions the amount of 'dick pics and vaginas' Liv is getting daily, she maintains this is the case. It's interesting as well that she mentions vaginas, which alerts us to the fact that masses of sexual content and body parts are circulating through these add networks on the platform, it becomes ubiquitous to Liv, but this doesn't mean that it doesn't carry risks for her.

For Liv, the benefits outweigh these risks. We came to see that Liv and her friends perceive the massive amount of dick pics she is receiving as a symbol of her popularity and desirability. The economies and power dynamics around receiving these images can be complex. Liv actively expects to get the videos and images because 'she's a really well-known person'. Dick pics have become markers of popularity for these particular girls, something to expect and perhaps even cultivate as a marker of esteem. Gerlitz and Helmond (2013) have introduced the concept of the 'like economy', which transforms likes on social media posts into a valued currency. Snapchat scores become a form of currency for Liv, who lives in a council estate near to the school, which may mean she has fewer resources available to her than some of the highly privileged young people that we studied in selective schools, but also even than some of the young people in her own highly stratified neighbourhood. For many young people in our study, there is a complex sexualised 'like economy' driven by the platforms, including likes on Instagram, but also metrics around how many contacts one has, which can be seen as a form of visibility and currency valuable to the young person. What is clear is Liv opening herself up to mass followers to gain high scores and this is a source of pride for her. This popularity metric of Snapscore points was also highly desirable for Venus as we saw in chapter 2. This is a very different type of capital than those performed by some of the elite

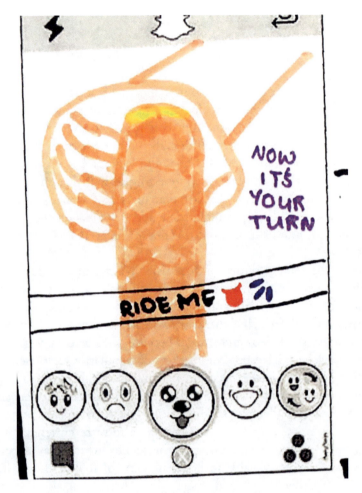

Fig. 7.3 Talia's drawings of image of transactional dick pic, with tounge and droplets emoji 'ride me; now its your turn'

young people who performed carefully curated feeds to their select friend group, recall Tilly from Lion's boarding school who shared a selfie of her paragliding in Switzerland.

Mass non-consensual spamming of dick pics—in the case of Liv, 200 a day on Snapchat—can be a by-product of this chasing of scores. For Liv the amount of 'attention' also becomes a marker of her popularity and

7 North West Secondary: Snapscore Micro-Celebrity ...

Fig. 7.4 Kira's drawing of masturbation videos

sexual attractiveness. While all the girls we've been looking at across this study who are opening their accounts to others are making themselves vulnerable to predators, Liv is the most extreme example we encountered of someone who is actively cultivating followers and for whom such status translates as high value within her peer group. Liv's age at 11, when these encounters are taking place, is what makes the situation more challenging to address. Indeed, while noting that she blocked 'older people', she did not report any of the content either to the online platform or at school, probably because she is not even legally supposed to be using the platform (the age to sign up is 13). It was clear that the importance of being on the site far outweighed any concern over unwanted sexual content and contact from adults. This issue of the user's age was addressed further by Kira:

> Kira: My little sister has Snapchat and she always gets pictures, she's only seven. And I literally have to go through her phone and like literally like...

> Liv: Oh no, I let my sister have Snapchat and...

> Interviewer: Do you ever tell your parents about that?

> Josie: I don't think it's that much of a big deal. I just delete it.

> Kira: My mum would just make me delete the whole thing. She'd say you're not having it. (NWS, Year 7, Girls).

Because of the age restrictions and the fact that they circumvent them, the young people become responsible for dealing with these issues for their own accounts but also their younger siblings. Kira talks about having to check her seven-year-old sister's Snapchat for her because if their parents knew they would make them both delete the App, which would be a terrible loss. When the interviewer asked 'what do you say to your seven-year-old sister' she responded:

> Kira: Usually she doesn't really open them, but when I do, because like I have to go through it and check it. Yeah, because like my sister's seven and obviously I don't want her to see any of that stuff, there's these accounts and their names is literally Anonymous Nudes, and then they just send like, my sister got added by one of them once, so I accepted it and then told them to never add this account again, and then I blocked him...then she adds all the random people, for some reason she adds all of them, so when they like try to add her she accepts all of them. I'm like what are

you doing? You don't know them. So I kind of argue with her about it because she's always adding them. (NWS, Year 7, Girls).

Here Kira who is 12-years old is monitoring and clearing the phone of her 7-year- old sister, to protect her from her parents taking away her phone. Through examples like this we can see how it is critically important to lower the age of RSE on digital sexual violence to Year 5 or younger when children are first getting onto these apps, in order to have in-depth conversations about privacy settings with them.

Year 9: What's App Wanking: Girls and Peer-on-Peer Sexual Harassment

The Year 9 girls, who were 14 years old, confirmed that they automatically add followers because they turn off their privacy settings on Snapchat:

Jules: On Snapchat um to get views you don't really have like privacy settings. You can block people and stuff, but when people add you it's like…

Esme: Like you just automatically add them back, you don't really think to remove that.

Jules: Well like Instagram you can have a private account though, and you can like kind of see their account.

Esme: Yeah, on Instagram if somebody you don't follow, or doesn't follow you…Messages go into requests.

Mila: Yeah, it's like a request folder, and you can go into that and see who is requesting to send you messages, and you can choose to like either ignore them or accept the message. (Year 9, girls)

In this excerpt, the Year 9 girls at NWS compare the visibility of Snapchat to that of Instagram, explaining it's easier to keep privacy settings on and see who the user is on Instagram. Unlike Snapchat, Instagram's built-in follow and message request folder settings offer less potential to add lots of unknown contacts for young people, and thus there is less chance of potential perpetrators accessing the teens' accounts.

With the 14-year-olds, more coercive elements of Snapchat came into fuller view, as they offered in-depth looks at the pressures girls can face on Snapchat. Mila, like Liv, had many Snapchat contacts, again derived mainly from Shoutouts:

> Mila: My friend Sam yeah, she um, she has a lot of people in her Snap, and she mentioned me and you just swipe up and they added me back on it, bare people just added me. Got sixty adds in like a minute, it was crazy, and I accepted some of them, and there was these weird people... (Year 9, Girls).

Mila explained that 'bare people' (meaning a lot of people) quickly added her; she expressed her amazement about getting 60 adds in one minute through her popular friend shouting her out. She went on to describe how this meant she'd been sent 'loads' of dick pics but also had been asked to send something back 'hundreds of times' (see Fig. 7.3).

> Mila: I've been asked, like seriously, probably hundreds of times because of how many people I have on my social media....you know on Snap you get added by random people and...
>
> Jules: Pop up to your story with like love heart eyes.
>
> Jenny: Yeah.
>
> Interviewer: Is it somebody you don't really know that well is asking you or someone you do know?
>
> Mila: I've had like a couple of people that I do know ask me, and then like loads of random people.

Interviewer: OK. So when somebody who you know asks you what do you do?

Jules: I don't send it to them, don't want to.

Interviewer: How do you manage it?

Tiffany: I'm just like nah.

Mila: You air them.

Jenny Yeah, you just ignore them.

Mila: You don't open it.

Jules: Just ignore.

Interviewer: So tell me what 'air them' means.

Mila: Basically they send you like, they poked your story, so like they send something to your story, you see that they've sent it, and you ignore it, you do not open it, you slide and check what they sent, then you like…

Here the Year 9 girls talk about how their strategy to 'air' or ignore the 'random' adult senders who pop up with love heart and tongue emojis on their Snapchat asking for nudes. They check the content in messages by sliding the message part way open to get the gist of it, but so it doesn't show as read to the sender, which is an invitation to keep sending. They don't respond but they also do not report any of this content.

While the volume from strangers may be annoying, they note that it is more difficult to manage these types of encounters with known boys in the peer group who send them dick pics or ask for nudes. One of the 14-year-olds, Alison, who had been quiet up to this point in the interview, told us about an incident involving boys she calls friends:

196   J. Ringrose and K. Regehr

Alison: So the boy on WhatsApp... he was high so he sent me a dick pic on WhatsApp. And a video of him like wanking.

LAUGHTER

Interviewer: What did you do?

Alison: I was just weirded out, I didn't block them or anything because they were my friends, but the next day I told them what they did. And they regretted it, like a lot.

Tiffany: Pretended to forget. I'm pretty sure he didn't forget that.

Interviewer: So you just thought that the best way was just to kind of like approach them?

Alison: Yeah.

Interviewer: Did they apologise?

Alison: Um, I think they just, they just really went really red and was like – fuck. They didn't apologise though.

Interviewer: OK, so what do you guys think about that type of like, what should happen around something like that happening?

Jules: I dunno, I think Alison dealt with it well.

Mila: Yeah.

Alison: Thank you.

Alison says she confronted 'them' at school indicating more than one boy was involved. She says they turned red and said 'fuck' and she surmised that they regretted it. Tiffany comments that she is sure they must have a memory of sending the video despite being high at the time and are merely pretending to forget. Alison confirms that they didn't apologise.

When we questioned this further, asking whether they think something, more should have happened, the other girls become defensive and say Alison handled it well, for which she thanks them. We felt there was a sense of pride from Alison that she had dealt with the situation on her own rather than seeking out support. There is no indication from the girls that they find this behaviour from boys problematic, harassing or abusive. We went on to try and unpack the episode further later in the interview during the drawing session, when Alison opened up more about the impact of the episode on her:

Alison: Think it's more of a big deal when you know them.

Tiffany: Yeah, same.

Jenny: Because it's like... you can't unsee it.

Tiffany: because it's your friend then like you're already close to them... they send you something like sexual, like weird shit...

Alison: Like its two people (boys) that go to our school, two people, close people to me, that have sent it...

Tiffany: I think it's worse when it's somebody you know, because like say they are, you're really good friends, and you've trusted them, and they do that, personally I think it's more of a big deal.

Mila: But if you're a friend and you say in a jokey way, like...

Alison: It wasn't in a jokey way!

Mila: Say something like wait a second, then they'll laugh it off in a way...avoid an awkward situation.

Alison: When it's like someone you don't know you can just go they're a weird person, and then just leave it... if it's just some random guy you're just like OK, I'm never gonna see them again. But if it's someone you know, and the fact that you'll see them again and...

Tiffany: Yeah, if they go to the same school as you then you see them every day, and it just reminds you of like what they did.

In this powerful excerpt Tiffany, Alison and Jenny discuss how hard it is when you've been sent images or videos by boys you know—'you can't unsee it'. They talk about how it is a violation of trust. Mila tries to say it could be a joke or laughed off, but rather than agree with her at this point Alison explains the dramatic effect of not being able to dismiss them as 'weird' because you know them, and Tiffany talks about the burden of having to see them at school every day. Here is a crystal-clear reminder that digital harassment from school based peers shapes everyday physical in person offline life for girls at school; it doesn't stay online.

Significantly, we see the institutionalised violence of the school setting when victims have to continue attending with those who have harassed them. This is very different than a workplace, for instance, where adults might have recourse to legal harassment policies. In the school space the limitation of bullying policies, which neglect the digital and physical dynamics of peer-to-peer sexual harassment, is highly problematic. Researchers note that punitive responses to harmful sexual behaviour (Lloyd, 2019) can also put the victim at further risk, which may go some way to explain why none of the girls thought reporting the incident to the school was an option. It may well be significant that there are three times more boys than girls in this school and this may make it more challenging to deal with homosocial peer culture, such as boys collectively sending harassing videos.

When there is such a lack of awareness of how to address such behaviour amongst young people at school the girls simply learn to accept it. Concluding the story Alison said:

Alison: You kind of just like go over it and forget about it, so you just don't do anything about it.

Interviewer: You felt you couldn't do anything?

Alison: Yeah, you don't do anything about it and then it goes away, and then you don't have to care about it or think about it. Like at first, when

I first started getting dick pics I'd be like disgusted, but then I just got so used to it, and every time a dick appears on my screen I'm like—great, again. It's normal. So even when I got it from my friends it was like...lovely. (Year 9, girls).

In this excerpt, Alison says she just wants to forget about it... since she cannot do anything about it and hopes it will just go away. The move from disgust to resignation is palpable and something we want our readers to really grapple with. In news media appearances and articles regarding this study we often pointed to this quote as one of the most powerful from the research: 'When I first started getting dick pics I'd be like disgusted, but then I just got so used to it... It's normal.' We see a vivid demonstration of how normalisation works. We will address the difficult dilemmas youth are in, feeling no support and no way to report, in our conclusion to this chapter.

14-Year-Old Boys: From Dick Pics to Pornbots—masculinity, Empathy and Solidarity

Turning to the boys, now, it is vital to begin by saying this type of sexually aggressive behaviour is certainly not the norm for all-boys: it is a minority of boys who harness technology to capitalise on elements or features that may enable them to access and harass girls. Many boys were deeply troubled by these issues and expressed frank concern and even indignation. Some boys at NWS had a critical understanding of nude image exchange. The Year 9 group said that peers who solicit nudes are not necessarily engaging in the practice for their own pleasure, but often as a means of engaging in masculine camaraderie. As Nico explains, 'People ask for nudes just so they can show their friends... like, I got this girl to do this and send it to me ah look I'm sick.' Nico went on to explain that this didn't particularly bring respect to these individuals but rather, their peers would 'pay attention' to them. Thus, for Nico and others in the group, they positioned the solicitation and sharing of nudes as an exercise in masculinity attention grabbing. A need for boys to stand out and be noticed by other boys, as we've seen throughout the book, particularly in the preceding chapter outlining these dynamics in an all-boys schooling environment.

What is different about a mixed school setting, however, is we found more evidence of empathy for girls. Nico went on to discuss an experience where a female friend received a dick pic from an unknown sender and 'found it scary'. He explained that she had been:

> Nico: sent a picture from some random guy…Yeah and I was with her, and someone sent a pic and she showed me it was disgusting. She did not react positively towards it. It was pretty bad. (Year 9, Boys).

Here, Nico empathises with his friend and takes the image-based abuse seriously. This is such an important reminder of the part played by friendship and solidarity in mixed gendered settings, and that genuine friendship does exist between heterosexual boys and girls in teen peer groups, despite the dynamics of abuse and lack of consent around dick pics that we've been discussing in the book. We argue these are the dynamics of empathy and support that need to be cultivated across all school settings through having discussions like these with boys.

This story about strangers sending unwanted sexual content prompted other boys in the group to discuss the types of unsolicited contact boys received, which they explained happened through 'group chats' on both Instagram and Snapchat:

> Jax: It's like one account, no followers. The account is like 'hey sexy do you want to see my nudes?' or 'take off your pants' and it's fake….It's like click this link if you want to see and you just delete.
>
> Interviewer: How old were you when you started getting these types of messages?
>
> Isaac: Two years ago. (Year 9, Boys).

We refer to this type of mass messaging of young people as 'porn push' often from 'pornbots' (Salim, 2023). Jax showed us his phone with a ream of messages dating back weeks to an Instagram group called 'take off my pants', which had responses such as 'why am I added to this stupid group?' The boys are critical of these practices, but the main thing is they still have all the messages and links on their phones, rather than removing or blocking them—in other words, they are using the same tactics as the girls did, of ignoring and normalising. The failure to block and report is a serious issue, as we touch on further in the conclusion to this chapter and the book as a whole.

The 'bots', as they call them, send nude female bodies as an enticement to 'click this link' which moves them onto other sites where they will be prompted to pay for content. Isaac suggests he had been pushed pornography by these bots as early as Year 7, meaning he was aged 11.

12-Year-Old Boys: Nudes for Science and Navigating Premium Account sex Subscriptions

Turning to the Year 7 boys at NSW who are 11–12 years old, we found they were both frank and funny, responding eagerly to our preamble to the interview about needing their views for our research study, saying 'Nudes for science! You should get that on a t shirt.' As tweens on the threshold of being teenagers, they were at vastly different stages of development, from nearly six feet tall with a deep voice already, to still small, with one boy whose voice had not begun to change, signalling the complexity of adolescent masculinities they were navigating amongst themselves and as they entered into digital sexual cultures. The boys were highly critical of the e-safety videos they had received, mocking the one called 'I saw your willy', which others in this study have also mentioned as particularly problematic:

> Benji: There's another horrendous internet safety video and they're like eight-year-old kids playing with each other's phone. And one takes a picture of the other one's junk.

> Ferdinand: The "I saw your willy" video.

Danny: I mean when I get older I probably would like I'm not lying I probably would. If I guess I was in a relationship or something like when you trust her and like cause we're going through puberty you get horny, like your hormones and stuff. So obviously like you, you like think about it and you probably will end up doing it. (Year 9, Boys).

Here Danny relates that he thinks sending nudes will be something he will do when he's older. They continued talking about how these practices were normalised from their social media environments, including the memes they circulate.

Ferdinand: The phrase 'send nudes' is in a lot of memes. People make fun of it.

Benji Like 'when she sends nudes and you're driving in a car' and it has a meme of like the car falling off a cliff and crashing down.

Danny: So yeah, it's basically become normal.

Memes were an important site of humour and learning for the boys in their social media networks, as has been previously researched (Whitehead & Ringrose, 2021). Despite nudes being normal, however, Ferdinand goes on to explain why he thinks sending them is stupid:

Ferdinand: Anyone who sends nudes I think is pretty stupid.

Benji: It can end up anywhere.

Ferdinand: And there's another meme where she says she just like she sends nudes and then it's like 'your turn' and this guy just laughs nonstop because like often a man will do it just to get nudes and then often forget about it and it's like a whole thing and it is really bad.

Ferdinand: They'll [boys] will be like ah send nudes… and then she ended up sending first and then the boy won't send anything back.

Anthony: Transfer nudes.

7 North West Secondary: Snapscore Micro-Celebrity ...

Benji: He's given nothing and got something.

Ferdinand: He's got them, he's going to use them or put them online or whatever… just knowing someone…can catfish you, knowing it's out of your hands. Knowing someone's got your nudes who you've never met is like really scary and it can end up anywhere.

Anthony: Like some people know it's illegal but others actually not. [inaudible].

Benji: What?

Loud Voices.

Ferdinand: It's illegal.

Danny: Sexting is illegal?

Here the boys talk about what they call 'transfer' nudes, which they appear to have also learned about from memes circulating in their digital peer networks. This transferring is what we refer to as transactional nudes, but they are clear that it is often the case that requests like this are malicious. They go on to say being catfished online is really scary. Like the boys in Stags, they are concerned about being lured into traps online. They do not, however, reference the legal term sextortion, when someone is blackmailed with the threat of disseminating their nudes if they do not pay up, with boys being the primary targets of organised sextortion attempts (Internet Watch Foundation, 2023).

Anthony then declares that some people don't know sending nudes is illegal, Benji seems surprised, yelling 'what!' and a loud discussion breaks out where they debate whether sexting is illegal, with Benji and Danny both shocked. This is a very interesting point to underscore the inadequacy of their e-safety lessons, which have left them completely confused about the law.

Danny went on to discuss how he is the only boy in the group who has indeed gotten a nude from a girl he knows. What happened is his cousin's (aged 14) girlfriend sent it to him 'by mistake' on a chat with them both. Danny says he discussed it with his cousin before deleting it.

> Danny: I didn't show anyone. I just told him, my cousin, cause like, it was weird. I was like your girlfriend kind of sent me a nude …But yeah I'm the only one that's received nudes but it wasn't on purpose anyway.

> Interviewer: How did it make you feel?

> Danny: Um, well I kind of know that happens because I've got three older brothers and like I know like about like sex and stuff. Cause of my older brothers, like I guess I've never been innocent…, I guess it did make me feel like oh I guess this is what I need to do when I'm older. (Year 9, Boys).

Here we can see how Danny talks about his future and what he'll need to do when he's older, referencing his older brothers, and how he's never been 'innocent'.

From here, like the older boys above, the younger boys swiftly moved on to the everyday nature of getting spammed by 'pornbots'. They talked about content coming through on PS4 and other gaming programs. For example, one explained that: 'When you go on PS4 a PS4 Girl who is18 or something, and then they'll text you and it'll be can you call me, and they'll send you a link to a website and you need to use your credit card to facetime them.' All the Year 7 boys had been sent these types of redirection links on social media or games and discuss being put in Instagram group chats with links to paid sex content (see Fig. 7.5). Like Jax who discussed being put into a group chat on Instagram entitled 'take off your pants', Danny explained being added to mass group messages with more than 200 mostly older people:

> Danny they just like pick like random 200 males like age range from like the youngest people like little kids to like any age. And then, yeah. And then sometimes like especially in the old people they would actually try to speak in the group chat. It's weird, but I guess you're speaking to somebody you don't know. (Year 7, Boys).

The boys recognised that some of these requests were from bots as the images indicate. Instagram bots are automated programs that perform tasks without human intervention. They can be used to increase engagement, gain followers, and generate traffic for accounts.

Elaborating further on specific examples of porn push they are targeted with, the boys described pay for content accounts on Snapchat, like those that came up in Chapter 6 at Stags School for Boys:

Fig. 7.5 Anthony's drawing of a post from xox,xox,xox account: 'follow for some nudes/send some news (sic),' which he describes as: 'Porn Bot account asking for followers'

Ferdinand: So there's this thing that people do like, like I said, like the porn stars, like the popular ones, they do like this thing and it's dumb. But like, they get money out of it, but basically it's like 'buy my premium Snapchat'. So it's a separate Snapchat but you have to pay for it like every month.

Danny: Like joining a YouTube channel. It's like a subscription.

Interviewer: Do you know anyone who has accessed those paid Snapchats?

Benji: No I've just seen it like being promoted. Like, like it's like them like this. They go 'buy my premium Snapchat to see the rest'. Only £4 or something.

Danny: There's like, so Belle Delphine [inaudible] um, so she has like a Patreon amd for like £100 monthly, you get to FaceTime me for like five minutes. [inaudible] And she's like, I'll even send you to explicit videos blah blah blah. It's like you're paying for her to show her body ...

Here the boys explain that they are targeted to buy premium Snapchat accounts to buy sex services.

Jordan: She's something called a gamer girl she like does cosplay and stuff. [inaudible] Like Hentai I guess. Hentai is a form of porn but it's cartoon. So she dresses up as characters like that and then...she said, okay, I'll start to sell my bath water and now she sells her bath water.

Benji: Fifty quid a pop.

Ferdinand: I just think it's such a weird concept. Gamer girls, as he said it's just people who dress up in like seductive cosplay and do like seductive videos on YouTube...She wears nothing then covers up certain bits. (Year 7, Boys).

The boys are being encouraged to buy sex subscriptions, through influencers like Belle Delphine on Instagram whose account links to a Patreon sign up. Belle Delphine capitalises on an anime style of 'cosplay' as the

7 North West Secondary: Snapscore Micro-Celebrity ...   207

boys describe her, wearing animal ears and fluffy tails in her nearly nude 'pornified' images (7.6) Delphine's account asks the user to verify they are over 18, but of course this is easy to bypass. The boys went on to marvel at the stunts that were common on such accounts:

> Jordan: Like they drink her bath water and it's genuine bath water and she got so much money off it. And now there's this thing, no one was ever gonna buy it, but it's £50,000 for an actual tub, like a massive thing of her bath water.

> Max: In one of her Instas—she's famous on Instagram - so like one of the Instagram posts, she's like not wearing a bra but she put, like an X there and an X there, on top of nipples, like yeah it's just weird. (Year 7, Boys).

One of the main elements about the porn influencer subscription sites is that they promote the taster material, such as posting Xs over their nipples, in a bid for users to pay, something that has become much more common since this study through platforms like OnlyFans. Even the bath water phenomenon is a tactical ploy (perhaps a play on thirst trap, which is slang for sexy selfies intended to attract viewers—the term "thirst" is a colloquialism that compares sexual frustration to dehydration, implying desperation.) The stunt is absurd and designed to raise the value of the influencer by attracting attention and drawing in more paid users. The boys do not need to sign up for the premium account and buy the sex, as they can simply consume the taster material. Ferdinand went on to again denounce the subscription sex as stupid:

> Ferdinand: I think it's stupid. I don't know, you're trying to create an intimate relationship, while getting paid. It's like being a prostitute.

> Jordan: Like a gold digger.

> Ferdinand: It's like using your body for business in a way like that is not great. It's using your body and sending naked pictures of yourself to people for money. And again, if that's how you want to live and you're

old enough to do it, fair enough. But, the fact is other people can access it through whatever way and that often ends badly.

Interviewer: Do you think some people are in a position where they feel like they more have to do that than other people?

Danny: Most of the people who are doing it, again like Belle Delphine, are rich already, they just want more money and publicity.

Interviewer: Okay.

Jordan: But yeah, some people would sell nudes. It's like an online strip joint because again, you're using your body to get paid and if you're like in university and you need money, it's a way to make a living. But again if other people can access it yes it's prostitution, it's not good.

The boys explain that they think these influencers are doing it for publicity and are already rich. They seem to vacillate between this being an acceptable way to make money, and a problem because you're using your body to get paid—'online strip joint' or 'prostitution' (see Fig. 7.6) and another calls the women with such accounts 'gold diggers', (Gold digger is a colloquialism to refer to a person, typically a woman, who engages in a type of transactional sexual relationship for money rather than love.) Gold digger is a sexist notion about female sexuality, that the boys apply to make sense of sex work. What is evident is that 12-year-old boys have first-hand experience with a platform economy of online sex work. They face pressures to buy sex and intimacy simply by virtue of using platforms like Snapchat and Instagram, and they are also concerned about catfishing and being drawn in by these schemes. Given how widespread these experiences are we think it is incumbent upon sex education in schools to step up and address the complexities of digital sexual cultures on social media platforms. Giving young people a clearer understanding of economic processes on social media and explaining sex work would enable young people to understand and manage these pressures without demonising female sexuality.

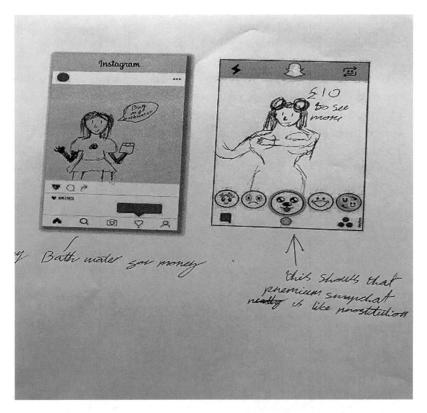

Fig. 7.6 Jordan's drawing of Belle Delphine selling bath water and premium Snapchat accounts as 'prostitution'

Conclusion: The Need for Better Sex Education and Support to Report Harmful Online Content

Despite having up to date sex education in their school (the sex education teacher facilitated the research visit) the young people at NWS were universally critical of the provision they were receiving. As we saw above, the boys ridiculed the anti-sexting film 'I saw your willy', which had nothing helpful to offer them regarding their experience of getting unwanted nudes from girls, nor porn push on their social media applications, which was happening regularly from age 11 for boys. As we also saw the young people were not sure about what was illegal and not. The boys talked about wanting much clearer sex education, including content they termed 'NSFW' (not safe for work), but of course what they actually mean is not safe for school. They are also concerned that their memes are not 'restricted' which would reduce their 'fun' (see Fig. 7.7).

The older boys were likewise scathing about their sex education.

Interviewer: Have you been taught about any other stuff in school in terms of like digital safety or sex education?

Isaac: It's like stranger danger.

Jax: No they shouldn't even bother with it.

Ryan: Some people are dumb enough to reply to strangers or send nudes to strangers or stuff like that.

Nico: But the thing is some people don't know at all, some people don't know how to react. So they just try to be polite but actually they're just getting themselves into a situation which is actually quite bad... Like this girl... she was like I don't want to talk to you you're an old guy and he was like oh I'll just wait until you grow up … until you're legal age. But that's still a bit weird because the guy is much older than her (Year 9 boys)

Recalling that Nico previously told us the powerful story of having been with his female friend when she received a dick pic and how traumatising it was for her, here he again interrupts Ryan, who says people are 'dumb' if they send nudes and recounts another episode of a girl being asked for nudes and not knowing how to react, and being too polite. Nico has a lot of emotional intelligence and really seems to empathise with his female friend's experiences in a way that we found very heartening. The implication from Nico is that the school needs to do much more to support girls in managing these issues, and we would add building up the types of understandings and empathy that Nico shows.

7 North West Secondary: Snapscore Micro-Celebrity … 211

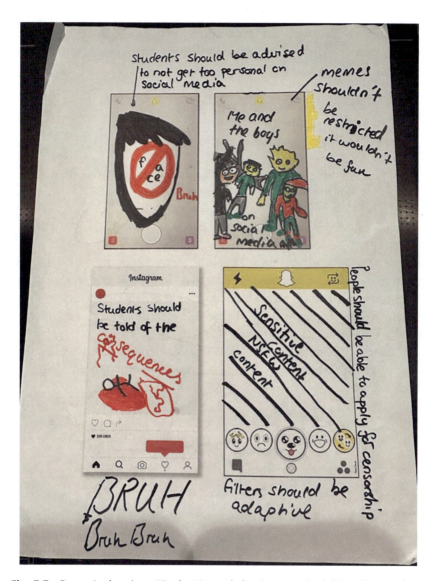

Fig. 7.7 Danny's drawing: "Bruh; Me and the Boys on Social Media, 'Students should be advised to not get too personal on social media'; 'Memes shouldn't be restricted it wouldn't be fun'; 'Students should be told of the consequences,' 'Sensitive content NSFW (Not Safe for Work) Content.'

Similarly to the boys, the girls noted that online safety assemblies with the message 'don't talk to strangers' are too superficial to make any difference at all:

Kira: We don't really learn about really a lot.

Liv: It's basic things, don't talk to strangers

Kira: Just like don't talk to strangers, don't send nudes, and don't talk to people you don't know.

Sierra: They should teach us just more like deeper into it. (Year 7 Girls).

The paradox of the education they are receiving is that the girls are ignoring all the e-safety messaging such as don't send nudes, don't talk to strangers, dismissing it in favour of turning off all the privacy settings on apps to gain more visibility, views, followers, friends and ultimately higher scores on social media apps like Snapchat.

Meanwhile, the older girls in NWS who had experienced a wide range of online sexual harassment commented upon the urgent need for better education, noting:

Jenny: Making sure people are educated in it would just make it easier for the person who got the pic, um, to deal with it. But like I feel like boys will just screenshot it.

Jules: And then they get spread about.

Tiffany: Call you a slag.

Mila: But if you don't do it [send nudes] it's all wrong.

Jules: You're like frigid.

Tiffany: If we do it we get called slags, whores, if we don't do it we get called frigid or

Mila: We need more PSHE days as well.

Jules: We've just got stuff which is like...

Alison: We've learnt about sex.

Jules: But we've never learnt about what to do in a situation when you're getting sent unsolicited images (Year 9 Girls).

These girls noted the urgent need to educate to move away from the messaging to simply not send nudes because they are pressured to do so, shamed if they do send images but also if they don't. They also talk about how when images are shared non-consensually, they are the ones that are called slags and whores. They explain never having learned about 'unsolicited images', terminology they've already picked up from the brief discussion with us. They argue they need support to deal with all these complex forms of what we have been discussing and identify as image-based sexual harassment and abuse.

To conclude this chapter we feel that our time at NWS helped us to dig even deeper into some of the problematic and coercive elements of Snapchat and Instagram that we've been mapping throughout the book. We felt the class dynamics at play in the school are significant. Liv lives on a council estate, her brother was in a gang, and she has amassed a high Instagram following due to her competitive dancing. She is already learning to gain value through the metrics of Snapchat and Instagram which is a precursor to actual monetisation of the self on social media platforms. As part of her drive to gain followers, Liv experiences mass amounts of non-consensual dick pics, transactional dick pics, and masturbation videos which she chalks up to being a hazard but also actual evidence of her popularity. When we came to the year 10 girls, we found they had moved from disgust when getting this content from strangers, to resignation when they received masturbation videos from their male peers at school. We witnessed a normalisation process where they've learned to accept sexual harassment as a part of life via being worn down around these practices on social media.

The boys in the school are experiencing the other side of the monetisation of feminine sexuality on social media, navigating porn push from an early age. They discussed influencer celebrities such as Belle Delphine, who has capitalised on an anime doll-like sexual aesthetic to sell her essence to those who will purchase her bath water. The absurdity of it all was commented with great reflection by the 12-year-old boys in this school.

Significantly, what was a constant across the boys' and the girls' groups was a failure to report any of this harmful content. We want to remind the reader that social media platforms like Snapchat's main source of revenue are from advertisements. In order to see more advertisements a user has to stay on the platform longer. The streaks and score points encourage high interaction as part of a fun, game-like environment. But being at risk of adult predators is the problematic element of this drive for high use. It does not even occur to these girls to report any of the content to Snapchat. Likewise, the boys do not report any of the porn push they receive, and they often have group messages, chats and links saved on their phones.

We are reminded of the main messages of this book: that these tech companies and applications need to be more accountable around these processes. Furthermore, these digital processes need to be front and centre in high quality sex education. Both boys and girls argued that they needed much more robust sex education that dealt with the types of social media dynamics they were actually experiencing instead of outdated 'horrendous' internet safety videos' as Benji called them. This is exactly the up to date and nuanced sex education aimed at preventing image-based sexual harassment and abuse which we outline in our conclusion.

References

Gerlitz, C., & Helmond, A. (2013). The like economy: Social buttons and the data-intensive web. *New Media & Society, 15*(8), 1348–1365. https://doi.org/10.1177/1461444812472322

Internet Watch Foundation. (2023). *Hotline reports 'shocking' rise in the sextortion of boys*. https://www.iwf.org.uk/news-media/news/hotline-reports-shocking-rise-in-the-sextortion-of-boys/

Lloyd, J. (2019). Response and interventions into harmful sexual behaviour in schools. *Child Abuse and Neglect, 94*, Article 104037.

Marwick, A. E. (2018). The algorithmic celebrity. In C. Abidin, M. L. Brown (Eds.), *Microcelebrity around the globe* (pp. 161–169). Emerald Publishing Limited. https://doi.org/10.1108/978-1-78756-749-820181015

Salim, N. (2023). A pornbot stole my identity on Instagram. It took an agonising month to get it deleted. *The Guardian*. https://www.theguardian.com/lifeandstyle/2023/feb/28/a-pornbot-stole-my-identity-on-instagram-it-took-an-agonising-month-to-get-it-deleted

Salter, M. (2016). Privates in the online public: Sex(ting) and reputation on social media. *New Media & Society, 18*(11), 2723–2739. https://doi.org/10.1177/1461444815604133

Walkerdine, V., Lucey, H., & Melody, J. (2001). *Growing up girl: Psychosocial explorations of gender and class*. Palgrave Press.

Whitehead, S., & Ringrose, J. (2021). Memetic masculinities: Exploring racialised homosociality and networked misogynoir in teen boys' Instagram social media diaries. In F. Blaikie (Ed.), *Global perspectives on youth and young adults: Situated, embodied and performed ways of being, engaging and belonging* (pp. 99–121). Routledge.

Open Access This chapter is licensed under the terms of the Creative Commons Attribution-NonCommercial-NoDerivatives 4.0 International License (http://creativecommons.org/licenses/by-nc-nd/4.0/), which permits any noncommercial use, sharing, distribution and reproduction in any medium or format, as long as you give appropriate credit to the original author(s) and the source, provide a link to the Creative Commons license and indicate if you modified the licensed material. You do not have permission under this license to share adapted material derived from this chapter or parts of it.

The images or other third party material in this chapter are included in the chapter's Creative Commons license, unless indicated otherwise in a credit line to the material. If material is not included in the chapter's Creative Commons license and your intended use is not permitted by statutory regulation or exceeds the permitted use, you will need to obtain permission directly from the copyright holder.

8

Swans School for Girls: Performing High Achieving Femininities: Sexy Selfies and Digital Dating Dynamics in an All-Girls School

Swans School for Girls is located in a highly desirable and exclusive suburb of London. Housed in a welcoming brick historic building, with a shiny new glass reception, the school was set amidst the large suburban homes in the area. Swans is a former girls' grammar school, now one of the most successful comprehensive schools in the country. Akin to the postcode lottery girls' school that was nearby to North West Secondary in Chapter 7, entry to Swans is restricted to the street you live in with parents making concerted efforts to live in the affluent catchment area.

Waiting outside for the designated time to start the sessions on a warm summer's day we basked under a tree on one of the picnic benches set up for students to enjoy. Swans was surrounded by a majestic brick wall with an iron gate, presenting an entirely different institutional environment than the chain linked and barbed wire fence we found at Outer Northern Academy in Chapter four. We conducted fieldwork visits twice at Swans School for Girls, once with the all-girls' part of the school interviewing Years 8, 9 and 10 (aged 12–15), and a second visit a couple of months later when we spoke to a mixed gender and sexuality diverse group in sixth form (aged 16–18) since the school admitted boys into the college. Swans as a school, then, represents the widest age school that we studied.

© The Author(s) 2025
J. Ringrose and K. Regehr, *Teens, Social Media, and Image Based Abuse*,
https://doi.org/10.1007/978-3-031-92322-7_8

217

By speaking with older sixth form girls who had attended the school since they were younger and boys who were more recent additions, we were able to gain valuable insights into their experiences of the mobile technology at ages 11–18, as they reflected upon experiences in their younger years.

In this chapter, we will delve into experiences of social media at an all-girls school. We will assess whether such single sex 'all-girls' spaces really shelter girls from issues like sexual harassment and violence when, as many girls explain, the only way they have to meet and interact with boys is online, much like the situation for the boys we met in Chapter 6 in Stags School for Boys. In addition to the high academic achievement focus of this former grammar school, we will document some of the online worlds created by the girls and how success is also based on generating a sexy self on Instagram and Snapchat platforms. Next, we will explore how they experience sexual images sent to them from the boys who are part of their mobile digital networks and how Snapchat and Instagram facilitate harassment and abuse. Finally, we ask the older sixth form students, given all the risks, why do young people stay on a platform like Snapchat? They respond by describing complex and ambivalent feelings: whereas on the one hand they know it can be bad, they also feel nostalgia for it, and they don't want to leave their contacts and networks built on the platform during their school years. Snapchat becomes habitual and there is a sense that if you don't use Snapchat it will result in social isolation. Overall, we argue that, although many parents seek to shelter and protect girls in 'all girl' spaces, such environments need to be thought through carefully in relation to digital networks and social media platforms because the same digital risks we found across all the schools are present and could even potentially be exacerbated in single gender environments.

Parental Surveillance and Meeting Boys Online

On our first visit, we are given an art room to conduct focus groups with girls in years 8, 9 and 10. In the breaks between our sessions, the staff go out of their way, bringing us tea and cake and checking to see if we are comfortable. These are staff with time and space to do extra, unlike the harried yet dedicated staff we worked with in some of the state schools in deprived areas.

The girls at Swans were largely enthusiastic and outgoing with many interested in our own backgrounds as researchers—where we went to university, and how we conducted our research. One of the girls in year 9, Helen, expressed wanting to become a sociologist and study gender herself. The girls started by explaining the dilemma that they must be extremely careful about what they post online and keep separate private accounts, because their parents are monitoring their social media:

Kerri: my mum follows me on Instagram.

Helen: Same.

Jo: It's really embarrassing, so she can see what I post, so I always have to be really careful, she's like oh let me comment on your picture, and I'm like – no!

LAUGHTER

Kerri: I make sure she doesn't like or comment because that's really embarrassing. But yeah, but like with like the privacy settings and stuff she's, oh I don't, she goes through all my followers, and she's like are you sure you know this person? And I'm like yeah, we met a couple of times. She always questions me on my followers, she's a bit strict about people following me.

Interviewer: OK, and you don't have like a second account or anything.

Kerri: Well I have a priv, but that's like fifteen people follow that and it's like most of my close friends, because like most people have like a main account and a priv, it's like probably about twenty-five people that actually like do stuff on it.

Interviewer: A priv is private?

Kerri: I make sure she doesn't follow my priv, because that's really embarrassing. (Swans year 9 girls)

These dynamics were like the types of protective environments we found at Lions boarding school where parents of girls in particular were monitoring their accounts in an attempt to protect them. Like at Lions, the girls in Swans are finding ways around this such as separate 'priv' private accounts.

The year 10 girls were similarly concerned with keeping content private from parents, with one girl Caroline claiming "I delete everything in case my mum sees". They also explained that creating an appealing social media presence was important because it was the only avenue available to communicate with boys:

Tamara: Online you make friends with them (a boy) they become like a mutual friend, and then when you meet them, they like become your friend, and you become friends with their friends.

Janice: A lot of the girls in our year they are friends with Cob School for Boys; they became friends with them through doing like a production with them.

Samantha: And if you didn't do the production then you're not really friends with any of those boys, you just sort of get cast out.

Tamara: That's how people meet the majority of the friends outside of school through some kind of joint activity or something.

Caroline: I just haven't spoken to a boy in like four years, so I don't know how people meet them! (Year 10, girls)

As we've noted, Swans is a very high achieving comprehensive school located an affluent neighbourhood. It also transpired that the school cultivated a partnership with a close by independent, fee paying school, Cobs School for Boys. Presumably, the relationship was to cultivate high cultural capital networks and experiences for the girls. Cobs and Swans were doing drama productions and other activities together, which is how the girls become friends with some of the boys. They also discussed associating with boys from the nearby comprehensive mixed gender state school, which we will call Hawkes Secondary as some of the girls had attended primary school with boys that went to Hawkes. Both schools are within approximately 2 miles from Swans. One of the girls in the Year 10 group claims, however, that she hasn't spoken to a boy in four years since she left primary school. The others mention that online space is very important because if they are not involved in some sort of joint activity then they never interact with boys.

Similarly the year 8 girls, who are 12–13-year-old girls explained how they would expand their social media contacts through boys they knew before attending the girls school, such as those they'd attended primary school with:

Interviewer: How would you meet boys online then?

Grace: I mean mutual friends.

Ruby: Friends of friends of friends.

Charli: Like primary school boys and then their friends that they've met in their new school…

Elizabeth: Yeah.

Charli: …and then you kind of just meet up with them and then they bring a few friends…

Steph: … then you find their Instagram and talk to them.

Charli: Or you put on a story and link.

Ruby: Like if you're linking someone I wouldn't really like send them stuff, but you post stuff for them, but it's not for them, but you know what I mean.

Beatrice: Because if you like send it to them it's like they'll think you're desperate.

Grace: Yeah, but if you like post it.

Ruby: It's being subtle.

Charli: Yeah, kind of being subtle, because you're linking them, and you're doing it for them. (Year 8, girls)

Here, the girls describe adding a Snapchat username to their Snapchat story for people to add them and 'link' (slang verb meaning to meet or connect with someone). This is akin to doing a Shoutout as you are advertising your username on your story. This is viewed as more acceptable than directly sending friend requests to boys, which would be seen as desperate or overly forward. There is an element of putting out attractive material and waiting to see who adds you, which they say is a subtle way to post 'stuff for them', with a boy in mind. The 12–13-year-olds are hyper aware of their online selves with specific imagined audiences and took great care in the production of their selfies.

Sexy Selfies

The girls offered us a critical analysis of what was going on in their peer networks, including pressures girls experienced to perform a 'sexy' persona online (Ringrose, 2011, 2013). They heatedly discussed what was acceptable for girls to post on their social media accounts and what was not ok, including an animated discussion about a friend in their school, Lily, who was an object of admiration, but also of jealousy and sometimes ridicule. The girls showed us successive images Lily had posted in a low-cut vest top in the mirror with Snapchat filter of dog ears and dog nose on her face, pouting and with a giant tongue licking the screen (Fig. 8.1).

The images we were shown from Lily's feed showcased her breast cleavage quite prominently and one had garnered 323 hearts or likes. The girls exclaimed 'she has three bras on to get her boobs this big', and they said that although she's using the fun Snapchat animal face filters for these images, the 'real' function of her bra selfies are: 'she's showing what she's got', saying the images were taken with the purposes of: one to showcase her 'tits', another her 'bum' and another her face. They also speculated that she used the dog nose Snapchat filter over her face because she was self-conscious around her 'pig nose', with one of the girls enjoying the dig at the revered Lily. At this comment, another

Fig. 8.1 Grace's drawing of Lily's mirror selfie with Snapchat dog ears filter in vest top

224   J. Ringrose and K. Regehr

girl protested at how the group was 'talking about girls' and 'judging them'. 'I'm not judging', responds another. 'it's just what it is'. Further, as if to say Lily is open game to criticism, one of the girls said: 'She's got 1300 followers and most people she doesn't even know'. They go on to show us and discuss the responses to Lily's cleavage post which garnered 323 likes. Comments included some from those who are known to Lily in real life: 'SO PRETTY! Miss you so much! Can't wait for this summer [three heart exclamation emojis]' and 'honestly one of the prettiest, nicest girls I've ever met [two red heart emojis]'. But there were other comments from unknown people such as: 'peng nice [three double pink heart emojis]', 'so fit [smiley face]'; with Lily responding 'thanksX', 'fave [two kissing heart face emojis]', 'prettiest', 'gorgeous', 'your body [heart eyes face emoji]'; with Lily responding 'merci [laughing face emoji] X'. There is also a request that simply says 'link? X'; to which Lily replies 'idku' (I don't know you). As noted, link is an invitation to communicate further, perhaps through private messenger, and link, as we heard from others, could also signal an invitation to meet offline. We don't know if the communication here went any further but what is critical here is that Lily is reaching an audience far beyond the cocoon of the girls' school, and even far beyond their neighbourhood and Cobs School for Boys and Hawkes Secondary school students.

In other photos, we saw girls who were experimenting with showing off their silhouette, girls at a sleepover photographing themselves in bed, or even the well-known squatting position looking over one's shoulder to accentuate the bottom. In many of these images, parts of their body are squiggled out using a digital photo editor (see Fig. 8.2).

When we asked the reason for the squiggles one girl responded with, 'it's to cross out the rude bits'. Another girl disagreed, explaining the doodle was an attempt to 'draw attention to that', and yet another theorises that the purpose of one squiggle is to hide the girls' 'belly'.

Another image shows partially bared breasts are covered up, with the flash over the face and a squiggle drawn to show the breast area. 9:30 pm has been written on the image, which has a 'sweet dreams' sticker pasted on it. While the earlier examples were breezed through as the girls showed us images using squiggles, this one generated specific comment and critique:

8 Swans School for Girls: Performing High Achieving … 225

Fig. 8.2 Charli's drawing of scribbles to focus on body parts

Grace: Uh Ah, did you see that picture that Danni posted on her private?

Charli: I know!

Grace: They were all like naked and they were just covering their boobs with their hands.

Steph: Apparently um…

Grace: And there's this one…So I've been having like a go at her for it. It's on her private.

Steph: Like this one.

Grace: The girls' privates are so weird. (Year 8, girls)

The girls make judgements upon Danni posting herself naked covering her breasts: 'I've been having a go at her for it'. Apparently, Danni's image crosses over the line of experimenting with a sexy femininity. They also mention her private account, which we heard about earlier to get around parental monitoring. You can create a limited group who sees this content rather than the entire contact list, who with Snapchat could be many unknown followers. They comment that Danni's privates are 'so weird', a signal they do not approve of the content she is experimenting with that relate to her body images. Charli noted social media influencers pose like this implying Danni to wanted to try out the same look, drawing the poses (Fig. 8.3).

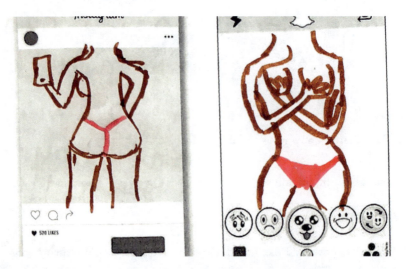

Fig. 8.3 Charli's drawing of mirror butt selfie (belfie) and figure covering naked breasts with hands

Our point in drawing attention to these practices is to show how girls are experimenting with their images online and how to present a sexy self to the outside world, given how important this is for forging heterosexual identity, that reaches beyond the all-girls environment through digital connectivity. The girls also drew messages and notes of advice around not caving to pressures to post the perfect body and face, or to pose in your underwear, and wrote warnings about making these types of posts (see Fig. 8.4).

Fig. 8.4 Ruby's drawing: 'Don't feel pressured to have pictures of yourself in underwear because it's how you're 'meant to look' or because someone tells you to

As with other schools, the Year 8 girls reported that expanding their networks resulted in them being added to unknown groups and chats on Instagram and getting DM requests that sent them links to porn and dick pics and asked them for nudes.

> Ruby: Like the people who usually get sent like pictures of their like penis and stuff, they're not, you don't really know them.

> Beatrice: Then they like send you links to porn and stuff.

> Charli: And they say if you follow me I'll give you like nude...

> Grace: I get added to group chats, like a massive group of just random adults who I've never even met before, and I'm like the only child. On Instagram. But it's like hi guys, do you want to see my nudes? And their profile picture is a massive picture of their [penis]...

> Charli: I got added to this group chat once, and it was like, you know the maximum is like 32 people, and I was looking through it thinking how did they get my Instagram, and literally everyone on there was adult. (Year 8 girls)

Looking around this group of eight girls we asked: 'How many people has this happened to?' Seven of the eight girls raised their hands, indicating they had been sent this type of what we call porn push. The girls wonder how adults get their Instagram and discuss the well-worn tactic of sending a dick pic and asking for a nude in return:

> Charli: If you start talking to like the wrong people, if you just randomly add someone on Snapchat, a boy you've never met...

> Charli: They can like start friendly, and then they'll be like oh yeah...

> Elizabeth: Yeah, they'll be like I'll send you something if you send me something back.

> Grace: One, I thought he was like a mutual friend, because one of my friends was like oh you've got to follow this guy, so I followed. And

then he sent me a chat and I thought, because you know when you add someone on Snapchat you start doing streaks, so I thought it was a streak, so I went on it, and it was just a pic of his like dick, and he was like oh come and suck my...and then I just blocked him.

Charli: It just depends, some people are more casual and chill about it than other people.

Steph: Some people will be like…

Charli: Ugh, it's a dick pic.

Charli: I think with nudes it's like drugs, everyone knows it's bad but they want to do it anyway. (Year 8 girls)

We hear about the transactional dick pic sent in a bid to get a nude back. The Year 8 girls work very hard to be nonchalant about dick pics, noting some people are 'casual about it', a similar narrative to what we found in Chapter 7 at Northwest Secondary, with Alison who said it had told us that receiving random dick pics had just become normal.

Boys Being 'Provocative' Online

In Year 10 the girls explained that while it was more common to receive loads of random dick pics from adult strangers or the porn push mechanisms described above, they offered a detailed look at how some boys in their digital peer groups (mostly from the neighbouring schools) would communicate with them. They explained how boys will send 'provocative' images first rather than sending an outright dick pic, which would be more extreme:

Zoe: The boys in our like year just send like provocative photos, they're not as like extreme.

Tamara: Explicit.

Interviewer: What is a provocative one?

Samantha: Like, I dunno, like their V line.

Denise: Or they'll be flexing their arms in the mirror or something.

Zoe: They would even put them on like their Snapchat stories, to show off. (Year 10 girls)

The girls carefully describe and draw the performative work the boys are doing to appear attractive, clenching their jaws and muscles or highlighting their abs or v-line (Fig. 8.5), trying to portray themselves as cool, 'sexy' and 'masculine':

Tamara: They're trying to be little like men, but like it's not really working because they're just sort of under-developed still.

Samantha: They go to the gym, they try to put on loads of muscle, but they don't actually understand the science behind muscle growth, so they're not really doing anything.

Janice: And they always feel they need to put it on their story, there'll be a picture of them in the gym mirror like flexing their arms... (Fig. 8.6)

Caroline: And it's not very big.

Zoe: ...and like I'm more muscly than them.

LAUGHTER

Denise: It's embarrassing.

Janice: His Instagram bio is Hit Me Up and then his only picture on there is a picture of his abs. (Year 10 girls)

The girls are somewhat scathing of the boys' attempts to display their muscles, mocking them, and noting that the girls have bigger arms themselves. It is interesting that the girls could engage in a much

8 Swans School for Girls: Performing High Achieving ... 231

more revealing discussion of boys' selfies and images than most boys in our study, who found it almost impossible to discuss their own image production in a self-reflective way. The girls go on to indicate that boys will try to reference a specific type of masculinity such as abs, V line, clenched jaw or bulge in their trousers:

Zoe: Or it'll just be a picture of a bulge under clothes or something.

Denise: Or the V line or the clenched jaw. Or like the shoulder or something.

Interviewer: Why the clenched jaw?

Denise: Because the jawline looks better. (Year 10 girls)

The girls discuss how these types of images are used as a form of banter by boys from Hawkes Secondary who they disparagingly call 'fuck boys' after asking if they can swear in the interview. 'Fuck boys' refers to boys who have lots of casual sexual partners, the masculine equivalent of a 'slut.' They also describe how they are aware boys will strategically work as a group to send images to one specific girl all at the same time or to a mass of girls simultaneously:

Milly: You've got like dares and stuff, when it's like oh yes, send this to this girl and see if she'll reply, and if she replies then we know you're a boy who's like a popular boy.

Tamara: They think it's funny.

Zoe: They like have a laugh.

Samantha: They have a competition, like how many responses you can get.

Milly: The boys will just be like oh...

Denise: They'll be hanging out.

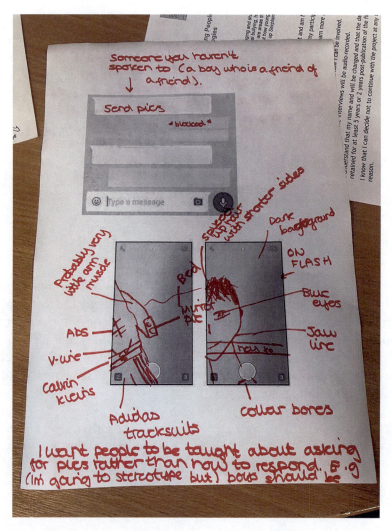

Fig. 8.5 Samantha's drawing of 'Abs, Jaw line, Collar bones. I want people to be taught about asking for pics rather than how to respond

Tamara: Yeah, and they'll all send a picture at the same time, and sometimes it's so bait because you'll get pictures from like three boys at the same time.

8 Swans School for Girls: Performing High Achieving ...

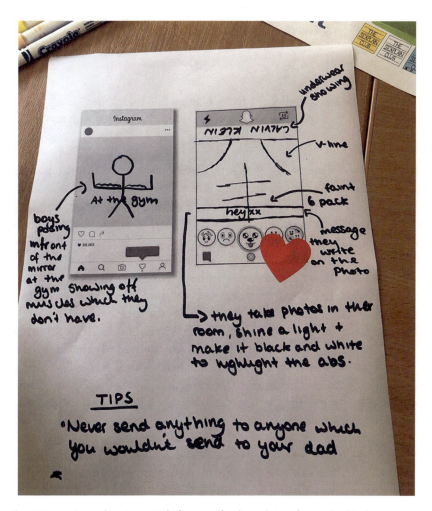

Fig. 8.6 Janice's drawing: stick figure of a boy doing front double bicep pose: 'posing in front of the mirror at the gym showing muscles they don't have'. Underwear showing, v-line, faint 6-pack 'they take photos in their room, shine a light and make it black and white to highlight their abs'. Tips: *Never send anything to anyone you wouldn't send to your dad

234   J. Ringrose and K. Regehr

Zoe: Yeah, you know that they're all friends.

Samantha: You know they are all together.

Milly: you know that they're having a competition, and then they'll just see, sometimes they'll all send it to one specific girl, and see who gets the response the fastest. (Year 10 girls)

Sending these images to a girl, Tamara explains, is 'bait' to prompt girls to respond and if they do the boys will send more explicit images. As Milly explains in her drawing, depending on which boy she responds to he might send a dick pic (Fig. 8.7). The intention behind sending these images is a form of aggression and taunting or 'lad 'banter (Haslop & O'Rourke, 2023), done for a laugh as Tamara explained in Fig. 8.8.

So these images are not simply harmless attempts to perform an attractive male muscularity with reference to boys' 'junk' they are group efforts to bait girls into responding. The girls also explained that they would ignore or block such images because if they screen shotted it, it would be a signal to the boy that she was interested, or alternatively that the girl is a snake who might tell on the boy for his behaviour. Responding to this they had developed ingenious methods such as having a second person take a screen shot of the phone when they opened the Snapchat streaks (which recall disappear quickly):

Milly: There's one boy in our year who sends like classic, hands down his pants, it's like half four, message to about a hundred girls. Yes. And um, like me and my friend do that to him, because his pictures would be funny.

Interviewer: OK, so you would have one phone ready, one person would wait to open and then you'd have a phone ready to take a picture of it?

Tamara: Yeah.

Interviewer: Presumably that can also happen the other way around.

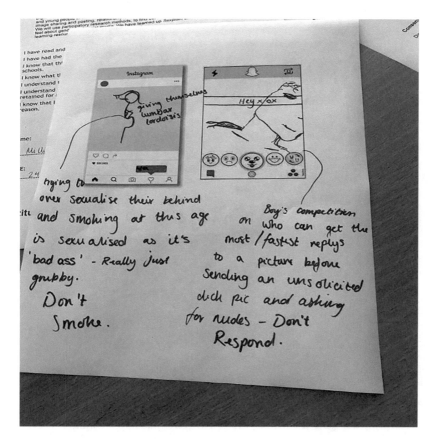

Fig. 8.7 Milly's drawing of jaw line image, 'boys competition on who can get the most/fastest replies to a picture before sending an unsolicited dick pic and asking for nudes. Don't respond

Tamara: Boys, they're not really bothered about it. They'll just screenshot and they don't care if you can see that they screenshot.

Denise: Girls we're a bit more worried about being called a snake.

Zoe: Boys it's like a trophy, for girls it's like shameful to share.

Tamara: For boys it's kind of like, it heightens them up, they are like oh I got a girl.

Fig. 8.8 Tamara's drawing of boys sending dick pics as 'banter'; shameful for girls to save them. Girls should be taught you don't need male attention

Zoe: [It's] normalised with boys to like behave that way, I think.

Samantha: Yeah. (Year 10 girls)

The girls discuss a boy who took a selfie in his bedroom mirror with his hands down his pants sending it as a Snapchat streak to hundreds of girls at half-four after school. They marvel at how 'comfortable' and 'casual' he seems about it, because it is *normalised for boys to behave that way*. They also discuss the strategies they've devised to document this without screenshotting it, so without him knowing, which would be a signal to send more material, or that they are a snake and will report him. As they explain, it is seen as shameful for girls to interact with, keep or share images of male body parts, whereas for a boy to have girls' nude images is a trophy, showing he can get the girls to send them to him:

> Samantha: Like boys in our year can be like oh look what I've got, and like want to like gas it up to his friends, to prove that you're like better than whatever he has. (Year 10 girls)

Significantly, the girls explain that its not just getting a nude from a girl that boys desire to prove their worth to one another, but these images are competitive, and boys will compare the nudes they get with one another even ranking them.

Trophy Dick Pics

While the year 10 girls said only boys could use girls' nudes as trophies, the year 8 girls disagreed. Charli had explained that some girls were more 'casual' and 'chill' about getting dick pics than others, and explained that if a dick pic was sent consensually then girls might save them:

> Grace: you know Emma, mmm, she's broken up with Andy, but she still keeps his dick pics on her phone.

> Interviewer: Keeps pictures of him on her phone?

> Grace: Yeah, she was going through her camera roll and I said what the hell? And she said oh look, it's Andy's dick. I was like OK. It's like you're not going out with him anymore, you can delete that. But she just keeps it on there.

> Interviewer: What do you think she keeps it for?

> Grace: It sounds kind of weird, but like a trophy, you know. She dumped him because he made out with Lisa and Deirdre, but I feel like deep-down she still wishes she was with him.

> Steph: Oh like I'm so popular, I've got like a dick pic, or I've got this...

Charli: So then you kind of have power over them, because you know…

Ruby: Yeah.

Beatrice: …you can expose them, and it's power (Year 8 girls)

Here the Year 8 girls debate whether girls are keeping a dick pick as a trophy or memento of a relationship or as a form of power they can use over the boy to expose him. We can see that Emma hasn't purposefully shown Grace Andy's dick pic but it pops up while they are scrolling through Emma's camera roll together. The dick pic is simply saved onto her camera role, the digital affordance of persistence we've discussed previously (boyd, 2010). Despite the girls noting that such images could be used against boys, we did not hear any accounts from this school of girls sharing boys' nudes around their network to shame them, unlike the common examples of girls nudes being widely distributed and shamed as we've been exploring throughout the book.

These girls also offered a complex look at how girls can manipulate boys' desire to receive nudes, as Grace told a story about a friend of hers who uses the promise of transactional nudes to get boys on Snapchat to send her images, then ghosts him (Fig. 8.9):

Grace: My friend, she came around to my house for a sleepover last week, like previously she'd already been talking to this boy who lived in Ireland, on Snapchat, just for like the sake of it, and then she was like oh wouldn't it be funny if we tried to get nudes of him and then not send them back. She was texting him, being like oh if you send them I'll send you stuff back, but she was like I'm not gonna send him anything, isn't that funny. And then he'd be like but don't screenshot it, because I've had it before and I got really upset when they never sent any back, and they screenshot it. And she was like don't worry, I will, I will, and then he sent them, and she said I'm not satisfied, send me another one, and then he sent her another one, and then she just left him and turned her mobile data off and just headed out for the rest of the day. And she was like oh I'm never gonna meet him, he lives in Ireland (Image 8.12).

Interviewer: So is this some kind of status thing then, that you could get a boy to do that?

Grace: I think she just found it funny, like it was something to do, you know.

Elizabeth: I don't think it's funny.

Charli: And not everyone like falls for that, if I told, if I said that to my boyfriend uh well they'd go like you won't send me one back, I'm not gonna send it to you, because they know like I wouldn't send it (Year 8 girls)

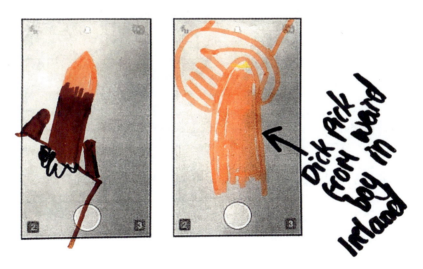

Fig. 8.9 Grace's drawing of 'dick pick from weird boy in Ireland'

Image-Based Abuse and Harassment

However, later in the interview, despite these discussions of the bravado of some of the girls, we heard painful examples of how girls' nudes were treated very differently by boys and used as a form of revenge. The Year 8 girls told us a story about their friend Jen whose nudes were 'exposed.'

> Ruby: Our friend kind of sent a nude and it went around the whole school.
>
> Charli: They screenshot it and sent it to one of our friends, who showed everyone.
>
> Beatrice: It got shared everywhere, so......and now pretty much everyone knows her, and it's like if you never met her it's just the girl with the nude...
>
> Ruby: She had a boyfriend at the time and she sent it to her boyfriend's friend, while her boyfriend was away on a holiday.
>
> Beatrice: Yeah, and then he showed the boyfriend and the boyfriend was like why did you send a nude to him? He (the boyfriend) was mad. He sent it to everyone. (Year 8 Girls)

Jen sends a nude to the boy's friend while her boyfriend is away on holiday. The friend shows the boyfriend and to punish her, the boyfriend then sends the image to 'everyone'. As the girls keep talking, more details about the exchange and the non-consensual spread of the image emerge:

> Interviewer: So who did he send it to?
>
> Charli: To literally everyone. Everyone.
>
> Grace: Everyone on his contacts basically.
>
> Elizabeth: And then someone from our school told Jen about it and some people have still got it on their camera roll.

Charli: In their pictures.

Interviewer: Oh they still have it on their phone?

Ruby: You know the day it went around everyone was talking about it, and I don't think she was in school.

Elizabeth: No, she didn't come into school.

Grace: She didn't come in school, but everybody was talking about it.

Elizabeth: She went to the police.

Interviewer: She did?

Grace: Yeah.

Interviewer: Can you tell us about that?

Charli: Well this girl who's close to her mum told her mum, and then her mum got really mad at her. And she took her Instagram away. And all of social medias, and went to the police, and like told the police about what had happened, and the threatening. Because one of them they got sent… shared …an adult found it and then shared it (Year 8, girls)

In this case, the image is sent to everyone on the boy's contact list and spreads through several forms of social media. WhatsApp images save to one's phone, so the girls talk about how this image is simply sitting on many people's phone due to the type of widely spread image based sexual abuse committed here. The police got involved because the image is found to have been shared by an adult. Drilling down into this the girls said they did not hear about the boy being punished, but rather the focus became on the adult having an image of an underage girl. Part of the issue here is the failing to address what is happening as peer-to-peer image-based sexual abuse, and the fact that the authorities only intervene when it constitutes child sexual abuse by adults. We also see the standard response to take away Jen's phone and 'all social medias', which is a reactive response, rather than educative and supportive as we will discuss in our conclusion.

Later in this discussion group, we noticed that one of the girls was looking very uncomfortable and had not spoken at all. When we asked her if she had something she'd like to contribute, after a pause she launched into another example of male rivalry inciting further forms of online sexual harassment:

Interviewer: Do you have something you'd like to share? What do you think?

Pause.

Ava: (slowly) I think it's happened to me. I was dating this boy, he said he was 13, and then I kind of, I kind of dated him, and then his best friend told me he's turning 15, so then, but then he used to send me nudes, and I didn't really like him as well, and he was also…he used to try to force me… but I didn't send, but everyone thought I did send him… and these rumours all spread around. A few people knew.

Interviewer: What was in the picture?

Ava: Dick pic…videos…Everyone told that I sent nudes to him but I never did….Because everyone was thinking like oh if he sent nudes she must have sent something for him to send nudes. And there was this Instagram page where you expose…they put something on you on there.

Interviewer: What did they put?

Ava: 'This girl is dating this 15-year-old and he sends nudes and she sends them back….' Because people think that when boys send you nudes you send them back. It's like an exchange thing. And then like…And then, and then if you don't send boys back nudes they'll tell all their friends oh she sent those, because they don't want to be all like…

Grace: A rejected person. (Year 8, girls).

Here Ava's contact details were posted to a public Instagram 'expose' page when she didn't send a nude in response to a transactional dick pic and request for nudes by one of the 'best friends' of her boyfriend, a boy attending Cobs School for boys. In our fieldnotes, we recorded feeling a deep sense of shame from Ava in discussing this with the group, and a sense of disbelief even amongst the girls in the group that she did not send him nudes of herself. It is also notable that Ava relates that this was a high profile boy whose 'father was a politician (a foreign diplomat) visiting London', whom she met via a boy she was dating at Cobs. She noted with relief that the politician's son had subsequently left the UK. It also emerged that after Ava rejected him, he sent similar material to several of her friends, who also blocked him.

This example highlights how unwanted dick pics can be double forms of abuse; as cyberflashing – being sent an unwanted image of a penis – but also as online sexual harassment - being pestered and pressured to send nudes back (McGlynn & Johnson, 2020). There is also an assumed implication of guilt and shame for Ava of having been caught up in this, Ava claims 'everyone was thinking … she must have sent something for him to send nudes.' It also emerges, however, that when she wouldn't provide him with an image a further level of abuse followed when the boy shared her public details on a local Instagram 'expose' page, claiming she sends nudes, as a way to shame her because he has been 'rejected'. There is no awareness of this constituting image-based sexual harassment and further abuse of doxing or posting private contact details about a person publicly online.

We came away from Swans on our first visit weighing up the dichotomies presented by the school. In some ways, the girls were empowered in the ways they were able to critically analyse their engagement with the digital space. Yet we also saw girls capitalising on boys' desire for nudes by tricking them to send dick pics and ghosting them; and although the girls did not threaten to share the images or shame the boys, this is non-consensual and a power play on the part of the girl in question.

On the other hand, the girls' had direct experience of image-based sexual harassment and abuse in their friend group as they discussed Jen who became known as 'the girl with the nude' after her image was shared widely and Ava who experienced harassment and doxing after refusing to reciprocate a transactional nude request. The girls are negotiating intimate digital sexual encounters, with boys some of whom have huge social capital setting them up for difficult contexts of abuse and little supports due to shame and stigma.

Sixth Formers and the Lingering Lure of Snapchat

It was a hot day further into summer when we next visited Swans to meet with the older students from the mixed gender sixth form who were between 16 and 18 years of age. It was interesting to see the different environment of the college building. In the all-girls younger years like most schools in England uniform was mandatory and all the girls were in their pleated kilts. In sixth form, the students wore street clothes and the boys and girls were intermingling in the open plan building. We spoke to eight students: five girls who sat together on one side of the table, and three boys accross from them, all eager to educate us on the rules of engagement for being middle class, 16–18-year-old digital natives. They quickly explained once again the limiting context of the girls' school and reliance upon social media:

Susie: I think it makes a big difference going to a girls' school.

Katie: Yeah, it does.

Dawn: Because unless you meet boys from like in different schools, like if you know them.

Cameron: like through like a club.

Dawn: Or primary school or something.

Joel: … the only other way is to meet them is through social media. (Sixth form, mixed)

The conversation quickly turned to the ways that Snapchat facilitates the spreadability of nudes:

Katie: kids should be taught about mainly Snapchat, because that is what people use to communicate.

Joel; When we first joined Snapchat is when we first got dick pics

Susie: It's really social like, because your friends are going, you kind of laugh about it, because you're like oh this person sent me this...

Katie: When you're young it's funny, but then you get to an age when it's like...

Joel: And you're just bored with it.

Dawn: It's really hard, because, I won't lie, it's sort of inevitable that you will either be sent, or send, a dick pic in your life. It's just...

Joel: It's just the internet. (Sixth form, mixed)

In this passage, the dick pic has become a normal 'inevitable' part of life youth are initiated into via Snapchat, as we've discussed in Chapter 2, through the quick add features and an ever expanding network of contacts. This group confirmed what we found in the wider study that unwanted dick pics were generally experienced as harassing by girls, and often accompanied by pressure to send something back. In this group of older teens, we were fortunate to have an openly gay participant, Joel, who spoke eloquently about his own relationship to technology and dick pics as part of the LGBTQ community. He described there being greater potential for consent and 'respect' as a young gay man:

Joel: Most of the time we don't share images [of ourselves], we were just all asked to, does that make sense?

Gary: Yeah.

Joel: Sometimes it's really, it's respectful. Yes, somebody I was talking to was like do you want to? And I was like not particularly, and he was like OK, that's fine. (Sixth form, mixed)

This conversation acts as an important reminder that young people have diverse sexualities (and genders), which shape their digital experiences. Whereas Joel is navigating a non-heterosexual ecosystem where he argues more possibilities of 'respect' are present around how image sharing is negotiated, he swiftly returned to a scenario involving a young heterosexual women in their school, whose nudes were non-consensually spread:

Joel: Well I remember there was a girl, somebody had gone onto their Snapchat and posted all of their nudes, frontals, onto their story, and a lot of people saw it.

Dawn: Someone had gone onto her Snapchat and posted them for her.

Katie: But without her knowing.

Susie: What you can do on Snapchat, you can take photos and because they delete automatically if you don't save it, you can save it to your memory, so you can access it again.

Joel: So what a lot of people do, in our generation, is they take like nudes...basically you take a photo, right, just basically a random photo. If I deleted that it would be gone forever. You can save it, right, so I've just saved it... I then can access it, and I can put it in this special folder, there's me without a shirt on...and you can export it to like My Eyes Only, which is this password protected folder, which is where a lot of people put their nudes. (Sixth form, mixed)

This story is significant for a couple of reasons. First, it underscores how Snapchat's disappearing images are not risk free, because images can be saved through screen shotting and spread on. But Snapchat also has a folder called 'for my eyes only', where people can keep their nudes. A special nudes folder surprises the interviewer who asks: 'So why would

8 Swans School for Girls: Performing High Achieving ... 247

you put it in My Eyes Only, and not just keep it, let's say, on your phone?'.

Dawn: Because people could go on your phone, because like you let people go on your stuff, and you wanna keep it like a special, if you are wanting to send something to someone you are not gonna scroll through all your saved, you just want to go to that folder.

Joel: They knew the password, got into it, and probably in spite, I think it was in spite, if anybody knows this story, in spite, put them on her story.

Cameron: it would have been a friend of hers most likely.

Susie: A girlfriend.

Jane: Maybe.

Joel: Or a boyfriend.

Katie: She took it down like almost straight away, within an hour I think, but um…

Joel: That's a lot of people,

Dawn: A lot of people can see it straight away, because it pops up, and so a lot of people screenshot it and then made stickers of her, um, …

Cameron: Her boobs.

Joel: But then they were obviously taken down and deleted, and I think she got bullied for it, I won't lie. I know she got nasty comments from it. (Sixth form, mixed)

Here, the girl in the story has shared her Snapchat password with possibly multiple people despite it being her own personal social media application. The rational given around the For My Eyes Only folder is so you won't have a nude lying around on your smartphone camera reel, but Snapchat is also not secure. Research has shown that control over technology use is a key element of peer-on-peer intimate abuse (Barter et al., 2017), but beyond sexual relationships young people share their devices and their passwords with friends. We can see how normal it is for the young people that the Snapchat password has been breached, showing that privacy functions may be futile in this type of context. We can also see how Joel who implies he 'knows the story' notes that it was a 'boyfriend' who posted the images of her breasts to 'spite' the girl, and others joined in screenshotting the image, posting stickers on it and spreading it further, it is a social and group act of abuse. Joel also describes the lasting repercussions since the girl was bullied and got nasty comments, despite being the victim of a form of image-based sexual abuse.

The students went on to further explain in a retrospective stance, that the reason teens send nudes is because it is often 'the only way of being like sexually active' when you are younger, and this is particularly the case in an all-girls' school:

> Heidi: Because when you're like 13, 14, if you were to ask your mum oh can I go around to a boy's house, it'll be like no. So that's why you would go online to do it. (Year 12)

Nonetheless they are acutely aware that this brings additional elements of risk for the girls in particular. Dawn recounts her experiences of handling the risk of permanence around nudes she sent in a relationship:

> Dawn: Well I did it (exchanged nudes) with my boyfriend then, and it's because like when I was younger I couldn't stay around at his, or go to his house, or he couldn't come to mine, so it was like that was the way to do it, sometimes, not all the time. Just like if it'd been like a really tough time or something.

> Interviewer: So because you were younger, and you weren't allowed to be at his house, that was your form of intimacy.

8 Swans School for Girls: Performing High Achieving ...   249

Dawn: It wasn't like really, really young, it was just like, yeah, it was still oh you can't go to his house like to sleep over.

Joel: The only way of being like sexually active.

Dawn: Yeah.

Interviewer: Are you still in a relationship with this person?

Dawn: No.

Interviewer: What did you do with the images once that relationship was over?

Dawn: Well I like when we broke up I saw him and asked him to delete it and watched him delete it, if he had saved any.

Interviewer: Oh, that's very responsible.

LAUGHTER

Dawn: The first thing I thought was - has he saved any, I don't want those to go around.

Interviewer: And what about your images of him?

Dawn: I didn't save any, it's just after you view it it's gone. (Sixth form, mixed)

Dawn consensually sends nudes to her boyfriend as means of being 'sexually active' with him as clarified by Joel. Interestingly Dawn notes that she would send nudes at points when things were more difficult in their relationship. We can also see that despite her having sent the nudes consensually while in the relationship, the fear of her images being shared after the relationship ends means Dawn went over to her ex-boyfriend's house and asked him to delete her nudes and watched him do so. That was how she had to manage the afterlife of her images, which he had kept. It is also notable that Dawn had not saved his nudes as they were sent through Snapchat and disappeared. Although the interviewer jokes about Dawn making sure her images are deleted as being 'responsible' this is in fact, precisely the point. Here, we can clearly see responsibilisation of girls for their nudes and for ensuring that they are not victims of image-based sexual abuse in a world that not only normalises these practices but then blames and shames girls and women for sexual activity (Karaian, 2014). Girls are also victim blamed despite suffering image-based abuse, they are judged responsible for their own abuse.

Dawn was also adamant that young people should have these avenues for communicating, however, advocating that "sexting" was a normal human activity just like 'real sex':

> Dawn: I think like sex isn't some like bad thing, it's a normal human…activity, it's not like it's weird, but I mean for example people who are in a relationship who can't be together because, I dunno, because of work or something, I don't think sexting is a bad idea, unless you know that you can't trust them, or if you've just met them …. there's always a risk like with sexting, like there's always a risk with social media in general, but there is always a risk that they can screenshot it and send it on to someone else (Sixth form, mixed)

Stop Snapping or Better Sext Education?

Given the risks of social media, particularly Snapchat, towards the end of the discussion, the interviewer asked the sixth formers: 'Why use it then?' That is, if the risks are so great, why continue to engage with the platform? They explained 'kids can't leave Snapchat because it is too hard to not be part of the group'. Teens cannot *not* use Snapchat because it is the dominant form of social networking and rejecting it will cause social isolation. They are also savvy in arguing that rather than stopping using technology or apps, the point is to create better education around these issues. As Dawn noted:

8 Swans School for Girls: Performing High Achieving ... 251

Dawn: It's kind of important maybe to tell the boys maybe not to like send them (dick pics) to random girls, if they're gonna go oh like I'm gonna like find this random girl and add her to Snapchat and send her something, maybe tell them not to do that... (Sixth form, mixed).

Joel was particularly adamant that better sex education would pave the way for better digital relationships, pointing out the inaccurate sex education they had had with someone from the local council visiting the school:

Joel: It was aimed towards the girls you need to give consent, you need to make sure you feel comfortable. And to the boys it was like never force any girl into it, make sure, it was very different.

Cameron: Disregarding the fact that it happens to the boys as well.

Dawn: It happens to boys as well.

Joel: To quote the lady that came in, you are men, you cannot be raped. That was like, the worst words that she said...

Dawn: We felt more educated than her.

Katie: She showed us the same video we'd seen since Year 8. The tea one.

Joel: The tea video.

Katie: Like if they try and give you tea...

Susie: Pours tea, [down their throat] when they are unconscious...

Katie: We've seen that tea video...

Joel: So many times.

Dawn: Probably every year, like twice every year...

Joel: Yeah.

Katie: …but we just need to know different stuff more. (Sixth form, mixed)

In this excerpt, Joel is outraged about the poor sex education, which neglects understandings about men as victims of sexual violence (typically from other men) with the commentator apparently claiming, 'men cannot be raped'; and also neglects LGBTQ experiences of sexual violence. They also discussed the overuse of the 'tea' video on sexual consent, which they'd seen repeatedly since Year 8. The tea video makes an analogy between drinking tea and having sex and that you wouldn't force someone to drink tea, so you shouldn't force sexual contact either. The tea video is widely recognising as glossing over many of the elements of sexual consent (Adams, 2021). Katie makes a plea for needing to know 'different stuff', arguing they needed something much clearer about digital consent:

Katie: You need to somehow get across to the boys, before they get this I don't care attitude, that it is unacceptable to send an unsolicited dick pic to a girl, because it's just, it's not, it's disrespectful…Not for any oh it will be shared and all of this fearmongering, you need to somehow get them to understand that it's disrespectful…

Dawn: Morally unacceptable.

Joel: So they should have the foundation in them, when they're younger, they could apply it to sexual relationships and stuff. (Sixth form, mixed)

The group explains that the education aimed at young people is all wrong, focusing on the potential risk of images being shared and the consequences of this, without teaching about the dynamics of consent that underpin such an outcome. Perhaps Joel's respectful gay nudes encounter we discussed earlier signals the types of 'safer sex' harm reduction practices we need for better youth digital intimacy, modelling different forms of masculinity. This is an area that needs development in our schools and society more generally and which should be extended to the education of heterosexual young people, particularly boys, around

8 Swans School for Girls: Performing High Achieving ... 253

their own body parts so they are clear that sending or sharing images without asking is abusive.

Returning to the Year 10 girls, they likewise echoed the critique of fearmongering, explaining how out of touch and 'hyperbolic' their sex education on digital technology was.

> Caroline: There's always that film about like the girl who posts something online, and she can't take it off...there's always that one.

> Zoe: And she ends up killing herself in the end.

> Denise: it's one of those classics...

> Milly: Yeah.

> Caroline: Because she's attacked by so many people, and then she's been sexualised because of that photo that she has posted, and then she's getting calls from random men sexualising her, she gets texts, everything, being bombarded with oh I will pay you if you sleep with me, and she feels as though her friends will leave, she can't tell anyone, and then she just...yeah.

> Zoe: It's very hyperbolic...

> Denise: It comes up on her brick phone as like...

> LAUGHTER

> Janice: We all laugh at it.

> Tamara: But the message does get across, we do know, you know, that if you post something on the internet it's gonna stay there. (Year 10, girls)

The girls mock the 'classic' anti-sexting videos they are shown with the out-of-date technology (brick phone and online message boards), an important reminder of how vital up to date and on-point messaging about platform-specific risks like Snapchat is for young people. While the girls note that these resources deliver the message that something 'stays' on the internet, they question this monolithic approach, also complaining about the messaging being based on fear-based scare tactics rather than preventative and educative, offering insight as what to actually do about it when things go wrong:

> Denise: Yeah, I think the school's attitude is more like we can't prevent you from doing this but we're going to show you what can happen when you do. So they tell us stories of like people who've had their career damaged by things they've found in the past. Even like with like racist or homophobic tweets and stuff like that.

> Interviewer: Is there ever a discussion of the implications for the person who shared it? Or is it always the fault of the person who took the photo?

> Zoe: We had some PDC (Personal Development and Citizenship) lessons about child pornography and stuff, the fact that if you share somebody else's…

> Samantha: You're the perpetrator.

> Tamara: …yeah, you're like in possession of child pornography if it's a nude of someone your age, then you'll face the same charges as an adult who did that. So we have looked at the implications, but not…not…

> Zoe: It's not the focus.

> Denise: Because the focus is kind of to dissuade us from in the first place doing that, because I think like, not to stereotype, but boys are often ones that leak the stuff, almost, like it's a stereotype, but, so they're the main focus, because we're an all-girl school, its like please don't send it, like this is what'll happen if you do, but if it does happen to you these are the sort of like websites that you can go to to try and get it taken down, blah, blah, blah, blah, blah. (Year 10 girls)

Interestingly the girls, much like the boys in other elite schools we've seen, have been told about the possible impacts of nudes on their future careers. Like the other schools we visited, the girls learn about child pornography and not to keep nudes in your possession or you'll be charged, with the implication here that their own nudes are child pornography. They mention the school telling them how to try to get images taken down, but they have never been taught about image-based sexual harassment or abuse. Coming to the final school of this study, a highly resourced all girl site, we find this omission highly concerning and something that needs to be urgently rectified across the entire school sector and the nation as a whole.

Conclusion

In this chapter we have presented compelling evidence that girls' environments need to be thought through carefully in relation to digital networks and platforms. What is of critical importance to grasp in relation to single sex schooling environments is that by limiting the capacity to interact with other genders in the school site, these environments create an over-reliance on the digital as the space for forging intimacy. Many of the girls in this school environment said point blank the only way they can meet a boy is online. Consequently, the social media applications become critically important for crafting a sexy self (especially for some of the younger girls at Swans). One of the main things that we've aimed to stress in this book is that girls should be free to experiment with a range of images of their bodies without fear of judgement or shaming, but this is not the media environment that they find themselves in; rather, they are surveyed and harshly evaluated and shamed for their images. In contrast, girls describe a digital landscape where boys are free to send images in harassing ways without fear of reprisal. The girls were resistant to these dynamics, they mocked the boys' images and attempts to be 'provocative', but they were also somewhat resigned to how 'normalised it was for boys to behave that way', as one Year 10 girl explained it.

We also discovered some complex dynamics around girls keeping boys' dick pics as well as manipulating boys to send them dick pics, demonstrating that girls can abuse their power over boys in some cases. Girls are willingly participating in online digital dating cultures and experimenting with their sexual power; something that adults do need to recognise and find ways of discussing in relation to issues of consent around images which impact girls and boys in a range of context specific ways. Nonetheless, we did not hear of any cases of girls spreading sexual images of boys without consent in Swans.

In contrast, the Year 8 girls had experienced several episodes of image-based abuse and image-based harassment. They told the story of Jen's nudes being leaked and her becoming known as 'the girl with the nude'. Ava also recounted a politician's son sending her dick pics and masturbation videos and publicly posting her details to an online site to punish her when she rejected him and would not send him nudes back. These examples demonstrate how girls in selective girls' schools often participate in digitally networked peer groups with boys with high social capital, who use privilege and entitlement to harass girls, and display misogynistic behaviour. The older group of mixed gender sixth formers recounted a similar case of a girl's nudes being posted to everyone after her 'For My Eyes Only' folder on Snapchat was hacked. The interviewer was aghast at this example, wondering why anyone would use this feature of the platform or stay on Snapchat, and these young people explained Snapchat participation was essential to avoid social isolation. These 16–18-year-olds went on to carefully explain that sharing nudes was an important developmental step, particularly for young people in gender segregated schools, because you cannot meet the person in real life, so the digital sexual connection becomes even more important.

Finally, the young people explained how misguided and out-of-date their sex education on consent was, which neglected discussions of LGBTQ intimacy and the possibilities of men and boys experiencing sexual violence. The e-safety and anti-sexting resources and videos they were shown, were woefully out of date, and used fear-based and shaming tactics. We learned once again that none of the young people had ever learned about image-based sexual harassment or abuse, despite our findings that many of the young people across genders and sexualities were experiencing these harms.

Overall, what the discussions at Swans demonstrate is that no young person—regardless of class or the amount of protection afforded by the school environment—is immune to these digital dynamics. From this perspective, we question the long-held assumptions about all-girls' schools as protected environments because they are separated from boys. Despite girls having more agency and space to navigate their daily in-school routines without managing heterosexual relationship culture, we argue this does not alleviate anxiety around their appearance, and perhaps we may be seeing a greater degree of fixation on the cultivation of a desirable online self in some instances. Because they are so reliant upon digital networks to explore intimacy, the protected physical space certainly does not safeguard the girls from online risks; in fact, gender segregation may increase online risk taking. As we've been arguing throughout this book, this is something that we as academics and educators need to heed in the development of educational resources that are context specific. So while privileged parents may seek to shelter their daughters by way of girls' only schools, the realities of their online interactions show that this environment needs the same types of caution and support as any other, and we hope that privileged parents and adults reading this see how a joined-up solution involving holding government and tech companies accountable, and better funding of the entire education sector is needed We urgently require educational resources that outline how platforms facilitate image-based sexual harassment and abuse and what we can do about it. We cover these issues in our next and final chapter, the conclusion.

References

Adams, B. (2021). Consent is not as simple as tea: Student activism against rape culture. *Girlhood Studies, 14*(1), 1–18. Retrieved August 20, 2024, from https://doi.org/10.3167/ghs.2021.140103

Barter, C., Stanley, N., Wood, M., Lanau, A., Aghtaie, N., Larkins, C., & Øverlien, C. (2017). Young people's online and face-to-face experiences of interpersonal violence and abuse and their subjective impact across five European countries. *Psychology of Violence, 7*(3), 375–384. https://doi.org/10.1037/vio0000096

boyd, D. (2010). Social network sites as networked publics: Affordances, dynamics, and implications. In Z. Papacharissi (Ed.), *A networked self: Identity, community and culture on social network sites* (pp. 39–58). Routledge.

Haslop, C., & O'Rourke, F. (2023). *Ladcultures: Social Networking Sites, 'Laddism' and Young Masculinities, 2020–2021*. [Data Collection]. Colchester, Essex: UK Data Service. https://doi.org/10.5255/UKDA-SN-855300

Karaian, L. (2014). Policing 'sexting': Responsibilisation, respectability and sexual subjectivity in child protection/crime prevention responses to teenagers' digital sexual expression. *Theoretical Criminology, 18*(3), 282–299. https://doi.org/10.1177/1362480613504331

McGlynn, C., & Johnson, K. (2020). Criminalising cyberflashing: Options for law reform. *The Journal of Criminal Law, 85*(3), 171–188. https://doi.org/10.1177/0022018320972306

Ringrose, J. (2011). Are you sexy, flirty or a slut? Exploring 'sexualisation' and how teen girls perform/negotiate digital sexual identity on social networking sites. In R. Gill and C. Scharff (Eds.), *New femininities: Postfeminism, neoliberalism and Iientity*. Palgrave.

Ringrose, J. (2013). *Post-feminist education? Girls and the sexual politics of schooling*. Routledge.

Open Access This chapter is licensed under the terms of the Creative Commons Attribution-NonCommercial-NoDerivatives 4.0 International License (http://creativecommons.org/licenses/by-nc-nd/4.0/), which permits any noncommercial use, sharing, distribution and reproduction in any medium or format, as long as you give appropriate credit to the original author(s) and the source, provide a link to the Creative Commons license and indicate if you modified the licensed material. You do not have permission under this license to share adapted material derived from this chapter or parts of it.

The images or other third party material in this chapter are included in the chapter's Creative Commons license, unless indicated otherwise in a credit line to the material. If material is not included in the chapter's Creative Commons license and your intended use is not permitted by statutory regulation or exceeds the permitted use, you will need to obtain permission directly from the copyright holder.

9

Conclusion: Image-Based Sexual Harassment and Abuse Affects Everyone So How Can We Best Support Young People?

2024 saw the rise of the 'Smartphone Free Childhood' movement in England, started by two concerned mothers, the campaign grew rapidly, and within a few months' parents from more than 20% of the nation's schools had signed a pledge to withhold smartphones from youth till aged 14 (Milmo, 2024). The grassroots organisation representing parents argues that smartphones "expose children to harmful content, raise the likelihood of developing a mental illness and are highly addictive" (Smartphone Free Childhood, 2024). Similar pledges exist in USA such as 'wait until 8th' which argues it "empowers parents to rally together to delay giving children a smartphone until at least the end of 8th grade" (Wait until 8th, 2024).

In England, the context for the research in this book, the Department for Education UK published guidance for schools in 2024 urging schools to implement policies that "create a mobile phone-free environment" to enable better educational outcomes and keep children "safe" (Department for Education, 2024, p. 3), based on claims that smart phone use is dangerous distractive, unhealthy, and lessening educational outcomes. Comparable guidance and legislation have been recently announced worldwide in countries such as France, Italy, Finland and

© The Author(s) 2025

J. Ringrose and K. Regehr, *Teens, Social Media, and Image Based Abuse,*

https://doi.org/10.1007/978-3-031-92322-7_9

261

the Netherlands and promoted by global agencies like UNESCO. In November 2024, Australia became the first country to pass legislation to officially ban under 16s from smartphones. This was amidst a global outcry that banning phones was not only impossible but irresponsible and could put young people at further risk. Thousands of Australian stakeholders responded to the legislation critiquing the ban as playing political football with children's lives, with Amnesty International noting, for instance, that a "ban that isolates young people will not meet the government's objective of improving young people's lives" (Sullivan, 2024).

We have raised many concerns about young people's safety throughout this book, yet we adamantly *do not* advocate a banning mentality around smart phones. While calls for 'digital degrowth' (Selwyn 2023) and attention to surveillance capitalism, and data extraction from young people are important, we do not think that banning policies will address these issues. The reality is that we have little conclusive evidence, either about effects of smartphone use nor the impacts of impacts of bans, or what the best practice for schools to adopt should be (Kemp et al., 2024; Rahali et al., 2024).

What we do know and have argued throughout this book is that abstinence approaches do not work. They have never been successful in mitigating other health issues such as underage sex or drug and alcohol use. Not only will bans create resistance from young people, but they also deter young people from help seeking when something goes wrong (Phippen, 2024). The associated attitudes from parents and teachers that using smartphones and accessing social media is only harmful and addictive tends to erode children's rights (Livingstone & Third, 2017). As Sonia Livingstone has pointed out (personal communication) while it is the tech companies that are failing to protect children from harm, it is children who will be punished through the mobile phoning bans, a sentiment with which we heartily agree.

In this final chapter of the book, we want to look at the multipronged improvements needed to counter the image-based sexual harassment and abuse we've documented. We do not promote simplistic solutions such as banning Smartphones, rather we take a nuanced approach looking at the law, regulation, corporate responsibility and education. First, we

9 Conclusion: Image-Based Sexual Harassment ... 263

consider recent changes to the Online Safety Act, and the creation of new cyberflashing and 'intimate image' offences, asking the question: will criminalisation abate image-based sexual harassment and abuse or not? Second, we scrutinise the culpability of big tech companies, asking: what needs to change to genuinely support young people in the fight against image-based abuse and on which platforms? Finally, we reflect on education, asking: what would need to improve at the level of government support, formal sex education and digital literacy curriculum but also informal education with family and parents? Overall, what we will we argue is that there is a need for a strong political will to stamp out *all sexual violence* in society (including digital and tech facilitated forms) across class, ethnic, religious and cultural boundaries. Before turning to these issues, we offer a whistle stop overview of the chapters in the book.

What Did We Find about Social Media Facilitated Image-Based Harassment and Abuse in the Seven School Sites?

In this book, we have demonstrated how the lack of consent inherent to some social media applications intersects with wider societal gender and sexual inequalities creating context specific vulnerabilities for young people. We took a platform-specific approach to the problem, explaining how some types of online harassment and abuse become *normalised* through specific features, showing for instance how adult predators, advertisers and influencers use the game-like affordances of Snapchat and Instagram to target youth. By working in seven distinct school settings and surveying the perspectives of nearly 500 young people, we captured a huge range of youth experiences social media, which was noted to be both fun and helpful but also risky and dangerous. From schools in deprived wards with high rates of poverty and crime, to elite, independent fee-paying school settings located in idyllic rural settings, to diverse inner-city schools where religious beliefs were prominent, each school offered distinct views into youth social media use and mobile peer networks. This wide lens enabled us to show how image-based sexual harassment and abuse traverses' class, culture, race and religion but lands in particular ways. This careful exploration of specific schooling cultures also enabled us to talk to young people about what they felt was working to support them and what was not and what they would like to see done differently.

In our first school-based chapter, Chapter 2, we looked at South East Community College, a highly diverse inner-city school, in special measures, in an area with high levels of deprivation, whose number of students receiving free school meals far exceeded the national average. We analysed youth as social media 'produsers' - that is, they both consume and create images in a complex interplay that can be risky. We saw that Snapchat was a platform that relies upon users expanding their networks, and a by-product of this was youth creating a gateway for adult predators by turning off privacy settings and receiving a steady stream of unwanted sexual content. Young people were often dealing with harassing and abusive dynamics on Snapchat without adult support. The girls described navigating racialised and sexualised slurs and slut shaming when their nudes were shared without their consent and some of the boys in this school frequented an online group page called 'the Neighbourhood Hoes', dedicated to exposing the nudes of girls and women in their local area. In contrast, we showed the ethics of care demonstrated by some of the girls who protected boys in their peer group who sent offending material. Indeed, we ended this chapter showing the strong resistant voice of a young feminist Janelle, who exemplifies both compassion and critical awareness, arguing schools should be educating young people about the different forms of online sexual assault and harm. We also found the school had dedicated staff seeking to improve sex education albeit with negligible resources.

Chapter 3 delved into an entirely different type of setting, an independent day and boarding school on the outskirts of London housed on an impressive campus, one of the most highly selective schools in the country, educating the children of international elites, politicians and celebrities. At Lions, we met privileged 13-year-old children, who were being taught to think carefully about how social media could put their own and parent's identities and resources at risk. The boys were highly risk adverse and judgemental about sexting, with one boy, Hugo,

9 Conclusion: Image-Based Sexual Harassment ...   265

concerned that association with nudes could hamper his possible future as a CEO. The school highlighted a dramatic difference between the maturity levels and intimate social media practices of 13-year-old boys and girls in this setting. Where the boys were mostly sheltered and naïve some of the girls were already receiving unwanted dick pics and requests to send nudes. Some girls were also highly concerned about how sexting could impact future relationships and marriage prospects. Most of the young people at the school felt their sex education was completely inadequate, and some of the boys noted they wanted boys to be learning more about digital sex issues earlier, so they would be less 'confused' and better prepared when things happened.

In Chapter 4, we moved back to an area of extreme economic marginalisation, Outer North Academy, situated in the bottom 10% for social deprivation of all wards in England with high knife crime, and many children receiving free school meals. We explored how Snapchat opened up young people to geolocation risk and violence in their neighbourhood through their mobile peer networks. An Academy school ONA had punitive measures such as confiscating phones and a social isolation unit. We met a young Congolese British girl, Venus, who had her mobile phone taken away by parents on advice of the school in response to a violent altercation via Snapchat. We saw how Snapchat's Snapmap tracking and Snapstory location feature were used to find Venus and physically attack her after a digital dalliance with a boy. Snapstories were also used to widely circulate racist and sexualised comments around the peer network in the school and we heard about an episode of peer-produced pornography where a 13-year-old circulated a Snapstory (video) of herself performing fellatio on an older boy. The young people were concerned that these types of issues were not being covered in their sex education at school or at home. We argued that parental and school responses such as taking away (or indeed banning) mobile phones as happened to Venus, or disciplining young people in prison like isolation units for 'perpetrators', were not offering adequate supports to youth. Rather we advocate for better digital literacy and sex education focused on consent.

In Chapter 5, we explored some of the challenges of digital sexual double standards and honour based gendered sexual shaming within the overtly religious context of Central Comprehensive, the most deprived school we worked in. Located in an inner-city borough, nearly 70% of the students at CC have English as a second language and a very high rate (nearly 65%) of students were eligible for free school meals. A large percentage of students were Bangladeshi Muslim, with many female students and staff wearing hijab. We examined a case where a Muslim boy, Amir, and his cousin sent a fake dick pic to a hijab wearing Muslim girl, Laila, asking her for nudes. When Laila sent a real nude of herself back, Amir showed their entire peer group at school. Laila's former friend group told us she had brought shame to herself, her friends, her family and her entire community, while the actions of the boys went largely unremarked. In contrast, we found some of the older boys in this school offered more compassionate narratives and concern, with Nico, for instance, expressing high awareness of the effects of sexualised violence upon girls at his school. We came away from this context very concerned about how many of the girls had internalised religious specific misogyny that underpins honour based violence. The point of this chapter is not to fuel Islamophobic narratives or suggest these communities are more backward, rather the opposite. We want to push for more context specific sex education that addresses cultural and religious specificity. There is an acute need for better culturally specific sex education for all young people; an abstinence approach denying them such education will only make gendered power inequalities worse.

In Chapter 6, we worked in another highly privileged site, Stags School for Boys, a selective all-boys school situated on a rural campus, with a partner girl school close by. Here, like Lions' boarding school, we encountered boys with high levels of access to resources and cultural capital. We found the boys were inundated with sexual content on social media, including what they call 'porn bots'—robots that target them with taster material with links to paid-for content, something we call porn push in this book. Boys noted that social media was normalising porn, making it 'easily accessible'. When it came to peer-produced nudes, however, boys were very careful about keeping a clean digital footprint and never having digital evidence of nudes on their phones, because their education had focused on mitigating the risks of possession of child pornography. They had devised workarounds like showing each other

9 Conclusion: Image-Based Sexual Harassment ... 267

girls' nudes on their physical phone screens rather than sending images which would create a digital trail. They are still, however, committing image-based sexual abuse although they don't realise this, and they hold judgemental and moralising views about the girls that have been abused in their peer networks. We discovered an urgent need for better sex education and found that when space is created for boys to have frank discussion around these issues, they can—and most likely will—open up. Tom and his friends reflected upon the need to stand up to the homosocial peer pressure they faced and felt that better digital sex education would help them do so. Overall, however, we wondered about how these 'single sex' environments create contexts of male entitlement and privilege and whether they are setting up boys to fail at heterosexual relationships later in life.

Chapter 7 looked at Northwest Secondary, a state school in a mixed urban area, with multi- million-pound homes located nearby a large council estate. NWS intake was impacted by postcode catchment dynamics. A well-regarded state girls' school was siphoning off higher achieving girls, with a result that the gender ratio in NWS was three boys to one girl. We looked at the case of 11-year-old Liv, who lived on the council estate, who was cultivating a micro-celebrity status through her Instagram following and accumulating a 'massive Snapscore' by adding copious contacts on Snapchat. This group also reported their younger siblings signing up to Snapchat aged seven and receiving a barrage of dick pics, and then relying on their siblings to clear their phones of explicit sexual content. In the peer-to-peer dynamics, we found a distressing episode of one of the 14-year-old girls, Alison, being sent masturbation videos by boys in her year group. Like the girls in South East Community College in Chapter 2, Alison protects the boys as her 'friends'. Alison did not report the episode as that would have generated further problems for her, since she will continue to see the boys every day at school. We also saw boys navigating porn push, paid for subscription sites, and having to manage inappropriate content that they did not want to see. They were concerned about catfishing but as with other schools, had only received e-safety advice about child pornography and not sextortion. The students did not report abuse to the platforms or peer harassment to schools because of coercive peer dynamics and backlash. Failure to report image-based harassment and abuse emerged strongly at this site but is also a factor across all the educational spaces we researched, a dilemma that needs to be urgently addressed.

In our final school-based chapter we examined Swans School for Girls, a single sex former grammar school, former 'single sex' grammar school now an all-girls comprehensive. Swans is in a very affluent borough, is top ranked nationally, and attracts high achieving students. We found intense levels of parental surveillance of girls' phones in this site, with girls discussing their strategies for dealing with the monitoring of their social media accounts. What became clear was given there are no boys at school the online environment was critically important for finding and connecting with romantic interests, as we saw was also the case in Chapter 6 at Stags School for boys. At Swans, the girls were creating online sexualised identities and developing digital dating rituals interacting with boys in neighbouring schools. The girls detailed how boys in their mobile networks created and used provocative images as lad banter, oftentimes to harass girls. In one episode, the son of a diplomat sent dick pics to a 14-year-old girl, Ava, asking her to send him nudes. When she didn't comply, he put her location details onto a website calling her a slut, which is a public doxing, and a form of online sexual harassment. In this school, we also met a mixed gender group of older students, sixth formers (aged 16–18) who reflected back upon their experiences of sexting when they were younger. They explained how out of touch their sex education had been as it completely neglected LGBT relationships. Across the board students at Swans complained about repeatedly seeing outdated videos with the anti-sexting messaging 'please don't send nudes' focused on girls in ways that neglected attention on masculinity or nuanced discussions of consent. The girls did actively deconstruct boys' digital sexual behaviour and its impacts upon them, but we found they were interacting with elite, high status boys and the protective walls of the school do not abate the online nor offline sexual risks they face. A major takeaway is that while putting your child into selective, highly ranked and elite settings may secure better exam results, it will not protect them from the scourge of digitally facilitated sexual violence. Single sex schooling creates contexts of isolation from real life friendships and relationships with differing genders that creates even more impetus for digital sexual relationships, which can, as we saw, go very wrong.

To summarise, our goal in conducting research across such diverse school spaces was to demonstrate how image-based abuse impacts all schools, young people, parents and communities. To prevent digital sexual violence we must therefore work at multiple levels paying attention to the barriers presented by the law, tech companies and of course the education sector. We will address each of these areas in the rest of this chapter.

What are the Implications of the Online Safety Act for Young People?

On March 19, 2024, a 39-year-old man became the first person in England and Wales to be convicted of the new criminal offence of cyberflashing. As reported in *The Guardian*,

> Nicholas Hawkes, from Basildon in Essex, sent unsolicited photos of his erect penis to a woman and a 15-year-old girl. The women reported Hawkes to Essex police the same day. Hawkes admitted to two counts of sending a photograph or film of genitals to cause alarm, distress or humiliation, and was convicted at the hearing on 11th March, 2024 (*Guardian* 19 March 2024).

This conviction followed on from a lengthy lobbying process as part of the Online Safety Act (2023) which began its progress through Parliament in 2021, culminating in the passage of the Act in October 2023. This Act adds two new offences to the Sexual Offences Act 2003; sending images of a person's genitals (cyberflashing) or sharing or threatening to share intimate images. As authors of this book, we saw this as a significant moment: as we discussed in the introduction, our research findings documenting the very high rates at which children and youth receive unsolicited male genital images on platforms like Snapchat was one of the primary forms of evidence used to create the new offence. It felt like a full circle moment, but we are also aware that it will take *much more* than legal reform to stamp out image-based sexual harassment and abuse in society. Changes to the law itself are never enough, and criminalisation often creates further problems, particularly for racialised and marginalised communities.

One of the main problems with the cyberflashing offence is that in order for the offender to be prosecuted the victim would have to report the crime to the platform and then to police. The 'complainant' would also have to *prove* in a court of law that the perpetrator had the 'intent to cause harm'. As legal scholars like Clare McGlynn (2022) have discussed at length regarding this offence, the focus on perpetrators' intentions makes it nearly impossible to prosecute. There is a need for the law to consider *consent* instead of *intent to harm*. As we've shown in this book, social media tech interfaces like Snapchat are set up to bypass consent. Improvements to the Act in January 2024 have supposedly reduced the emphasis on proof of intent to harm, but this element still plays a significant role when sexual violence is brought into a court of law.

From an educational perspective, then, does a cyberflashing offence simply play a symbolic role to define something as criminal? Does that create a crisis of legitimacy for the criminal justice system when the court system cannot actually prosecute or hold up the law? In a political and legal context where, according to the violence against women and girls' charitable sector, real life physical rape has been effectively decriminalised (Centre for Women's Justice et al., 2020), we need to ask what impact the creation of new digital sexual crimes is going to have? Is it merely paying lip service to the campaigners? How will it work in practice?

These are important questions to consider given what has been called a crisis of violence against women and girls in the UK, where we've seen mass public protests about the failure of policing to protect women and girls against sexual violence, including 'femicide' or the murder of women and girls by men (Femicide Census, 2021). Heterosexual domestic and intimate partner violence accounts for a huge bulk of sexual violence, in addition to sexual harassment in public places (street harrassment), as well as rising rates of tech facilitated sexual violence (Henry & Powell, 2018) and online misogyny, which commentators note is linked to algorithmically promoted social media content aimed at radicalising boys and men (Bates, 2021).

Age is also critical in relation to the law. It is significant that one of the images sent by the convicted cyberflasher was to a 15-year-old girl, who is a minor and who is subject to different legal provisions of protection and criminalisation herself. The article in the *Guardian* about the new cyberflashing offence did not connect these dots, which we've been aiming to do in this book. What if, for instance, the sender had been an 'underage' boy, and an image of his genitals constitutes child pornography, and would therefore be subject to child sexual abuse laws and protections? Criminologists have noted that police rarely prosecute children under child pornography laws when they involve 'sexting' or self -produced images between youth. So will juvenile offenders fall between the cracks? How would we respond to some of the complex situations in this book where teen boys have sent girls unwanted dick pics and masturbation videos, or threatened girls if they do not send nudes, and other scenarios which are harassing and abusive? We saw time and again that young people did not understand cyberflashing as a problem with consent. It was normalised both when coming from random adult strangers but also when it happened amongst their friend group.

We found the focus on young people's nude images as illegal, along with policing measures in schools, often served to exacerbate issues, leaving young people afraid and unsupported. Across most schools we found young people expressed confusion over the law. They were often aware of child pornography being illegal and the risk in making or possessing images. But they had little awareness that non-consensual image sharing was illegal; the e-safety advice given in schools had apparently focused on not making child porn images with a focus on girls' nudes, largely neglecting boys' behaviour, including boys making and sending their own nude images or pressuring girls to send nudes or distributing images of girls without consent. Most of these cases, as we saw, were never reported to the school and kept secret from parents due to societally imposed sexual double standards and shame facing girls around their images.

We also saw that much of the unwanted sexual content is spread through predatory mechanisms such as what we've called 'porn bots', which young people often don't report. Criminal law against individual cyberflashers cannot address the harmful technological platforms that we've been referencing in this book, which make it easier and easier for youth to be targeted as they open themselves up to wider and wider networks of unknown users.

The new cyberflashing law will therefore have negligible impacts for young people at the level of legal prosecutions, due to child pornography laws and a failure to grapple with the technological platforms. The same issues apply to the Act's second addition to the Sexual Offences Act 2003, 'sharing or threatening to share intimate photographs or films', since the criminal law doesn't apply to those under 18 years of age. As noted by Setty et al. (2024)

> Outdated laws surrounding illicit imagery of minors (designed pre-smartphone era and intended to address adult offending toward children) are used to prohibit all image sharing among young people and preclude a more nuanced discussion around preventing, identifying and responding to risk and non-consensual online sexual behaviours through a harm-reduction approach.

We therefore question criminalisation *alone* as a strategy and ask how we can bridge the gap between adult image-based abuse laws and child pornography laws. We argue there is a need for a multipronged approach involving government support across sectors of education, communication and justice, as well as an acceptance of corporate responsibility from big tech that doesn't rely on reactive regulation from government to try to stem the flow of digital or tech facilitated sexual violence and image-based sexual harassment and abuse.

How Could Social Media Companies Better Address Image-Based Abuse?

Throughout this book, we've been describing how social media platforms facilitate abuse through features and affordances which leave young people vulnerable to risk and harm. In the public report that we

9 Conclusion: Image-Based Sexual Harassment ... 273

launched with Members of Parliament in 2021, our main recommendation was that social media platforms should work with child e-safety design to improve the online safety of young people. We made four specific recommendations for Snapchat deemed the worst offender for enabling image-based abuse. We recommended that Snapchat should:

1. Maintain a record of images, videos and messages.
2. Create clearer and more extensive privacy settings.
3. Create more rigorous identity verification procedures.
4. Develop innovative solutions to prevent image-based sexual harassment and abuse and improve reporting functions.

Our findings and recommendations were picked up by several UK media outlets. The headline from the *Daily Mail* (6 December 2021) was 'Crackdown on "cyberflashing": Social media firms face call for action as it emerges that some children are sent sexual images daily.' The *Guardian* (6 December 2021) headline read: 'Three in four girls have been sent sexual images via apps, report finds'. The *Guardian* story focused on the crisis of under-reporting, noting 'reporting to Snapchat was deemed "useless" by young people because the images automatically delete.' 'Half (51 percent) of the respondents who had received unwanted sexual content online or had their image shared without their consent admitted doing nothing about it.' The *Guardian* quoted Jessica to underline how neither reporting online nor talking to adults was working for youth:

> Prof Jessica Ringrose of the UCL Institute of Education, one of the report's authors, said, 'Young people in the UK are facing a crisis of online sexual violence. Despite these young people, in particular girls, saying they felt disgusted, embarrassed and confused about the sending and receiving of non-consensual images, they rarely want to talk about their online experiences for fear of victim blaming and worry that reporting will make matters worse.' (ibid.)

Both the *Daily Mail* and *Guardian* published statements from Snapchat:

> Snapchat said while it doesn't keep a library of every image sent on the platform, it does save all reported content to enable investigation.

The sender is not alerted that someone has used the reporting tool. A spokesman said: 'Any sexual harassment is deplorable and we work with the police and industry partners like Childnet to keep it off Snapchat.' (*Daily Mail* 6 December 2021)

A spokesperson for Snapchat said: 'There will always be people who try to evade our systems, but we provide easy in-app reporting tools and have teams dedicated to building more features, including new parental tools, to keep our community safe.' (*Guardian* 6 December 2021)

Here Snapchat has circumvented the main finding of the report: that young people do not report on their platform, saying that they have 'easy in-app reporting tools', and that they save all reported content. They have ignored the discussion with young people that reporting doesn't work, given content disappears, and the fact that young people don't find the reporting tools 'easy.'

Statements from Meta and Instagram followed suit:

A spokesperson for Meta, the holding company formerly known as Facebook which operates Instagram, said the safety of young people using its apps was its 'top priority'. 'If anyone is sent an unsolicited explicit image, we strongly encourage them to report it to us and the police,' the spokesperson said. (*Guardian*, ibid.).

Instagram said: 'Keeping the young people who use our apps safe is our top priority, and we have measures in place to protect them.' (*Daily Mail* 6 December 2021)

Like Snapchat, Meta offer a pat response, encouraging young people to report abuse. These responses underscore the issues we are facing in society with big tech. The abuse is *effectively ignored*. The concerns of nearly 500 young people in our study that reporting was largely ineffective, are rendered invisible by the statements the social media company issued to the press. Nothing was done to support them.

Recall our survey findings that 62% of unsolicited sexual images and/or videos, 60% of pressure for nudes, and 33% of images being shared beyond the intended recipient were on Snapchat. Has Snapchat really thought through the scenarios of distress that we documented—for instance of a 13-year-old being contacted via Snapchat by an adult man unzipping his trousers? Remember we showed how youth are highly invested in keeping up streaks and achieving high Snapscores, sometimes through Shoutouts, which means they will turn off privacy settings and accept masses of unknown contacts via wider Snapchat networks. We also explained the difficulty that girls had reporting Snapstreaks because they disappear, and they didn't want to alert the senders that they'd read offending content or kept it, since the sender is notified of screen captures, even if they are not alerted that the user has used the reporting tool. We carefully documented the processes through which this happens. The failure to keep images or have a way to account for cyberflashing remains a critical issue on the platform. It is something that has not been addressed and will not be solved by a criminal offence on cyberflashing. Hence our specific recommendations that Snapchat keeps records of images as well as designing child friendly warnings, perhaps to pop up during usage rather than only at the point of joining the application.

In Chapter 4, we showed examples of Snapchat's geolocation tracking feature, the Snapmap. We discussed examples of 12-and 13-year-olds' Snapmaps, which showed densely populated maps on their phones with the live physical location of many of their friends. We found digital tracking led to a physical attack on 13 year old Venus, with the consequence that she had her phone taken away, effectively isolating her. Snapchat relies on its tracking feature and location feature being off at the default settings as a defence against the widespread use of this feature amongst young people. We suggest messages could pop up when the tracking function is turned on in the app. Snapchat appears to be using the default settings on their apps to claim that the app is private, but we have discussed throughout this book how the game-like functions of the app mean these are overridden by young people. These are the social elements that interact with technology and need to be accounted for.

We want to underscore, however, that Snapchat generates nearly all of its revenue from advertisements (Lebow, 2024). This means that it has to keep users on the platform for the maximum amount of time to see the ads. Snapchat uses gamified features to keep users engaged, which is its main agenda. The volume of users and time spent on the app is what counts, and the Snap management are likely not eager to interrupt this flow with safety messaging, as we saw from their inadequate and superficial responses above.

There were also important issues around the porn push which we found on Instagram. Our study took place in 2019–2020 and the biggest issue for boys in particular was being sent mass group messages with porn links or encouraging them to buy sex subscriptions on Instagram. It took two further years, however, for Instagram to introduce a filter for abusive messages in 2021 (BBC, 2021). In the public announcements for this change introduced by the company it was noted that Instagram launched a tool to enable users to automatically filter out abusive messages from those they do not follow. It was noted that the change: 'Follows a number of footballers speaking out about experiencing racist, sexist and other abuse on Instagram.' (BBC, 2021); 'The tool focused on message requests from people users did not already follow "because this is where people usually receive abusive messages" (BBC, 2021). It is notable that high profile celebrities had to experience abuse through DM functions on Instagram before Instagram took measures against it. While Instagram has recently introduced teen accounts to stop young people being contacted by unknown users many have raised concerns that young people already circumvent age restrictions and separate accounts will not address issues of porn push content in the platform for all users (Zahn, 2024).

At this juncture in the conclusion to this book, we need to ask wider questions about the tech industry. What responsibility do they have and how will they be regulated? How can parents or concerned citizens have a say in shaping how technology can be better? What are the mechanisms for holding social media companies to account? What are the strategies for insisting platforms embrace what Sonia Livingstone (2023) calls 'safety by design'? How could corporate responsibility be enforced? How can we raise public awareness about this?

We argue social media companies need to build in innovative solutions to their applications to prevent image-based sexual harassment and abuse: not only to rely on reactive reporting functions, but also to improve the functionality of platforms. And, while the Online Safety

Act is important, to try to enforce standards on social media platforms does not go nearly far enough and we need to advocate for solutions that intervene at the root of the problem and are *pro-active* rather than *reactive*. These companies' ethical responsibility is to look at the way in which their technologies make harmful content accessible, and worse how such content is algorithmically targetting children. We recommend that community guidelines are reviewed and that new affordances are implemented to make it easier for children to block and report harm.

However, without being held to account to implement such measures by the state or international bodies or the public at large, these companies are doing the bare minimum. They are providing gateways to abuse and harm. Some social media platforms are creating the opportunities for data mining, privacy leaks, phishing, hacking, and all manner of digital sexual crime. Snapchat, for instance, has repeatedly refused to address issues of child sexual abuse and grooming and we would therefore endorse the banning of a specific platform like this one; but we advocate taking a nuanced approach to each social media type. Our indictment of this platform comes only after years of research to document its failure to improve.

Indeed, the massive profits such social media companies are taking while enabling these harms need to be addressed and to become the focus of political will, rather than only looking at individual perpetrators via cyberflashing and intimate image offences; or in the repeated calls for parents to monitor their children's mobile phones and accounts more closely; or calls for a new type of phone without the problem apps on them; or the widespread generalised discussion of banning of mobile phones in schools. These types of reactive measures distract the public from more concerted attention to accountability from specific tech companies and apps profiting through their platforms. We of course disagree with these distraction techniques, and we also want to push for better quality education and digital literacy for everyone on this issue. We conclude the chapter by focusing on how we think the education sector could improve.

How Can We All Do Digital Sex Education Better?

In the opening of this chapter and throughout this book we've shown how banning social media, taking young people's social media or phones away from them, and rigid surveillance, infringes upon young people's rights, and doesn't offer a long-term solution to the underlying issues fuelling image-based sexual harassment and abuse. The banning mentality pits adults against children and is a harmful dynamic. We want instead to bring everyone to the table to find solutions to support smart use of smart phones.

Throughout this book we also found that young people were calling out for better education on these issues. Young people repeatedly pointed out they were not educated about social media in relation to online harms and abuses in ways they could relate to; rather, they were given limited information about child pornography, and fear-mongering abstinence messaging not to produce sexts themselves. A wealth of international literature has found that abstinence messaging—in effect urging youth to not express digital sexuality (don't sext)—does not work (Woodley et al, 2024). What it does do is force issues underground, so when young people experience harm they feel shame and do not feel that they can tell anyone about it. We saw practices such as having multiple accounts to conceal activity from parents. In other cases, siblings were called upon either to help their younger siblings navigate risky apps like Snapchat, or to help if something went wrong online.

Despite, therefore, the government's recent efforts to turn back the clock on RSE in England, that we outlined in our introduction, we advocate that the Department for Education (DfE) improves and enhances its approach to Relationships, Sex and Health Education, by fully considering digital dynamics. First of all, the DfE guidance needs to remove all victim blaming rhetoric from guidance and curriculum. The DfE (2019) guidelines stated during the time of our study in 2019 and continue to state in the 2025 updated version that children should be taught 'not to provide material to others that they would not want shared further and not to share personal material which is sent to them' (Department for Education, 2025: 15). This puts the onus back on to those who create sexual images to prevent themselves being abused. As we have shown throughout this book, this abstinence approach (do not provide material to others) fails to identify issues of pressured 'sexting' and neglects that the harm lies in the non-consensual sharing of images; it sends the message to children that victims of coercion are responsible for changing their behaviour, rather than those who are harassing or acting non-consensually. The updated 2025 guidelines do pay more attention to consent, saying "keeping or forwarding indecent or sexual images of someone under 18 is a crime, even if the photo is of themselves or of someone who has consented" but still focus on the serious consequences of acquiring or generating indecent or sexual images of someone under 18, including the potential for criminal charges and severe penalties including imprisonment (Department for Education, 2025: 15). As we've noted the focus on how generating sexual images is illegal rather than spelling out the details of consent around image sharing fails to adequately address the complexities of peer-to-peer intimacies and relationships (Finkelhor et al., 2023).

We advocate for the inclusion of the terminology of digital consent and image-based sexual harassment and abuse into policies and curriculum so schools, families and young people gain fluency with these concepts (Ringrose et al., 2024). We also need to raise awareness about the new sexual offences of cyberflashing and non-consensual sharing of intimate photographs and videos. This would be a huge step forward, as these offences offer the gradation and nuance of content of what is in images and how they are being used, rather than the overarching category of child pornography.

We found teachers in the schools we researched were working hard to address the gaps in sex education but state schools, unsurprisingly, had fewer resources than the independent sector. However, the elite schools focused on digital safety in instrumental ways to safeguard future career and status and were not unpacking important issues of digital consent. Indeed, they were often reproducing harmful gender norms. It follows that we recommend all schools include training for teachers and school staff to identify and respond to image-based sexual harassment and abuse (see Association of School and College Leaders, no date). In the state sector, the government must provide schools with the financial

280   J. Ringrose and K. Regehr

means to secure appropriate staffing, training and high quality evidence-based resources to teach gender and sexual equity to tackle the roots of sexual harassment. It puts schools in a bind to make the RSE curriculum subject 'compulsory' but not have a mechanism for it to be prioritised or timetabled in schools everyday workings and again to not offer teacher training support and infrastructure in RSE, which is critical for all young people's well-being and futures.

In our survey, we found that only 2% of respondents who reported issues of online harm reported these issues to schools. This was largely because they felt the so-called safeguarding procedures in schools would increase the risks they faced. Most young people do not feel secure to report at school because the safeguarding strategies deter them by making what has happened even more public and exposing them further than they already are. It may also incur victim blaming and slut shaming for girls in particular, possibly opening the victim up to further abuse. These types of conundrums propel us forward with our main message that schools need to get on top of digital sex ed messaging in ways that fully grapple with consent and abuse.

Given we also found youth rarely report issues to social media platforms further support on how platform-based reporting works would be helpful. There is also a need to direct youth to online support services such as Report and Remove from the Internet Watch Foundation. Explaining what to do if image-based sexual harassment and abuse has occurred is key. Signposting young people to helplines can also be very useful offering the much-needed confidentiality and anonymity that young people may need to begin discussing these harms.

A different relation to policing in schools would also help. We found police educational efforts, such as ill-advised large-scale fear-based assemblies delivering the message not to sext, were met with frustration from youth. Messaging that is about girls not producing child pornography images focusing on the illegality of these images, needs to change to a focus on the wider social dynamics and issues around consent and images. We saw in Chapter 2 that the girls felt that the police educational work going on in their school was completely ineffective; they would never go to the police officer who worked there, even if they realised they could potentially help, because the officer told them what 'not to do'

9 Conclusion: Image-Based Sexual Harassment ... 281

and that if girls produced images it was illegal, but 'don't really explain the consequences or risks of what you're actually doing... they are not really helping to understand.' The girls said they would be too scared to ever approach this officer. This is a missed opportunity around the nexus of policing and schools, which we hope can be addressed. Setty and colleagues (2024) have offered a framework for improving school/police relationships, arguing:

> schools are in a unique position to be able to deliver preventative education and to intervene in response to incidents of harmful sexual behaviour in ways that can help tackle the issues through promoting sexual citizenship and the rights of young people to live safe and healthy lives. Schools can provide young people with alternative perspectives and a firm foundation upon which to build, as an example of how society can be arranged to ensure the safety and growth of all young people.

We therefore advocate for schools to take a victim-centred and trauma informed approach, since we found young people are not reporting their experiences of sexual harassment and abuse because they fear victim blaming and shaming and that reporting their experiences will make matters worse.

We also saw that young people learn the law around distribution of sexual imagery as wrong and bad—that they should not 'leak' nudes so send them to one another digitally. Some in our study acknowledged that these practices of viewing and sharing images of women's and girls' bodies was wrong, but many participated anyway. We looked at some of the complexities they expressed around what Sidsel Harder (2020) calls 'digital bystanding' of image-based sexual harassment and abuse online. Some boys at Stags School had learned it was illegal to send images digitally as they could be prosecuted through child porn laws, so they shared the images on their phone screens instead. They are still committing image-based sexual abuse. We contend this harmful sexual behaviour is accepted because they have only learned about child pornography laws and the imperative not to be found in possession of images. They have *not* learned to frame what they are doing a matter of consent, and as image-based harassment and abuse. With an instrumental and divided approach to sex education and e-safety where digital crime is not covered in enough depth, these boys are learning how to keep their own footprint crime free, but not the respect and care of others' images.

Girls were adamant that the messages needed to shift from a moralising judgement and regulating of girls' bodies to a focus on boys' attitudes and behaviour. Janelle at South East Community College talked about feminism and standing up for girls' and women's rights against sexual violence; girls at Swans wanted education that addressed 'toxic masculinity. We found important instances of consensual sexting amongst the older young people at Swans. Dawn maintained girls' and women's rights to sext, but also insisted that boys be taught early on that it is unacceptable to send an image of your penis without consent. Joel explained he had experienced more consensual exchange of dick pics in the gay community but reminded us that schools also need to address sexual violence for LGBTQ youth and include up to date gender sensitive messaging. Some of the youngest kids at Outer Northern Academy had also advocated strongly for the need for more gender and sexuality tolerance and inclusion, remember12-year-old Fera who argued "children should learn about how LGBT people should be accepted" including in Muslim culture.

There is an urgent need to consider boys' roles in either perpetuating or contributing to a (largely heterosexual) culture that normalises image-based sexual harassment and abuse. Participants discussed the ways in which parental and educational interventions need to refocus attention towards eliminating the systemic gender norms that motivate boys to engage in these harmful forms of image-based sexual harassment and abuse. Schools need to be pro-active in educating about cyberflashing and having frank discussions about ethics and consent rather than shame and blame tactics. What supports are there around transforming homosocial masculinity cultures that objectify and dehumanise girls? We saw some very important examples of empathy and concern from boys in our study. But we also found that boys were able to critically discuss and challenge what they called 'subconscious pressures' they put on one another to appear powerful and desirable to girls. When boys are given a chance to discuss and think about how some of their masculinity norms and behaviour is unethical, there is reflection and reconsideration.

In these ways, students actively suggest strategies for raising awareness about image-based sexual harassment and abuse through education, thereby combatting it. We want to close this chapter by reminding our readers that education does not only mean the formal state-regulated curriculum. Young people need education, guidance, support and understanding from their parents/guardians and families as well. Students outlined the lack of support they feel from parents as well as schools and told us how they turn instead to other young people including siblings. Because sex education and e-safety in schools is so variable, as we've shown, parents cannot rely on schools for digital literacy, nor is it appropriate to put all the onus on schools and teachers to solve these issues. The complexities outlined throughout this book show that all teens are impacted by image-based abuse. These issues are intensified by issues of class, race and gender but regardless of the school or community, no kids are safe. Thus, we want to encourage parents that rather than putting all your energy into sheltering your individual child, instead let us collectively band together to make social media safer for all kids. We must hold the government and internet companies accountable.

This means pressuring government and social media companies to be child responsive—giving teens the critical tools to safely engage with their platforms. This might take the shape of platforms providing more information and pop ups to inform children of the new criminal offences in country-specific ways, for instance. What we are advocating for is society wide education that pinpoints the abusive and often gendered nature of IBSHA. Adults, parents, teachers and schools need to grapple with these gendered and sexualised power relations in the online environment and recognise how these harms travel offline—permeating experiences in and around schools, as we have demonstrated in this book. It is only by acknowledging the degree and severity of abuse happening online, and how it disproportionately impacts girls as well as gender minority and LGBTQ youth, that we can collectively challenge normalised forms of abuse and support all young people in navigating the complicated terrain of digital sexual cultures.

What we have demonstrated throughout the book, is that young people are keen to voice their concerns, often insisting that what is happening is not right or fair. Our work as educators, parents and activists, is to *balance* the need to keep young people safe online through protections, with a keen awareness of and adherence to young people's rights. We need to be collaboratively creating educational and support systems with and for young people will enable genuine shifts towards equity and better digital lives for all.

References

Association of School and College Leaders. (no date). *Resources: Understanding and Combatting Youth Experiences of Image-Based Sexual Harassment and Abuse.* https://www.ascl.org.uk/Microsites/IBSHA/Resources

Bates, L. (2021). *Men Who Hate Women From incels to pickup artists, the truth about extreme misogyny and how it affects us all.* Sourcebooks.

BBC. (10 February 2021). *Facebook 'horrified' by online abuse of Premier League footballers.* https://www.bbc.com/sport/football/56007601.amp

BBC. (21 April 2021). *Instagram lets users filter out abusive messages, BBC Technology.* https://www.bbc.co.uk/news/technology-56831119

BBC. (24 January 2024). *'MP urges social media ban for under16s'.* https://www.bbc.co.uk/news/av/uk-politics-68085378

Centre for Women's Justice, End Violence Against Women coalition, Imkaan, and Rape Crisis England & Wales. (2020). *The decriminalisation of rape: why the justice system is failing rape survivors and what needs to change.* https://rcew.fra1.cdn.digitaloceanspaces.com/media/documents/c-decriminalisation-of-rape-report-cwj-evaw-imkaan-rcew-nov-2020.pdf

Daily Mail. (2021). Crackdown on cyberflashing. https://www.dailymail.co.uk/news/article-10278283/Crackdown-cyberflashing-Social-media-firms-face-call-action.html

Department for Education. (2019). *Statutory guidance: Relationships education, relationships and sex education (RSE) and health education.* https://www.gov.uk/government/publications/relationships-education-relationships-and-sex-education-rse-and-health-education/relationships-and-sex-education-rse-sec ondary

Department for Education. (2024). *Mobile phones in schools guidance for schools on prohibiting the use of mobile phones throughout the school day.* https://assets.publishing.service.gov.uk/media/65cf5f2a4239310 011b7b916/Mobile_phones_in_schools_guidance.pdf

Department for Education. (2025). *Relationships education, relationships and sex education (RSE) and health education statutory guidance for governing bodies, proprietors, head teachers, principals, senior leadership teams, and teachers.* https://assets.publishing.service.gov.uk/media/689c57087b2e384441636190/RSHE_Statutory_Guidance_-_July_2025.pdf

Femicide Census. (2021). https://www.femicidecensus.org/reports/

Finkelhor, D., Turner, H., Colburn, D., Mitchell, K., & Mathews, B. (2023). Child sexual abuse images and youth produced images: the varieties of image-based sexual exploitation and abuse of children. *Child Abuse & Neglect, 143.* https://doi.org/10.1016/j.chiabu.2023.106269

Guardian. (2021). Three in four girls have been sent sexual images via apps https://www.theguardian.com/media/2021/dec/06/three-in-four-girls-have-been-sent-sexual-images-via-apps-report-finds

Guardian. (2024). Court jails first person convicted of cyberflashing in England https://www.theguardian.com/uk-news/2024/mar/19/court-jails-first-person-convicted-of-cyber-flashing-in-england

Harder, S. K. (2020). The emotional bystander—Sexting and image-based sexual abuse among young adults. *Journal of Youth Studies, 24*(5), 655–669. https://doi.org/10.1080/13676261.2020.1757631

Henry N., & Powell A. (2018 Apr). Technology-facilitated sexual violence: a literature review of empirical research. *Trauma Violence Abuse, 19*(2):195–208. https://doi.org/10.1177/1524838016650189. Epub 2016 Jun 16. PMID: 27311818

Kemp, P., Brock, R., & O'Brien, A. (2024). Mobile phone bans in schools: Impact on achievement. British Educational Research Association, https://www.bera.ac.uk/blog/mobile-phone-bans-in-schools-impact-on-achievement

Lebow, S. (2024). *Guide to Snapchat: Audience stats, ad opportunities, and trends for marketers.* https://www.emarketer.com/insights/snapchat-user-statistics/#:~:text=Snapchat's%20advertising%20revenues,growth%20of%208.7%25%20over%202024

Livingstone, S., & Third, A. (2017). Children and young people's rights in the digital age: An emerging agenda. *New Media & Society, 19*(5), 657–670. https://doi.org/libproxy.ucl.ac.uk/10.1177/1461444816686318

Livingstone, S. (2023). *How can we make the internet safe for children in practice?* https://blogs.lse.ac.uk/politicsandpolicy/how-can-we-make-the-internet-safe-for-children-in-practice/

McGlynn, C. (2022). Cyberflashing: Consent, Reform and the Criminal Law. *The Journal of Criminal Law, 86*(5), 336–352. https://doi.org/10.1177/002 20183211073644

Milmo, D. (2024). MPs urge under-16s UK smartphone ban and statutory ban in schools. *The Guardian.* https://www.theguardian.com/technology/article/ 2024/may/25/mps-urge-under-16s-smartphone-ban-statutory-ban-schools

Online Safety Act. (2023). https://www.legislation.gov.uk/ukpga/2023/50. Accessed December, 1, 2025.

Phippen, A. (2024). Why bans on smartphones or social media for teenagers could do more harm than good. *The Conversation.* https://theconversat ion.com/why-bans-on-smartphones-or-social-media-for-teenagers-could-do-more-harm-than-good-224005

Rahali, M., Kidron, B., & Livingstone, S. (2024). Smartphone policies in schools: What does the evidence say? *LSE.* https://eprints.lse.ac.uk/125554/ 1/Smartphone_policies_in_schools_Rahali_et_al_2024_002_.pdf

Ringrose, J., Mendes, K., Horeck, T., Desborough, K., & Milne, B. (2024). Equipping Young People to Navigate Post-digital Sexual Violence. UCL Institute of Education. https://discovery.ucl.ac.uk/id/eprint/10186206/

Selwyn, N. (2023). Digital degrowth: Toward radically sustainable education technology. *Learning, Media and Technology, 49*(2), 186–199. https://doi. org/10.1080/17439884.2022.2159978

Setty, E., Hunt, J., & Ringrose, J. (2024). *Policing harmful sexual behaviour among young people in schools.* https://www.surrey.ac.uk/sites/default/files/ 2024-03/policing-harmful-sexual-behaviour-guidance.pdf

Smartphone Free Childhood. (2024). *About.* https://smartphonefreechildhood. co.uk/about

Sullivan, H. (2024). Australia passes world-first law banning under-16s from social media despite safety concerns. *The Guardian.* https://www.thegua rdian.com/media/2024/nov/28/australia-passes-world-first-law-banning-under-16s-from-social-media-despite-safety-concerns

Wait Till the 8th. (2024). *About.* https://www.waituntil8th.org/

Woodley, G. N., Green, L., & Jacques, C. (2024). 'Send Nudes?': Teens' perspectives of education around sexting, an argument for a balanced approach. *Sexualities, 0*(0). https://doi.org/10.1177/13634607241237675

Zahn, M. (2024). *Instagram imposes new restrictions for teens. Will they work?* https://abcnews.go.com/Business/instagram-imposes-new-restri ctions-teens-work/story?id=113804044

Open Access This chapter is licensed under the terms of the Creative Commons Attribution-NonCommercial-NoDerivatives 4.0 International License (http://creativecommons.org/licenses/by-nc-nd/4.0/), which permits any noncommercial use, sharing, distribution and reproduction in any medium or format, as long as you give appropriate credit to the original author(s) and the source, provide a link to the Creative Commons license and indicate if you modified the licensed material. You do not have permission under this license to share adapted material derived from this chapter or parts of it.

The images or other third party material in this chapter are included in the chapter's Creative Commons license, unless indicated otherwise in a credit line to the material. If material is not included in the chapter's Creative Commons license and your intended use is not permitted by statutory regulation or exceeds the permitted use, you will need to obtain permission directly from the copyright holder.

Index

A

Academy school 83
Age restrictions 155
Age verification 85
Algorithm 8, 16, 157, 177, 182, 271

B

Banter 114, 268
  lad banter 14
  lad banter 234
Bare 194, 277
Belfie 186
Bitmoji 7, 85, 88, 104, 116
Bot 38, 153, 201
  porn bots 153, 200, 204, 266

C

Catfish 203

Child pornography 12, 13, 114, 136, 137, 173, 255, 266, 267, 271, 272, 278–281
Child sexual abuse 13, 102, 241, 271, 277
  grooming 277
Comprehensive school 123, 217, 221
Criminalisation 13, 263, 270–272
Cultural capital 266
Cyberbullying 78, 79, 117, 146
Cyberflashing 4, 10, 12, 80, 175, 243, 263, 269–272, 275, 277, 279, 282

D

Dick pic 4, 5, 10, 12, 14, 44, 51, 52, 60, 72, 78, 79, 104, 106, 129, 130, 133, 164, 165, 167,

© The Editor(s) (if applicable) and The Author(s) 2025
J. Ringrose and K. Regehr, *Teens, Social Media, and Image Based Abuse*,
https://doi.org/10.1007/978-3-031-92322-7

168, 178, 182, 184–187, 189,
194, 195, 200, 210, 213, 228,
229, 234, 237–239, 243, 245,
255, 256, 265–268, 271, 282
transactional dick pic 12, 72
Digital bystanding 281
Digital literacy 9, 15, 19, 57, 104,
120, 126, 178, 265
Doxing 97, 98, 243, 268

E

e-safety 19, 65, 79, 117, 201, 203,
212, 256, 267, 271, 273, 282,
283

F

Femicide 270
Femininity 132, 135, 143, 144, 178,
214, 226
Feminism 1, 60, 264
Free school meals 27, 123, 264–266

G

Gender and sexuality diverse (GSD)
85
bisexual 85
gender fluid 85
Genders 14, 18, 20, 26, 28, 85,
120, 135, 137, 150, 157, 159,
174, 178, 217–219, 244, 246,
255–257, 263, 267, 269, 280,
282, 283
Cis gendered 124
Geolocation/location tracking 87,
88, 265, 275
Grammar school 181, 217, 218, 268

H

Heterosexual 111, 124, 159, 227,
246, 270, 282
heterosexual matrix 124
Homosocial 114, 159, 164, 171,
177, 198, 267
Honour based violence 125, 266

I

Image-based abuse and image-based
harassment (IBSHA) 256
Image based sexual abuse 4, 9, 14,
116, 124, 133, 137, 143, 144,
163, 241, 250, 267
Image based sexual harassment 115,
146, 255
Image based sexual harassment and
abuse (IBSHA) 6, 9–12, 137,
167, 213, 214, 262, 278, 283
image-based sexual harassment 1
online sexual assault 57
online sexual harassment 57
revenge porn 48
Independent school 19, 63, 149
Influencer 8, 15, 153, 206, 207,
208, 226
Instagram 5, 8, 9, 17, 18, 30, 33,
37, 41, 48, 57, 65, 70, 72, 79,
98, 128, 152–155, 157, 177,
182, 185, 187, 189, 194, 200,
204–206, 208, 213, 218, 228,
241, 243, 263, 267, 274, 276
status update 70
Internalisation 79, 143
Intimate image offences 277
Isolation units 120, 265

Index 291

L

LGBTQ 85, 118, 245, 252, 256, 282, 283

M

Masculinity 4, 110, 139, 159, 160, 177, 178, 199, 201, 231, 252, 268, 282
homosocial 111, 142, 282
male victimisation 109
male victimisation 115
toxic masculinity 282
Micro-celebrity 182, 267
Misogyny 1, 16, 47, 112, 125, 256, 266, 270
misogynoir 47
Mobile phone banning 265
Monetisation 213

N

Normalisation 84, 112, 182, 199, 213
Nude 4, 8, 12, 14, 19, 30, 38, 44, 47–50, 54, 59, 65, 67, 69, 70, 72, 73, 76, 79, 80, 91, 104, 106–111, 115, 116, 124, 125, 128, 131, 133, 140, 142, 143, 149, 150, 159–162, 164, 166–169, 171–175, 177, 178, 184, 185, 195, 199, 201–203, 207, 210, 212, 213, 228, 229, 235, 237, 238, 240, 243–246, 248–250, 252, 255, 256, 264–268, 271, 274, 281
transactional nude 203, 238

O

Online Safety Act 11
OnlyFans 207

P

Patriarchy 60, 125, 143
Platform affordance 17, 57, 161
Platform economy 208
Platform feature 6
Porn 156, 172, 228
Pornbot 9, 177, 199

R

Radicalisation 271
Rape culture 1, 108
Reporting 4, 6, 9, 42, 58, 86, 95, 141, 198, 273–276, 280, 281
Responsibilisation 250

S

Safeguarding 162, 280
Safety by design 13, 18, 276
Selfie 28–30, 37, 64, 65, 70, 80, 126, 128, 186, 190, 207, 222, 223, 226, 231, 236
Abs 232
Belfie 226
Jaw line 232
mirror selfie 226
6-pack 233
V-line 233
Sex education 1, 11, 14, 15, 19, 25, 27, 28, 53–57, 63, 78, 79, 81, 117, 118, 123, 124, 126, 137, 143, 171, 172, 176, 178, 182, 183, 208–210, 214, 251–253, 256, 263–268, 282

Index

abstinence approach 12, 16, 54, 103, 137, 262, 266, 279
digital sex education 266
Sexism 1, 3, 16, 84, 99, 110, 112, 118, 120, 143, 145
Sex subscriptions 17, 18, 154–157, 201, 206, 276
Sexting 3, 12–14, 53–55, 66, 69, 70, 74, 76, 117, 124, 133, 136, 203, 214, 250, 264, 265, 268, 271, 282
Sextortion 8, 38, 166, 203, 267
Sexual consent 11, 124, 177, 178, 252
Sexual double standards (SDS) 1, 3, 4, 30, 46, 57, 59, 72, 80, 111, 112, 123–125, 141, 143, 144, 167, 169, 271
sexually promiscuous 65
sexually shame 47, 124
sexual reputation 169
sexual shaming 47, 110, 143
shame 80
sket 108
slut shaming 1, 108, 124, 125, 280
victim blamed 116, 125, 250, 280
sexual double standards (SDS) 110, 124, 150
Sexualisation 11, 74
Sexual violence 3, 9, 15, 117, 141, 144, 157, 193, 252, 256, 268–270, 273, 282
intimate partner violence 270
sexual harassment 270
Single sex 149, 178, 181, 218, 255, 267, 268
Smartphone 25, 88, 103, 278

Snapchat 4–10, 17, 18, 32–35, 37, 39, 41, 42, 44, 53, 57, 70, 72, 79, 84–88, 91, 93–95, 98–100, 103–105, 116, 117, 120, 126, 128, 152–155, 157, 177, 182–185, 188–190, 192, 194, 195, 200, 205, 206, 208, 209, 212–214, 218, 222, 223, 226, 234, 236, 238, 244–246, 248, 250, 253, 256, 263–265, 267, 269, 270, 273–275, 277, 278
quick add 34, 95, 116
shoutouts 33, 93
snapcodes 34
snapmap 88, 103
snapscore 34
snapstory 48
streak 35
Snapmap 7, 86, 88, 97, 104, 116, 265, 275
Snapscore 33, 57, 92, 93, 152, 182, 184, 189, 275
Snapstory 40, 99, 100, 116, 265
Snapstreak 275
Social media 2–4, 10, 13, 15–17, 19, 25, 26, 32, 53, 56, 60, 67, 68, 70, 73, 79, 80, 85, 86, 88, 89, 93, 100, 102, 103, 125, 126, 128, 143, 145, 151, 156, 164, 175–177, 182, 183, 189, 202, 204, 210, 212–214, 218–222, 226, 241, 247, 250, 255, 262–266, 268, 270–272, 274, 276–278, 283
social media subscription 102
spam accounts 74
Social media drawing templates 25, 32, 53

Sociologist 219

Urban Dictionary 47, 98

T

Tech facilitated sexual violence 9, 13, 270, 272

TikTok 16

Transactional dick pic 79, 106, 143, 185, 190, 229, 243

V

Victim blaming 14, 130, 137, 143

V-line 230

VPN 155

U

Unsolicited dick pic 1, 11, 41, 72, 167, 235

W

WhatsApp 5, 6, 56, 125, 161, 241

Printed in the United States
by Baker & Taylor Publisher Services